Billy Miske
The St. Paul Thunderbolt

Clay Moyle

Win By KO Publications
Iowa City

Billy Miske: The St. Paul Thunderbolt

Clay Moyle

(ISBN): 978-0-9799822-4-8
(hardcover: 55# acid-free alkaline paper)
Library of Congress Control Number: 2011942999
Includes footnotes, appendix, and index.
© 2011 by Clay Moyle. All Rights Reserved.

No part of this book may be reproduced, or transmitted in any form or by any means, graphic, electronic or mechanical, including photocopying, recording, taping, or by any information storage retrieval system without the written permission of Clay Moyle.

Cover design by Gwyn Snider ©

Manufactured in the United States of America.

Win By KO Publications
Iowa City, Iowa
winbykopublications.com

Dedicated to my parents, Ben and Marliss Moyle,
for their loving guidance and support.

ACKNOWLEDGEMENTS

There are many parties that I owe my thanks to for their contributions to the completion of this book. I'd like to start by thanking Billy Miske's grandsons, Bill Miske and Robert Booth, for allowing me to interview them and providing copies of articles and photographs. They are both extremely proud of their grandfather's legacy and justifiably so.

I would also like to thank my friends and fellow authors Colleen Aycock and Tracy Callis as well as journalist Tami Beaumont and my aunt, Sheila Rabe, for all their editorial assistance and advice during the course of this project. Their input was invaluable and greatly appreciated. Another friend and author, Bill Paxton, was also kind enough to read a draft of the story and provide valuable input.

Debra LaFontaine, a Minnesota based researcher, was extremely helpful in tracking down additional information concerning Billy's past, and a real pleasure to work with. David Toms was kind enough to provide proofreading services and helped me find a number of errors that I was able to correct. Any remaining errors that may be found will surely be the result of additional work that I did after his proofreading efforts were completed. If you are looking for a great proofreader I highly recommend that you consider David's services.

I would also like to thank my friend Adam Pollack for offering to publish the book. Adam has already written six wonderful books chronicling the boxing careers of six heavyweight champions and is hard at work on his next one about Jack Johnson.

Others who contributed in some manner to the book, whether it be by providing valuable information or photographs, and that I would like to thank include: David Bergin, George Blair, Monte Cox, Lawrence Davies, Craig Hamilton, Steve Compton, Henry Hascup, Brendan Henehan, John Ochs, Charles Saunders, Don Scott, Harry Shaffer, Gregory Speciale, Christopher Tarr, Tony Triem, Jake Wegner, and the folks with the King County Library System who helped me gain access to so many reels of old newspaper microfilm.

Lastly, I must once again thank my wife Margaret and our children, Grace and Caleb, for their patience and understanding while I worked on this book. If I have left anyone out who contributed to this work in some manner I offer my sincere apology and beg their forgiveness.

Contents

Foreword by Jake Wegner   6

1. Becoming a Fighter   7

2. Early Days in the Ring   14

3. Jack Dillon and "Battling" Levinsky   23

4. Injured Left Hand   32

5. Fulton, Dempsey and "Gunboat" Smith   45

6. Work or Fight   55

7. Billy Learns His Fate   64

8. The Elgin Six   77

Photographs   84 – 105

9. Training for the Title Fight   106

10. Referee Controversy   116

11. Outcome of the Fight   121

12. The Comeback Trail   129

13. Gibbons Establishes His Superiority   140

14. A Title Fight in Shelby, Montana   156

15. Dempsey versus Gibbons   164

16. "Get Me a Fight!"   174

17. Billy's Last Christmas   185

Epilogue   191

Appendix: Billy Miske's Record   193

Index   200

Foreword

It was a great honor when I got the call to write the Foreword for this book by my fellow friend and historian, Clay Moyle. Already known for his in-depth research and spot-on facts as seen in his previous work, "Sam Langford- Boxing's Greatest Uncrowned Champion," it made me extremely excited when Clay first shared with me that the next subject of his research was to be The Saint Paul Thunderbolt, Billy Miske. As one of boxing's all-time greats, Miske's accomplishments as a fighter are well-noted, but it is perhaps his accomplishments as a man, that have come to define him as one of greatest stories in all of sports. For it is not only what he achieved in the ring that made him great, although that aspect alone has made him a Hall of Famer, but also his tragic, yet heart-warming story outside of the ring that so touches every person that hears it. It makes women emotional, and inspires men to dig deeper and become better men; regardless of their walk of life—*and who doesn't like a story like that?* It is for these reasons that Hollywood has yearned to bring it to the big screen, and that Fox hit gold with it in 2008 as one of their highest rated episodes of their mini-series, *Amazing Sports Stories;* and it is for these reasons that I know his story will also serve as the antidote to readers everywhere when life deals them a blow and their outlook seems dim. For when those times come, as they invariably do, this book will glow from your mantle and inspire you to pick yourself up, take inventory, and to move on—and we all can use that.

But every great story needs a story-teller; as no biography can be fully enjoyed unless the reader can have full-faith in the facts told by the author, and as a historian from Miske's home state and a lifetime student of his career, I can well attest that Clay Moyle has spared no detail, and has indeed scored a knockout. For us enthusiasts, this is one count we hope never to wake from.

Thank you to Clay Moyle for resurrecting the storm and the thunderbolt that Billy Miske was.

Jake Wegner - Boxing Historian and President of the Minnesota Boxing Hall of Fame.

CHAPTER 1

Becoming a Fighter

In the summer of 1919, Billy Miske was a 25-year-old professional fighter, six feet tall and 175 pounds, a young man with "an Adonis build, and the muscles of Hercules."[1] He had always prided himself on his physical condition, and had been held up as an example of clean living.[2] They said he was a scrappy and aggressive fighter with a bright future, so the news from the doctor that he was suffering from a kidney disease, and in all likelihood had less than five years to live, must have come as a complete shock.

At the time Billy received this dire news, he was married with two very young boys and living in St. Paul, Minneapolis. Rather than share the news of his deadly disease with the public, Billy chose to reveal the true nature and extent of his condition to only a couple of very close friends, on the condition they keep the information to themselves. Not even his own wife realized just how sick he was. This is the story of Billy's life and boxing career and how he chose to respond to the fatal diagnosis he received that summer.

There was disagreement over Billy's nationality for a number of years after he began receiving attention in the sporting world. Some folks said he was of German descent, some Polish, while still others said he was a Bohemian. Billy finally settled the issue, claiming he was a Prussian. "My real name is Miska," Billy said, "but my father found that people in this country could not pronounce the name correctly so he allowed it to become Miske by default, as it were."[3] Words that end in "e" in German are pronounced with an "a" or "ah" or "uh" sound.

Perhaps it was this Prussian heritage that partly explained Billy's character. He certainly possessed the "Prussian virtues" of discipline; sacrifice, reliability, honesty, modesty and diligence, among others, virtues some believe were part of the reason for Prussia's rise in the eighteenth and nineteenth centuries.[4]

Billy's story began in the year of 1894. The only son of German 'emigres' Herman and Bertha Miske, William Arthur (Billy) was born in St.

---

1 *Denver Post*, February 19, 1916 photograph caption.
2 *Denver Post*, Miske Tackles Dick Gilbert Tomorrow Evening at N.A.C. February 28, 1916.
3 *Lincoln Daily Star*, Billy Miske vs. Battling Levinsky, Ten Rounds, at New York City. December 31, 1916.
4 Howard, Michael. *The Lessons of History*, Yale University Press, New Haven, Connecticut, 1991.

Paul, Minnesota on February 16 of that year.[5] He had two sisters, Florence, who was born in March of 1895, and Mildred, who was born in 1912. His father immigrated to the United States in 1884 as a 12-year-old. Herman was a big fellow, standing 6'2" tall and weighing over 200 pounds. He received an appointment as a patrolman for the St. Paul Police Department on August 9, 1900, and went on to serve for the next 27 years, the last three as a constable.

St. Paul is located in the southeastern part of the state and sits just across the Mississippi River from Minneapolis. They are referred to as the "Twin Cities" and have enjoyed a friendly rivalry for many years. St. Paul began as a trading and transportation center and was once a very busy steamboat port and became the capital of the Minnesota territory in 1849.

As a result of its northerly location and the lack of large bodies of water to moderate the air, St. Paul is subjected to cold Arctic air masses, especially during the winter months of December, January and February. The winters are frigid and snowy, while the summers are often comfortable and warm, but can also be hot and humid. The city experiences one of the greatest ranges of temperatures on earth, and the average annual temperature of 45.4 degrees gives the Minneapolis – St. Paul area the coldest annual mean temperature of any major metropolitan area in the continental United States.

Life for folks in the United States during Billy's childhood was much different than it is now. He and his sisters, as all children, were at a high risk of not even surviving past the age of ten. In 1900, twenty percent of newborns died before reaching age five. In general, life expectancy during Billy's time in the early 1900s was much lower than what we enjoy today because of our public health, nutrition and medicine practices in place, much of which was unavailable during that period of time.

The family lived at 549 Pine Street, in a residential area of what was then downtown St. Paul, at the time Billy was born. But over the course of his childhood they lived at many different St. Paul addresses (such as 404 Blair Street, 610 North Western Avenue, 538 Sherburne Street, 811 Van Buren, and 758 Blair Avenue). These locations were primarily in blue-collar neighborhoods among closely built, modest wood-frame and brick houses. Many of the men in these neighborhoods worked for, or were associated in some manner, with the St. Paul and Pacific Railroad, which became a part of the Great Northern Railroad, now Burlington Northern. Many others earned their living as sheet metal workers, shoemakers, blacksmiths, janitors, or some other form of manual labor. The area was commonly referred to as "Frogtown," though officially known as the Thomas-Dale District. Some said the *Frogtown* term originated from the fact the area was first settled by the French. Another theory was the name may have come

---

[5] Ramsey County Public Health Department birth records.

about as a result of the fact so many railroad workers lived in the area and the couplers on the railroad cars were called "frogs." The area, however, was also heavily populated by folks of German, Irish, Polish and Scandinavian descent and *frogtown* is an English version of the German word *froschburg*.6

Billy dropped out of school at a young age, possibly as early as 15 when he began working as a clerk for the Great Northern Railroad. The following year, he held a job in the mailroom of the *St. Paul Daily News*. He also spent some time working in the railroad machine shops repairing railcars. After that, he spent two years with the Northwest Bell Telephone Company installing cables and boxes for the phones used by the police on the street corners.

It was while working in the shops of the railroad with Mike and Tom Gibbons, two neighborhood brothers who went on to become well-known professional boxers themselves, that Billy first conceived the idea of becoming a professional fighter.

Mike Gibbons, the elder of the two brothers, was the first of the pair to establish his name in the fight game. A master of the art of scientific boxing, he was hailed for years as the uncrowned champion of the middleweight division, and was known as "The Phantom" because of his wonderful defensive skills. Mike is credited with establishing St. Paul as a boxing capital in the decade before 1920, and there were many who followed who patterned their style after him.7

Mike's success in the ring influenced Billy, along with others from the state of Minnesota such as Mike O'Dowd, Jock Malone, Johnny Ertle, and Jimmy Delaney to become fighters. Commenting on Mike's influence and his own decision to become a boxer, Billy said:

> I was a naturally strong kid. My work as a mechanic and as a lineman for the telephone company developed my muscles, and I could lick most of the fellows of my weight in our neighborhood. Then, when Mike became famous, I decided I'd like to be a fighter too. So, I joined the Dreamland Athletic club in St. Paul and used to put on the gloves with the professionals who trained there and I soon picked up a slight knowledge of the game.8

Like many others in the St. Paul area, Billy also acquired a love for the outdoors at an early age, and especially enjoyed hunting and fishing. He maintained that his love of the outdoors was one of the factors which influenced him to choose boxing as a profession. In fact, when one reporter asked him why he decided to become a boxer, Billy said:

---

6 *Frog Town or Thomas Dale*. Ramsey County Historical Society, Saint Paul, Minnesota.
7 Blair, George. *Mike Gibbons. The St. Paul Phantom*. Self-Published, Minnesota, no date.
8 *Kingston Daily Freeman*, Billy Miske Is Real Lover Of Boxing Game. February 14, 1917.

I am strong for the outdoor life and no other line of business allows one the outdoor exercise that boxing does. I consider boxing the greatest of all sports and think that every boy in the country should learn to box, not so much for the pecuniary benefits that are derived from this particular line, but for the health and vigor that one derives there from. Life is one continual struggle for supremacy and that everyone should be fitted physically is my belief.9

At the time Billy decided to make boxing, or "prize fighting" as it was referred to at the time, his chosen profession, it was illegal in the state of Minnesota. The anti-prize-fight law was enacted by the Minnesota state legislature in 1892 at the request of acting Governor William Merriam. He ordered the law after two St. Paul promoters had arranged a world championship middleweight contest between Australian fighters, Bob Fitzsimmons and Jim Hall during the summer of 1891. Local reform elements threatened the governor with impeachment if he didn't put a stop to the fight so the governor ordered it to be cancelled.

The promoters refused and threatened legal action. Their attorneys correctly pointed out no law against prize-fighting existed in the state. They maintained their stance to stage the fight right up until the governor surrounded the arena with state militia on the date of the fight.

During the winter of 1892, the state legislature, at the urging of the governor and others, passed a law making professional boxing in the state a felony. The law stated any person (boxer, manager, promoter, referee, trainer or second) found guilty of having any connection with a prize fight was subject to a sentence of one to five years in prison, a fine of $1,000, or both.10

The potential penalties turned out to have about as little success in preventing organized fights from taking place as prohibition had on the consumption of alcohol in the 1920s. The law only forced promoters to become more creative, arranging for "sneak" fights to take place in small halls, gymnasiums, barns, and even wooded areas when the weather allowed. The only advertising of these events was by word of mouth. Newspaper editors of Minnesota and St. Paul cooperated with promoters by withholding all publicity until the day after the contests. Of course, "sneak" fights were not unique to the state of Minnesota. They were taking place all around the country in locations where the sport was outlawed. The attendance of bouts was understandably much lower because of the need for secrecy and as a result the purses for fighters were generally small.

Billy's first professional fight was recorded in March of 1913 in Superior, Wisconsin against a man named Soldier Gregory. He knocked him out in four rounds. But the main thing he remembered about the fight

---

9 *Denver Post*, Miske Recommends Boxing For All Youngsters. February 25, 1916.
10 Barton, George. *My Lifetime in Sports*. The Olympic Press, Minneapolis, Minnesota, 1957.

was he didn't receive a dime for it. In fact, he hardly considered it a professional bout as a result, and the experience convinced him he needed a manager. He selected John "Pearl" Smith for the job.11

Smith was a former resident of Superior. He once demonstrated a lot of promise as a baseball pitcher and the local newspapermen thought sure he would one day display his talent in the big leagues. For many years he held the amateur record with a baseball throw of 394 feet. By the time he and Billy paired up, Smith had already made his fortune in the Minnesota iron mines, had a home in Los Angeles, and was a large stockholder in the Mendota Coal & Coke Company.12 He also found time to serve as wrestling instructor at a St. Paul Y.M.C.A. and later claimed it was there he had "discovered" Billy.13 His relationships in Superior, Wisconsin, where boxing events were being successfully staged, made him a good choice for a manager at the time.

All of Billy's earliest recognized, professional contests took place in Superior, Wisconsin, a city located on the northwestern tip of Wisconsin, just across the bay from Duluth, Minnesota, and approximately 150 miles from St. Paul. While prizefighting was also illegal in Wisconsin, the officials in Superior recognized that fights were going to take place regardless of their stance on the matter. As a result they took a more practical approach than the officials in Minnesota and staging boxing events there wasn't as difficult. They chose to allow fights, but insisted they be supervised in a manner to ensure fighters were evenly matched, the length of fights was regulated, specific rules were followed, and there was no trouble surrounding the event.14 As a result, a number of well publicized contests involving leading fighters from the state of Minnesota took place in Superior, Wisconsin.

Perhaps the difference between the two states stance on fighting at the time was best conveyed in an article written by T.S. Andrews titled "Boxing versus Prizefighting".15 In the article Andrews quoted one A.B. Nichols who said, "I've noticed many articles of late regarding prize fighting and boxing, and I want to say that there is all the difference in the world between the two." Nichols had witnessed a prize fight in 1873 between Tom Allen and Mike McCoole, a bare knuckle fight under the old London prize ring rules where a round did not end until one man was knocked down and the time between rounds lasted only 30 seconds. "That was a real prize fight and without gloves and padded ring," said Nichols. "I've attended many contests under the new rules with big gloves and must say

---

11 *St. Paul Pioneer Press.* Unknown article title, November 12, 1916.
12 *Superior Telegram*, Pearl Smith to Play Matty. Former Superior Man to Oppose Big League Star in Indoor Game. December 22, 1913.
13 *Salt Lake Tribune.* Miske Coming Rapidly. August 6, 1916.
14 *Superior Telegram,* Unknown article title, July 5, 1913.
15 *Racine Journal-News.* Boxing versus Prizefighting. March 11, 1913.

that the present day boxing is like a pillow fight between children compared to that prize fight that I saw near St. Louis," he added.

To Nichols' way of thinking, the present-day bouts were real boxing contests and nothing more. He felt the "big" gloves, padded ring, rounds limited to two or three minutes with a minute rest between rounds, and stoppage of contests once a man demonstrated his superiority over another made it more of a clean sparring contest.

During much of Billy's childhood the acting president of the United States was Theodore Roosevelt (1901 – 1909). Typifying those tougher times, the former Spanish-American war hero boxed at Harvard University during his college days, and sparred regularly with men such as the U.S. middleweight champion Mike Donovan during his presidency. He regularly invited boxers to the White House, and knew them all, including the heavyweight champion of the world, John L. Sullivan.

Roosevelt expressed the following view on the sport of boxing in 1896 when he held the position of Police Commissioner of New York:

> I like to see a bout between two evenly matched men. There can be no harm in such an exhibition. In my opinion it is much better for a man to know how to protect himself with his fists than to resort to firearms, knives or clubs. I believe the sport should be encouraged, it is a manly sport.[16]

Later, while he was the governor of New York, he approved a bill that made prizefighting in the state illegal. However, he explained his only objection to it was the "crookedness" involved with the sport at the time.

Roosevelt continued his practice of sparring until suffering a detached retina that left him blind in his left eye. One of his favorite sayings was to "speak softly and carry a big stick." He certainly wasn't the only person in the country at the time who thought boxing should be encouraged.

Roosevelt's successor, William Taft, who served from 1909 to 1913, was a large man who evidently also believed there was a time and place for action. Shortly after his college days a newspaperman by the last name Rose wrote a vicious article about Taft's father, who was a prominent judge. Taft was warned Rose was a strong and rugged fighter, but he approached him on a busy street corner, and after confirming he had the right man, gave him a thorough beating.[17]

The enactment of the Frawley Law in New York, in 1911, created the first state athletic commission in the United States, and had a large role in the legalization of boxing. Under Chapter 79 of the Laws of 1911, the New York State Athletic Commission came into existence, and boxing, or sparring matches, as opposed to prizefights, were placed under the commission's purview. The Frawley Law specified fights not ending in a

---

16 Kendall, Dr. Walter G., *Four Score Years of Sport*, The Stratford Company, Boston, MA 1933.
17 Lindop, Edmund, *White House Sportsmen*, Houghton Mifflin Company, Boston, MA 1964.

knockout would be declared a no-decision. The thinking was this would minimize the possibility of corruption in decisions. However, this proved to be ineffective when newspapers declared official decisions, and people who wished to gamble would simply agree to abide by "newspaper decisions." Corruption plaguing boxing judges was in effect transferred to the reporters covering the fights.[18]

The establishment of an athletic commission to oversee boxing in the state of New York was viewed as a success though, and by early 1913, numerous states across the country were seeking legislative approval of bills patterned after New York's laws to legalize boxing in their respective states.

As early as March, it was being reported a proposed measure to legalize boxing in Wisconsin was certain to become law. Later that month a court decision had been rendered permitting bouts to take place.[19] Minnesota passed its own boxing bill in early April approving six-round contests with eight-ounce gloves, and established a state athletic commission to supervise the contests. They also added the requirement of a 10% tax on the gate receipts from those events.[20] There had been talk of a 5% tax, but it ended up being 10%, and remained that way until the mid - 1950s when it was reduced to 5%.

Billy fought as a middleweight in 1913. His opponents during the year included Soldier Gregory, Theodore "Thor" Thompson, Danny Ritt, and Bill Scott. As previously noted, he knocked out Gregory in four rounds, captured a ten-round newspaper decision over Thompson,[21] stopped Ritt in two rounds, and effectively drew with the more experienced "Steamboat" Bill Scott. The *Superior Telegram* named Scott the winner by a shade.[22] Another paper reported while neither man showed class, and Billy failed to exhibit much cleverness, he did most of the forcing, landed more blows, hit the hardest, and outpointed and outslugged Scott.[23]

Billy became an immediate crowd pleaser in Superior for his aggressive style and willingness to mix it up with his opponents. *The Superior Telegram* said that considering the fact he was still a kid (19-years-old), had little experience and knowledge of the science of the sport, his showing against Scott was good. He was lauded for his willingness to work and a bright future was forecast for him. Once he learned to direct his blows and save some of his wasted energy, their reporter felt he would be able to stand up with the best of them.[24]

---

18 Rodriguez, Robert G. *The Regulation of Boxing*. McFarland Publishing, Jefferson, North Carolina. 2009.
19 *Superior Telegram*, How States Stand on the Boxing Measure. March 24, 1913.
20 *Superior Telegram*, Minnesota Assembly Passes Boxing Bill. April 2, 1913.
21 *Superior Telegram*, Sheehan, Miske, Brady are Winners in Snappy Boxing Show at Grand. April 30, 1913.
22 *Superior Telegram*, Fast and Furious Bouts Feature Stellar Card at Curley's Arena. October 1, 1913.
23 *St. Paul Pioneer Press*, Billy Miske Goes Ten Slugging Rounds with Scott at Superior. October 1, 1913.
24 *Superior Telegram*, Unknown article title, November 1, 1913.

CHAPTER 2

Early Days in the Ring

In February of 1914 Billy worked out regularly in St. Paul under the guidance of Mike Gibbons and picked up a lot about the finer points of the game.[25] That month he tackled one of the country's top welterweights in a more experienced fighter named "Spike" Kelly and made a very good showing. Kelly, a Chicago based welterweight, had been fighting professionally since 1909 and had given Mike Gibbons a tough fight only four months earlier. Billy earned a draw according to the *Duluth News Tribune*, and lost by a shade according to the *Superior Telegram*.[26] The *Duluth News Tribune* said Kelly had butted Billy with his head with such frequency he should have been disqualified. Their reporter felt the training in the Gibbons' brother's camp had benefited Billy greatly, noting he used both hands to advantage, and dodged with a fleetness of foot surprising to those who remembered him as a flat footed fighter only six months prior.[27]

Still trying to find his way as a professional fighter, Billy secured the services of a new manager by the name of Hugh McMahon. McMahon arranged for a trip east to provide him with additional exposure and experience. McMahon was considered an excellent judge of boxing talent, and had been former lightweight "Battling" Nelson's chief advisor when Bat was a world champion.[28] But before embarking on the adventure Billy fought Mike Gibbons younger brother, Tommy, in a matchup of two young talented St. Paul middleweights on March 24 in the opening of Hudson, Wisconsin's new arena before a crowd of 5,000.

Tommy was three years older than Billy, and like his brother Mike, was a very talented and clever fighter. He was undefeated after 12 professional fights. Tommy weighed approximately 157 pounds to Billy's 163.[29] The contest generated a considerable amount of interest among St. Paul fight fans and over 2,000 traveled to Wisconsin by train to attend.[30]

Billy had been after a match with Tommy for some time, but he came away disappointed when afterwards Tommy received a popular newspaper decision victory, winning seven of the ten rounds.[31] It had proved a lively contest, the two men going toe to toe, but while Billy was credited for the

---

25 *Superior Telegram*, Billy Miske Dead Sure He's Going to "Spike" Kelly. February 16, 1914.
26 *Superior Telegram*, Kelly Shades Miske. February 18, 1914.
27 *Duluth News Tribune*, Miske Gets Draw With Spike Kelly. February 18, 1914.
28 *Pottsville Journal*, Fight Fans To See Biggest Bouts Ever Staged Here. May 26, 1914.
29 *St. Paul Pioneer Press*, Biggest Event of its Kind in This Section in Quarter Century. March 23, 1914.
30 *St. Paul Pioneer Press*, Preparations Completed for Staging First Fight Program of New Club. March 22, 1914.
31 *Superior Telegram*, Mike and Tommy Win Hudson Bouts. March 25, 1914.

gameness he exhibited, he was outclassed by Tommy. Tommy's superior left jab and infighting skills gave him the edge.[32] So Billy headed east with McMahon to lick his wounds and continue improving his skills.

The eastern campaign consisted of 11 fights in the state of Pennsylvania against nine different men over a seven-month period, from May of 1914 to January 16 of 1915. It proved somewhat successful in terms of establishing Billy's name in the east and enabling him to further hone his craft.

The campaign began with a match against a well-regarded middleweight from Philadelphia named George Ashe. Ashe, who was born in Russia as Abraham Rivkind, had fought a bout ruled a draw with the highly-regarded Jack Dillon the previous year and Billy's showing against him established his credibility with the local fight fans. Reports of the fight result differed depending upon the source, but the *Pottsville Journal* wrote that Billy "showed he was a boxer of class by defeating George Ashe."[33]

His second fight took place in Pottsville against a seasoned middleweight from Allentown, Pennsylvania by the name of Jack McCarron. Born as Philip John McCarron in Allentown, Pennsylvania on August 10, 1890, McCarron was a protégé of the former light-heavyweight champion "Philadelphia" Jack O'Brien, and earlier in his career had been touted as a second coming of the great middleweight champion Stanley Ketchel. He had also been referred to as the "$50,000 beauty" because it was understood the agreement between he and O'Brien was for McCarron to fight for him for a certain number of years for the sum of $50,000. [34] Coming into the contest with Billy, Jack had suffered only two defeats in 25 bouts. He'd shown well against Mike Gibbons in May of 1913, and defeated him in November of 1912. Although McCarron earned the decision in the match versus Billy on May 26, 1914 in the view of most, Billy was the aggressor and almost knocked him out.[35]

His subsequent successes in the region against other veterans such as Kid Griffo, "Thor" Thompson, Jimmy Dougherty, Ralph Erne and Billy Maxwell (twice) won him many fans and inadvertently led to a match with the one and only Harry Greb. Like Billy, Greb's professional career began in 1913. A remarkable boxer, and undoubtedly one of the greatest pound-for-pound fighters of all time, Greb was an unusually clever fighter, who exhibited outstanding footwork, and was dubbed the "Pittsburgh Windmill" for his perpetual-motion style of fighting. On the night of January 12, 1915, Harry substituted as Billy's opponent in the main event at the Fairmount Athletic Club in Philadelphia for a black welterweight named Tommy Coleman who was suffering from an abscessed tooth. Harry gained an early

---

32 *St. Paul Pioneer Press*, Mike and Tom Gibbons Demonstrate Superiority Over Christie and Miske. March 25, 1914.
33 *Pottsville Journal*, Miske–McCarron Bout Stirs Coal Region Fight Fans. May 2, 1914.
34 *Chester Times*, Local Fight Manager Calls O'Brien's Hand. April 27, 1912.
35 *Pottsville Journal*, Fight Fans See Slashing Bouts At The Academy. May 27, 1914.

advantage, but Billy won the last round by a large margin, rushing from his corner, not allowing Harry to get set, and showering him with hard hooks to the head, to gain a draw.[36]

It was later claimed Harry had been at a disadvantage accepting the fight on short notice, and wasn't in condition, but Billy disputed this saying:

> We trained in the same gymnasium and Greb was ready for a fight. He substituted for Coleman. I was told not to fight him off his feet in the first three rounds. I did not, but I certainly gave him a bad beating in the fifth and sixth rounds. He's strong and aggressive, but very awkward.[37]

Four days later, Billy faced Jack McCarron for a second time at the National Athletic Club in Philadelphia and lost a tough six-round newspaper decision. McCarron had used his elbows several times during the contest, drawing blood from Billy's mouth at one point, and he'd managed to get the better of Billy by staying on the inside and smothering Billy's attack.[38]

Billy and Hugh McMahon then severed their relationship, and Billy returned home and reunited with manager John "Pearl" Smith in the hope of furthering his career in the Midwest region. He defeated three Chicagoan middleweights, Mike Hirsch, Gus Christie, and Eddie Nearing, in Milwaukee and Hudson, Wisconsin to set up an early April meeting with his former friend and fellow St. Paul native Mike O'Dowd. The victory over the highly regarded Nearing was especially impressive, as Eddie had only suffered a small number of defeats in over 70 contests at the time. Although he was only 23 years old at the time he fought Billy, the Chicago based middleweight had an impressive resume and had crammed an awful lot of fights into a seven and a half year professional career, and it wasn't often he came out on the short end of a fight.

Mike O'Dowd, "The Fighting Harp", was a rugged, aggressive, slugging type who wore his opponents down with a steady pounding.[39] Two and a half years later he knocked out Al McCoy to capture the world middleweight title and become Minnesota's first world champion. Mike was approximately a year younger than Billy, and was an outstanding football and baseball player. But like Billy, Mike was drawn to the boxing game, and began his professional career in February of 1914 in Superior, Wisconsin. He won his first eight bouts in Wisconsin before dropping a newspaper decision to Willie Schaeffer, and then defeated both Walter Monaghan and "Stockyards" Tommy Murphy.

---

36 *Philadelphia Public Register*, Greb and Miske Draw. January 13, 1915.
37 *St. Paul Pioneer Press*, Miske and Snider Home. Early November 1915.
38 *Philadelphia Public Register*, unknown article title. January 17, 1915.
39 Blair, George, *Mike "The Harp" O'Dowd. World Middleweight Champion*. Privately published, no date.

Once Billy returned to the Midwest there was quite a bit of interest in matching the two rising stars. Although Billy had a great advantage in reach over the smaller man, O'Dowd's supporters pointed to his recent performance against the middleweight Tommy Murphy and believed Mike's punch, superior speed and footwork would offset the advantage, and when Billy consented to make 158 pounds by 3 p.m. on the day of the fight, promoter Mike Collins scheduled a ten-round match to take place in Hudson, Wisconsin between the pair on April 6.[40] O'Dowd was expected to come in at 152 pounds.[41]

Each man had a number of loyal followers and there were a lot of bets placed at even money on one or the other. The match attracted as much interest as any bout staged in Hudson, drawing a crowd of approximately 3,500, but some said it should have never taken place, Billy's physical advantages being too great for Mike. The two fighters had been friendly once, having trained together for several months early in their careers, but reportedly had a falling out as a result of a heated sparring session. Still, it's likely they would never have fought one another if it hadn't been for the pleading of their respective friends.[42]

When they came together in the ring Billy towered head and shoulders over Mike.[43] It was also estimated he may have outweighed Mike by as many as eight pounds.[44] At least one other report had Billy at 158 pounds to Mike's 155.

The first two rounds were relatively even, but in the third session O'Dowd tired of the long left he found continually in his face and started rushing Billy. O'Dowd's rushes were met with numerous blows to the jaw, and for the next three rounds Billy took the lead, opening a cut to Mike's eye and drawing a stream of blood from his nose. He had Mike groggy several times.[45]

Mike reversed the tide in the seventh and eighth rounds, opening an old cut over Billy's eye that seemed to greatly bother him.[46] But Billy came on strong in the ninth round and landed a right uppercut which caused Mike to wince. The bell saved Mike at the end of the round.[47] The tenth and final round found both men swinging wildly, trying for a knockout, but they were badly tired, and when the bell sounded they fell into the others arms, and hugged each other, Billy kissing Mike on the cheek.[48]

---

40 Blair, George, *Mike "The Harp" O'Dowd. World Middleweight Champion*. Privately published, no date.
41 *St. Paul Pioneer Press*. Miske – O'Dowd Bout Causes Great Interest. March 1915.
42 *Minneapolis News*, Dillon and Miske Win Battles in Hudson Ring. April 7, 1915.
43 *St. Paul Pioneer Press*, Welters Fight Hard. April 7, 1915.
44 *Minneapolis News*, Dillon and Miske Win Battles in Hudson Ring. April 7, 1915.
45 *Minneapolis Journal*, Miske Trims O'Dowd. April 7, 1915.
46 *St. Paul Pioneer Press*, Welters Fight Hard. April 7, 1915.
47 *Minneapolis Journal*, Miske Trims O'Dowd. April 7, 1915.
48 *Minneapolis Tribune*, Billy Miske Defeats Mike O'Dowd in Terrific Opening Bout. April 7, 1915.

Billy was awarded the decision, winning six of the ten rounds, three going to Mike, and one being even.[49] The fight had lived up to its advance billing, a good fight all the way, but once again proved the old adage that a good big man can usually beat a good little man.[50]

O'Dowd's boxing career continued until 1923, after which time he became a partner in a coin-operated phonograph-machine franchise. In 1936 he purchased a large nightclub in the heart of downtown St. Paul and operated the business until 1955 when he sold it and retired. He passed away in 1957 at the age of 62, a short time after suffering a serious heart attack.[51]

After Billy's victory over O'Dowd, Smith began lobbying for a ten-round rematch with Tommy Gibbons, and in the meantime arranged for Billy to meet George "Knockout" Brown in Platteville, Wisconsin thinking a victory over the tough Chicago middleweight would strengthen Billy's case for another meeting with Gibbons. Brown, whose real name was George Contas, was a left-handed fighter, and one of the earliest successful southpaws in boxing history. Left-handed fighters present a challenge for most right-handed fighters because everything is backward from what they are used to, i.e., they fight with their right foot forward, and jab with their right hand rather than their left. All of a left hander's punches come from the opposite direction than which a fighter is trained to look for. The term "southpaw" can be traced back to baseball in the 1880's when baseball diamonds were normally set up so the batters would face east, to avoid looking into the afternoon sun. The pitcher's left hand, or paw, would thus be on the south side of the diamond, therefore the term "southpaw".[52]

While the *Racine Journal* reported the April 27 meeting between Brown and Billy a draw,[53] the *St. Paul Pioneer Press* named Billy the winner of seven rounds, the other three being even. "Miske landed the heavier blows and showed great cleverness," and "did all the leading and landed some heavy jolts, especially in the early rounds, but Brown soon learned to clinch when Miske started fast milling and saved himself a worse beating," they reported.[54] Smith returned to Minnesota with newspaper clippings stating the Platteville fans liked Billy and his style, and was given five of the ten rounds, with four judged even.[55]

On May 24, 1915 a "sneak" fight took place at Matt Dietsch's hall in St. Paul that resulted in the death of one of the participants, a 19-year old St. Paul native by the name of John Simmer. Simmer's foe was named John Neu. Two days after the death it was reported that in addition to Neu, who

---

49 *St. Paul Pioneer Press*, Welters Fight Hard. April 7, 1915.
50 *Minneapolis News*, Dillon and Miske Win Battles in Hudson Ring. April 7, 1915.
51 Blair, George, *Mike "The Harp" O'Dowd. World Middleweight Champion*. Privately published, no date.
52 *Fightbeat/Fighterworld*, Southpaws: Doing It Right The Wrong Way, May 2005 by Monte Cox.
53 *Racine Journal*, Miske and K.O. Brown in Draw at Platteville. April 29, 1915.
54 *St. Paul Pioneer Press*, Miske Wins From Knockout Brown. April 29, 1915.
55 *Minneapolis Tribune*, Coburn's Column, May 4, 1915.

was being held without bail pending an investigation of a grand jury, eight other parties, including Billy had been placed under arrest. The eight were all said to be connected in some way with the management of the fight, and were charged with aiding and abetting a prize fight contrary to law. In addition to Billy, the eight included Eddy Reddy, the former manager of the Gibbons brothers and the referee for this fight, the promoter P.J. Deitsch, Adam Neu, F.C. Schaaf, Joseph Bauer, Walter Nelson, Hugh McFayden and J.C. Cusick. They were released on bail in the amount of $25 until their court appearance.

The police initially received information the fight was arranged to settle a grudge and it was understood one of the two men would be knocked out. Simmer's brother, George, said his brother had been allowed to remain unconscious on the floor for 30 minutes before any attempt was made to get any medical aid. It was a brutal fight and his brother was groggy and helpless in the fifth round, when he was compelled to continue so Neu would have the chance to deliver his knockout blow. Neu denied it was a grudge match, and said he would never put on the gloves again.[56] He never did.

While the grand jury continued its investigation, five of the men, including Billy, pleaded guilty to the charge of aiding and conducting the prize fight on May 28.[57] On May 31 the *Minneapolis Tribune* reported that since prize fighting was legalized by the last session of the state legislature the death could not be placed in the category of a crime.[58] During the course of their investigation the grand jury subpoenaed 20 witnesses and ultimately ruled an accidental fall had been the cause of death. All the witnesses testified the fatal blow hadn't occurred from the fist of John Neu, but rather from Simmer's head hitting the floor when he fell.[59] Billy and the others involved were ordered to pay a fine of $25 each and subsequently released.[60] Reddy's involvement in the incident didn't prevent his appointment as matchmaker for the St. Paul Athletic Club on June 22. [61]

Billy received his much desired opportunity to even the score with Tommy Gibbons in a ten-round event when matchmaker Jack Reddy headlined the pair in the first legal fight card in Minnesota in 23 years under the recently approved boxing bill. The fight was scheduled to take place on July 12 of 1915 in the St. Paul Auditorium, and was sponsored by the Capital City Athletic club. The event was promoted by Mike Collins, the first man to obtain a promoters license in the state after boxing was legalized there. Mike Gibbons was initially offered the opportunity to head the card in honor of the recognition the city had received as a result of his

---

56 *Minneapolis Tribune*, Nine Arrested Following Death of Prize Fighter, May 26, 1915.
57 *Minneapolis Tribune*, Five Plead Guilty in Fatal Boxing Match Case, May 29, 1915.
58 *Minneapolis Tribune*, Spirit of the Press, May 31, 1915.
59 *Minneapolis Tribune*, Fighter's Death Held Accidental by Jury, June 2, 1915.
60 *Minneapolis Tribune*, Boxer Match Injury Ends With Fines Imposed On Seven, June 4, 1915.
61 *Minneapolis Tribune*, Eddy Reddy Will Be Matchmaker for the St. Paul Boxing Club, June 22, 1915.

boxing skills, but he had to decline since he was still nursing injuries suffered in a recent bout with Leo Houck.[62]

It was agreed the contestants would weigh in under a limit of 163 pounds at 3 o'clock on the date of the match. The Auditorium had a seating capacity of 7,000 and ticket prices were set from $1 to $5. Ticket sales didn't live up to expectations. The evening's entertainment drew a total of approximately 3,800 fans, resulting in total receipts of $5,706.10, out of which Tommy received $1,526.50 and Billy $1,000.

Once again Billy found himself on the short end of the newspaper decisions from the reporters at ringside. The *Evening Tribune* reported Tommy "easily outpointed" Billy,[63] while the *St. Paul Pioneer Press* said "Tommy easily and decisively out boxed and outfought Billy." They noted Billy was game, took the punishment "unflinchingly," kept coming in for more and tried his best to land his heavy right, to no avail except a few times. Their writer felt Tommy might have been able to put Billy away in the eighth or ninth rounds if he had desired to do so, but chose to coast after building up a big lead on points.[64]

There was certainly no shame in losing to Tommy. "Battling" Levinsky, a man who had over 280 fights in his own professional career, said in terms of boxing ability only, he rated Tommy Gibbons as the best man he ever met, and a master at rolling with punches to avoid getting hurt. He also maintained Tommy was the quickest thinker he ever boxed, and said when he saw an opening he didn't lose an instant in shooting for it.[65]

Billy resumed action a month-and-half later in Dubuque, Iowa in a rematch with Gus Christie. The *Racine Journal* reported the contest as a decisive victory for Christie, saying he took seven of the ten rounds, boxed better than ever, and had Billy all but out within eight rounds.[66] A Minnesota paper reported it a draw, and said if there was a shade in the bout it was in Billy's favor, as he showed all kinds of cleverness in covering up and blocking Christie's bull rushes, while displaying a powerful left.[67]

Jack Lester was Billy's next opponent. Lester, born John Jubeck, was a Polish-American who stood approximately 5'9" to 5'10" tall and weighed in the 185 to 190 pound range. A one-time protégé of former heavyweight champion Tommy Burns, Lester was a rugged fighter who had faced some of the better men in the game including the likes of Billy Papke, Sam Langford, Sam McVea, and Jack Dillon among a number of others.

Despite the impressive list of opponents on his resume, Lester appeared badly overmatched on September 10 at the St. Paul Auditorium, where he was knocked out. Billy floored Lester a total of five times, the last one

---

62 *St. Paul Pioneer Press*, Tom Gibbons to Meet Bill Miske in Opening Card. July 1915.
63 *Evening Tribune*, Big Crowd Sees Boxing. July 13, 1915.
64 *St. Paul Pioneer Press*, T. Gibbons Wins Over Bill Miske. July 13, 1915.
65 *Washington Post*, Great Fighter Finds Smiles Most Effective. April 15, 1928.
66 *Racine Journal*, Gus Christie Wins Over Bill Miske of St. Paul. August 25, 1915.
67 *Unknown Minnesota newspaper*, Christie – Miske Battle is a Draw. August 25, 1915.

occurring about a minute into the second round and resulting in the latter being counted out.

The state boxing commission was convinced Lester had laid down for the fight and ended up barring him from any further bouts in the state. His $225 purse was also withheld and donated to a state charity. There were some reports of side betting on the fight, so the commission also quizzed Billy and his manager, Pearl Smith, but ruled Billy had no awareness of any wrongdoing on Lester's part and had expected a tough fight.[68]

On October 15, 1915, Billy married a local St. Paul girl, named Marie Przyblek[69], in a private ceremony at St. Adalbert's Catholic Church. Marie, who was born in Poland, immigrated to the United States with her parents in 1912. She was a singer and actress when she met Billy, had a beautiful voice and Billy always received great pleasure in listening to her sing.[70] She was an energetic and feisty individual and stood approximately 5'4" tall, with wonderful soft skin, and an infectious smile. She described the courtship between herself and Billy as a romance out of a storybook and fondly remembered her excitement and the butterflies which would form in her stomach whenever she saw the young man she later described as a kind and generous gentleman.[71]

While Marie was Catholic, a special dispensation had to be obtained by the couple to be married in the church rectory since Billy was Lutheran.[72] It was announced the new couple would embark on a honeymoon trip to Chicago and up the great lakes of Eastern Canada, and then return to St. Paul to reside with Billy's parents at 758 Blair Street. They planned to purchase a cottage the following spring.[73]

Undoubtedly a little rusty after returning from his honeymoon, Billy immediately embarked upon a trip to Winnipeg, Manitoba in Canada to face veteran middleweight George "Knockout" Brown in a 12-round go. The two men failed to make much of an impression upon the Winnipeg fight fans who had anticipated a spirited performance. It was only after the pair was threatened with the withholding of payment if they didn't mix it up, that the action increased over the last three rounds. The local press called the bout a draw, and said as a boxing match Miske might be given a shade, while as a fight Brown deserved the honors.[74]

A month later, on December 3, 1915, Billy's manager matched him with light-heavyweight Terry Kellar for ten-rounds before the Twin Ports Fight club at the Superior, Wisconsin Opera House. The event marked Billy's

---

68 *Minneapolis Tribune, Boxing Bosses Make Ertle Sure Champ*, September 15, 1915.
69 Last name spelling from Billy and Marie's marriage certificate.
70 Blair, George, *Billy Miske, The St. Paul Thunderbolt*, Privately published, 1988.
71 January 10, 2010 phone interview with Billy Miske's grandson, Robert Booth.
72 Email from Bill Miske, Billy Miske's grandson.
73 *St. Paul Pioneer Press*, Miske to Sign Life Contract. October 1915.
74 *Manitoba Free Press*, Middleweight Battlers Fail to Make Impression Upon Winnipeg Fans. November 2, 1915.

transition from middleweight to light-heavyweight as his body continued to mature and it had become too difficult for him to make the middleweight limit.[75] The two men agreed to weigh in at 168 pounds at 3 o'clock on the day of the match.

Billy earned a close newspaper decision over Kellar. In the sixth round he landed several hard left hooks to Kellar's jaw, and had him hanging on for the last half of the round, coming very close to knocking him out. But Kellar weathered the storm and actually came back to win the ninth round. In the tenth and last round both men stood toe to toe slugging it out while the crowd yelled their approval. At the end of the fight Kellar patted Billy on the head and said, "You're some kid, believe me." Billy grinned and replied, "And you're the toughest scrapper I've ever met."[76]

Two weeks later Billy Hoke, the matchmaker of the Minneapolis Boxing club, found himself in a bind when a fighter named Fred Lang injured himself and was unable to fight Jack Clements on December 17. Miske agreed to take Lang's place in the 10-round event and would enter the ring weighing 172 pounds to Clements' 178. It was an unfortunate turn of events for Clements, who had only two previous professional bouts.

Billy provided a lackluster performance over the first five rounds of the bout, but began to pick up the pace in the sixth round. The bell saved Clements in the seventh frame, and Billy put him away with a right to the jaw the first minute of the eighth round.[77] The referee, George Barton, didn't even bother to count when Clements went down, and just motioned for Clements seconds to come to the aid of their man. Clements displayed his gameness, but was no match for Billy in any department in the opinion of Fred Coburn of the *Minneapolis Tribune*.[78]

Billy concluded 1915 with a second round knockout of an Indiana fighter named Frank Hoe before the Marshfield Athletic Club in Marshfield, Wisconsin. It was a scheduled ten-round contest, but an aggressive Hoe was knocked to the canvas twice in the first round, and Billy finished him off in the second round with a right to the jaw, followed by a body shot, and a left to the chin.[79]

Overall, 1915 had been a relatively successful year for the young fighter and his successes in the light heavyweight class foretold of a bright future. There were serious discussions underway concerning the possibility of a match for Billy with the king of the light heavyweights, Indiana's giant killer, Jack Dillon.

---

75 *St. Paul Pioneer Press*, Miske is Matched to Fight Kellar. November 1915.
76 *St. Paul Pioneer Press*, Miske Earns Shade Over Kellar in Slashing Match. December 4, 1915.
77 *St. Paul Pioneer Press*, Billy Miske Stops Clements in Eighth. December 18, 1915.
78 *Minneapolis Tribune*, Matt Brock's Whirlwind Finish Earns Him a Draw With Miller, December 18, 1915.
79 *St. Paul Pioneer Press*, Hoe Takes Count In Second Round With Billy Miske. December 29, 1915.

CHAPTER 3

Jack Dillon and "Battling" Levinsky

By 1916, Billy had made a name for himself in the ring. That was the year he first faced two light-heavyweight legends in Jack Dillon and "Battling" Levinsky.

Although not universally recognized, Jack Dillon, who was known as "the giant killer," was generally acknowledged as the light-heavyweight champion of the world in January of 1916. As a result, when his manager Pearl Smith matched Billy to fight Dillon on January 28 in Superior, Wisconsin, and the articles stipulated the men weigh in at 175 pounds at 3 o'clock the afternoon of the fight, many believed he'd badly mismatched his man.[80]

But, confidence was one of Billy's greatest assets, and Smith had a very strong belief in him as well. In reply to his critics Smith said:

> You have to meet these tough ones some time. Miske is going good right now, can take the punishment if he has to, and is hitting pretty hard himself. I know Bill is going to have a tough battle but I also am positive he will be there when the tenth rolls around and these scoffers will give Miske the credit he should receive.[81]

Smith had carefully reviewed Dillon's record and the results of his matches with a number of opponents he and Billy had in common such as George "Knockout" Brown, Gus Christie, George Ashe, Ralph Erne and Jack Lester. He compared the results of Dillon's fights against these men to Billy's, and the findings only increased his confidence in Billy.

Jack Dillon, was born Ernest Cutler Price, in Frankfort, Indiana on February 2, 1891. As a young teenager he was fond of horses and began to visit the Maywood Stock Farm located a short distance from his home. The owner, Sterling Holt, took a liking to the boy and allowed him to work there performing menial tasks. The farm was the home of a beautiful stallion Ernest admired named Sidney Dillon. He dreamed of one day owning a stable of his own thoroughbreds.

There were a number of men employed on the farm, and in their spare time they used to put on boxing gloves and have informal matches among themselves. Though just a youngster, Ernest had a strong build, and was invited to participate. He turned out to be a natural and, by age 15, was the

---

80 *Lincoln Daily Star*, Dillon is Matched to Meet Billy Miske. January 15, 1916.
81 *St. Paul Pioneer Press*, Miske's Manager Says Scoffers To Get Big Surprise. January 1, 1916.

farm champion. One day, 17-year-old Ernest was approached by an Indianapolis based fight promoter and offered $20 to fight a preliminary bout on April 18 of 1908. He accepted and on the day of the fight when the referee asked him his name he replied, "Sidney Dillon." Somehow the referee bungled the first name and when the young fighter was announced to the crowd it was as Jack Dillon of Indianapolis. He fought under the name from then on.[82]

By January of 1916, the 25-year-old "Hoosier Bearcat," as Dillon was also known, had already engaged in at least 172 professional fights. Standing 5'7" he began his career as a lightweight, before moving up to the middleweight division where he terrorized the weight class for many years. Eventually, it became too difficult for him to make the weight with his muscular frame. He was forced to move into the light-heavyweight ranks. But, Dillon was no stranger to fighting men in the weight class. He'd fought a number of light-heavyweights while only a middleweight himself, his manager finding it difficult to match him with men his own size. In 1969 *The Ring* magazine writers named him the greatest light-heavyweight of all time.[83]

Billy knew he faced the toughest test of his young career when he stepped into the ring with Jack Dillon. The folks who attended the bout in Superior, Wisconsin got the surprise of their life, however, when Billy shaded Dillon in the ten-round event, in the opinion of a majority of newspapermen at ringside.[84]

The *Racine Journal* called the contest a draw, while noting by rounds Billy had a slight shade. They reported that Dillon carried the fighting to Billy, trying mostly for body blows, of which few landed, and Dillon was saved by the bell in the eighth when he was dazed by a rain of blows to the face.[85] Billy also delivered what was later described as the most effective blow of the fight when he landed a right uppercut to the chin in the tenth round and rocked Dillon.[86] Dillon claimed he'd been suffering from an illness and unable to perform at his best.

Billy travelled to Denver next for a match on February 29 with "Fighting" Dick Gilbert. Gilbert, who had been campaigning as a professional since 1909 didn't enjoy a particularly distinguished career, but he fought and lost to many of the top men of his era including the likes of "Battling" Levinsky, Jack Dillon, "Gunboat" Smith and Jack Dempsey. The Denver media was impressed with Billy's physique and his personality, noting his face usually featured a big smile, and he wasn't a big brainless

---

[82] Bearcat of the Ring, *Fight Stories*, 1931 by Tom O'Neill, pages 41-74.
[83] *The Ring*, The Ring All-Time Greats, March 1969, pages 42 & 78.
[84] *Eau Claire Leader*, Billy Miske Returned Winner Over Jack Dillon at Superior. January 29, 1916.
[85] *Racine Journal*, Dillon Gets Draw With Billy Miske. January 29, 1916.
[86] *Denver Post*, Gilbert Meets Tough Gent When He Boxes With Miske. February 20, 1916.

brute as so many fighters were pictured.[87] They held him up as an example of clean living.[88]

Billy weighed 173 pounds for the fight, while Gilbert appeared to be close to 180. Billy pounded on Gilbert for 15 rounds and earned a clear cut decision victory, the *Denver Post* describing him as a "well pastured colt as he stepped around the ring at the National Athletic club."[89] Gilbert continued to fight for another three years before hanging up the gloves. He ultimately enjoyed a fair amount of success as an actor, appearing in 52 films from 1921 to 1951, as well as a number of Laurel and Hardy and Our Gang television series comedies. He passed away on May 6, 1960 at the age of 70.

Billy enjoyed a well-earned rest for the next couple of weeks but then began training for a rematch with Jack Dillon, to take place in Minneapolis on April 14. When the month of April arrived the local fight fans were excitedly anticipating the matchup. Dillon reiterated the stance he had taken after their first bout, once again claiming he'd been in poor shape, and he had underestimated Billy. The fact he knocked out big heavyweight Tom Cowler in two rounds in New York only two days after the first bout with Billy didn't help his case, though. Dillon hoped to earn a more lucrative match with either Mike Gibbons or Frank Moran should he decisively defeat Billy. Many people at the time were of the belief Dillon could defeat any of the heavyweights in action at the time, with the exception of the champion, Jess Willard.[90]

Dillon's manager, Sam Marburger, promised a victory for his man over Billy. "Jack was a sick man when he met Miske at Superior," said Sam, "and when we get into the ring with him on the 14th Mr. Miske is going to see an altogether different boxer than the one he met in Wisconsin a few months ago. Dillon was ill and underestimated his man. He will defeat Billy just as sure as he lives, and then watch us get Mike Gibbons and either make him meet us or get out of the boxing business."

Marburger went on to say Miske was one of the best men Dillon had ever boxed, but said he was willing to bet $1,000 Dillon would stop Billy this time. Told of this, Billy's manager, Pearl Smith, responded, "Every man has got to meet his master, and Dillon's master is William Miske of St. Paul."[91]

But, Jack Dillon turned the tables on Billy on April 14, 1916 before the hometown fans, easily outpointing Billy over ten rounds, and winning a popular newspaper decision. The bout was described as tame throughout with a lot of clinching, where the two men repeatedly held one or both arms

---

87 *Denver Post*. Billy Miske Executes Ten Miles of Arduous Rock Work. February 27, 1916.
88 *Denver Post*, Miske Tackles Dick Gilbert Tomorrow Evening at N.A.C. February 28, 1916.
89 *Denver Post*, Miske Wins From Gilbert in Thrilling Battle at N.A.C. March 1, 1916.
90 *Minneapolis Tribune*, Dillon Says He Will Knock Out Moran if Bout is Put on Here, April 5, 1916.
91 *Minneapolis Tribune*, Mike Gibbons Says if Jack Dillon Clears His Record He Will Fight Him.

of the other in order to prevent, or hinder their ability to punch the other. Dillon had been the aggressor and landed the cleaner and heavier blows.[92]

Fred Coburn of the *Minneapolis Tribune* called Billy's performance disappointing, and said although Billy was clearly the crowd favorite at the beginning of the fight it wasn't long before the locals were hissing him for his constant clinching tactics. Billy didn't win a round out of the ten in Coburn's opinion and seemed intent only on staying the distance with the rugged Dillon.[93]

Billy had thought Dillon was greatly overrated after their first meeting, but changed his mind after their second bout. "If he would take care of himself, he would be the greatest in the ring," said Billy.[94]

Far from discouraged by the setback, Billy and his manager traveled east, where they spent the next 17 months building Billy's reputation as a coming champion. The campaign began with a ninth-round knockout of Jack Hubbard in Brooklyn, New York on June 22 at the Clermont Avenue Rink.[95] Although he was game, Hubbard was knocked to the canvas for a count of nine twice in the first round, and another long count in the eighth session, before Billy put him down for good in the ninth round with a right hand blow to the pit of the stomach.[96]

This was followed by a ten-round bout against a classy middleweight named Johnny Howard. Howard, whose real name was Tkac, was born in Bayonne, New Jersey on February 1, 1893. He got his professional start as a 19-year-old teenager with a four round victory over Mike Lynch. Over the course of the next 10 years, he averaged a fight a month and boxed against some of the greatest fighters of that era, including Harry Greb, Jack Dillon and Leo Houck, among others. On May 5th of 1914, Howard had given Mike Gibbons all he could handle during a ten round contest fought in Brooklyn before the Broadway Sporting Club. Gibbons ultimately defeated Howard, but only by a small margin, and Mike was reportedly very tired at the end of the bout, while Howard appeared relatively fresh.[97] Although Howard was a middleweight, he would often box out of his weight class. In 1917, he lost a 12 round decision to light-heavyweight-champion "Battling" Levinsky. He retired in 1922 after 121 fights and was eventually inducted into the New Jersey Boxing Hall of Fame.[98]

Johnny and Billy fought in Brooklyn at the Clermont on August 31, 1916, and Billy knocked him to the canvas in the third and ninth rounds for counts of nine, before finally delivering the knockout blows in the tenth and

---

92 *Lima Times Democrat,* Jack Dillon Defeats Billy Miske. April 15, 1916.
93 *Minneapolis Tribune,* Dillon Beats Miske But Fight is Disappointing, April 15, 1916.
94 *St. Paul Pioneer Press,* Fighting Billy Miske of St. Paul is the Newest Attraction for the Boxing Fans. November 12, 1916.
95 *Nevada State Journal,* Jack Hubbard Loses to Billy Miske. June 23, 1916.
96 *Brooklyn Daily Eagle,* Frank Moran Will Re-enlist If Uncle Sam Needs Him Again, June 23, 1916.
97 *National Police Gazette,* Mike Gibbons Has Trouble In Beating Johnny Howard, May 23, 1914.
98 New Jersey Boxing Hall of Fame.

final round.[99] Billy followed up with a sixth-round technical knockout of veteran Jim Barry on September 21 in the same venue.[100]

Billy then received an opportunity to fight another great light-heavyweight named "Battling" Levinsky. Levinsky, born Barney Lebrowitz, began his career fighting under the name Barney Williams. He was born in Philadelphia, Pennsylvania on June 10, 1891, four months after Jack Dillon. Levinsky stood 5'11" tall and while his career didn't begin quite as early as Dillon's, he started boxing professionally in February of 1910. Like Dillon, he fought often, participating in at least 175 bouts, an incredible average of 25 fights per year over the first seven years of his career! He would go on to have nearly 300 official professional fights before he hung up his gloves after a career spanning twenty years. Famed *The Ring* magazine editor and founder Nat Fleischer rated Levinsky the sixth greatest light-heavyweight of all time.[101]

When Billy and Levinsky met at the Clermont in Brooklyn on October 12 of 1916, Levinsky and Dillon had already fought each another nine times over a five-year period. While Dillon held a decided advantage in the series, Levinsky had finally broken through and won a 10-round newspaper decision over him in July of that year. The pair fought a draw two months later, and some folks began mentioning Levinsky as a possible challenger for Jess Willard's heavyweight title.

While Levinsky lacked Dillon's punch, he was generally thought of as one of the cleverest fighters in the game, and was typically the aggressor in most of his contests. But he met his match when he faced Billy for the first time on October 12. Billy weighed in at 178 pounds, while Levinsky came in at 180.[102] The two men started slowly, feeling one another out, and there was little action in the first round. But toward the end of the second round, Billy landed a heavy right to Levinsky's jaw and did all the leading thereafter.

Billy shook Levinsky up with heavy rights to the head in the fifth and made his knees sag in the ninth when he caught him with another heavy blow flush on the chin. Levinsky tried to rally in the tenth and final session, but Billy "gave as good as he got," and clearly earned the honors. The crowd was well pleased by the action and the management immediately matched the pair to meet again two weeks later.

In the meantime, Levinsky and Dillon fought for Dillon's light-heavyweight title on October 24 in Boston, Massachusetts. Levinsky came away with the decision and was acknowledged as the new light-heavyweight

---

99 *Philadelphia Press*, Billy Miske Stops Howard. September 1, 1916.
100 *Milwaukee Free Press*, Miske Stops Barry. September 23, 1916.
101 Fleischer, Nat, *50 Years at Ringside*, Fleet Publishing Corporation, New York, 1958.
102 *Brooklyn Daily Eagle*, Boxing News. October 13, 1916.

champion of the world. Since he was already under contract to face Billy again only six days later, he had no real choice but to go through with it.[103]

The two resumed hostilities in the same venue on October 30 and once again Billy dominated the fight. "(Levinsky) met his master in every department of the game and was outclassed in practically every one of the ten rounds."[104] The *Brooklyn Daily Eagle* said Billy was unquestionably a comer, and wasn't only clever, but carried a punch in either hand.

Levinsky put one over on Billy near the end of the fight, but Billy didn't realize it until he had returned to his dressing room. In the ninth round, Billy hurt Levinsky badly, and he realized how weak the latter was when they clinched. But, the bell rang to end the round before he could do anything about it.

When the tenth round began Billy rushed across the ring and Levinsky began to laugh as he fell into another clinch. When they broke, Levinsky was laughing so hard he dropped his hands to his side.

Billy wondered what was so funny. The first thought which went through his mind was perhaps there was something wrong with his trunks, and when the spectators began laughing as well he was afraid he was the goat. So, the next thing he knew he was laughing along with everyone else. He didn't know why, but he didn't want anyone to think there was a joke going on and he was slow to see it. So, he let Levinsky laugh his way through the round. Then, Levinsky laughed for real, because he knew his plan had worked and he was able to last the round.[105]

Although Billy had clearly won the fight, and Levinsky, himself acknowledged it was the case, it didn't affect the title, because it was officially considered a no-decision bout.[106] Billy had to be content with the knowledge he had just defeated the light heavyweight champion of the world.

Ten days later, Billy stopped Tim O'Neil in the sixth round when the latter's seconds threw in the sponge after O'Neil was floored for the second time in the round.[107] Jack Dillon had failed to stop O'Neil within the distance only three weeks earlier.

On November 12 of 1916, an interesting article appeared in the *St. Paul Pioneer Press* about Billy, courtesy of one Robert Ripley. The following is an excerpt from the article by Ripley, who later achieved worldwide fame for his '*Believe It or Not!*' newspaper panel series, radio and television shows featuring odd facts:

> My oh my! What a mean trick this young St. Paul gentleman played on "Battling" Levinsky. The famous perpetual mitt mixer of Dan

---

103 *Washington Post*, Great Fighter Finds Smiles Most Effective. April 15, 1928.
104 *Brooklyn Daily Eagle*, Billy Miske Again Defeats Levinsky. October 31, 1916.
105 *Des Moines Register*, Miske Unable to Box For Few Weeks. February 11, 1917.
106 *Washington Post*, Great Fighter Finds Smiles Most Effective. April 15, 1928.
107 *New Castle News*, Billy Miske Stops O'Neil. November 10, 1916.

Morgan's has been working and fighting almost every day for years making a "rep" for himself. He even goes out and whips Jack Dillon to a referee's decision. Everyone is a-talking of a Willard-Levinsky match. And just as the noted Hebrew battler is about to hook up with the big champion for the big battle that means so much glory and $$$, why along comes this mischievous Miske and gives him the whipping of his life.[108]

On November 17, Billy continued his winning ways, earning a newspaper decision over rough "Caveman" Bob Moha before the Broadway Club of Brooklyn. Prior to the match, Billy admitted he wasn't fond of the idea of meeting Moha, but said he preferred to take his chances against him in the ring rather than suffer from a suspension by the Boxing Commission for avoiding him. Billy wasn't the only fighter who didn't relish the idea of facing Moha at the time. According to Hyatt Daab of New York's *Evening Telegram*, "He is so good that ducking matches with the "Caveman" has become one of the most popular pugilistic pastimes." Moha's manager, Pat Callaghan, felt Miske would be an ideal opponent for his fighter.[109]

Moha, born as Robert Mucha in 1889, was only 5'4" to 5'5" tall but very stocky and muscular with a broad back and deep chest. In fact, his short height and build reminded some of the original Joe Walcott, "The Barbados Demon," and they took to referring to him as "The White Walcott." Bob was a Milwaukee-based fighter who had been fighting professionally for ten years and held his own with many of the top middleweights and light-heavyweights of his era. Gus Christie, who was no slouch in the ring himself, said Moha was the best man of his inches he ever met.[110]

Bob's resume included victories over the likes of former middleweight champion Billy Papke, "Battling" Levinsky, Mike "Twin" Sullivan, Gus Christie, and "Cyclone" Johnny Thompson, among others, and he'd fought and lost to some of the best in the business including Jack Dillon, Harry Greb and the Gibbons brothers.

Billy won every round of the ten-round contest and Moha "held like a leach" in the final frame to avoid a knockout.[111] He was better at infighting and his longer reach allowed him to land solid punches to Moha's head.[112] Billy weighed 171 pounds to Moha's 167. New York fight fans were singing his praises.

---

108 *St. Paul Pioneer Press*, Fighting Billy Miske of St. Paul is the Newest Attraction for the Boxing Fans. November 12, 1916.
109 *Evening Telegram*, Moha Battles Miske at Broadway Tonight. November 17, 1916.
110 *Milwaukee Journal*, Gus Christie's Quarter Century of Service Recognized by Club, February 20, 1944.
111 *Indianapolis Star*, Billy Miske Beats Moha All The Way In Bout. November 18, 1916.
112 *New York Times*. Too Much Miske For Moha, November 18, 1916.

Billy travelled to Philadelphia next where he earned another newspaper decision victory over Larry Williams on November 27 in a short six-round bout, knocking Williams down in the second and fourth frames. Williams was forced to hang on to Billy in order to avoid suffering a knockout.[113]

On December 13th, the *Minneapolis Tribune* reported that Frank Tyrell, the recently appointed matchmaker for the Twin City Boxing club, hoped to sign Billy for three fights before Minneapolis and St. Paul fans, his opponents to include Frank Moran, Tommy Gibbons, and either Fred Fulton or Carl Morris. If he was able to get Billy's name on a contract, he hoped to secure Frank Moran for a match with him on January 5 of 1917. "Miske is one of the best heavyweights in the game and I feel sure he can give Moran all he wants. I want Miske to fight Moran, then Tom Gibbons and then Fulton, if Fulton cares to. If not, we'll try Carl Morris," said Tyrell. "Miske is a vastly improved fighter and is almost big enough now to meet any of the heavyweights," he added.[114]

A day later, on December 14, John P. Dunn, announcer for the Brooklyn's Broadway Sporting club advised that a match had been made between Billy and Jack Dillon to take place on December 19. While Dillon had suffered defeats to Levinsky (twice) and Mike Gibbons since his last meeting with Billy, he'd also put an end to all the talk about Frank Moran challenging for Jess Willard's title when he clearly out-boxed the slower heavyweight in late June.

When Billy and Dillon stepped between the ropes on December 19, Billy weighed 174 pounds to Dillon's 173 ¼ pounds. Afterward, some thought Billy had earned a narrow victory, while just as many thought Dillon deserved a draw. The New York fight fans who had witnessed Dillon's dismantling of Frank Moran were extremely impressed with Billy's fighting abilities. It was the first time they'd seen Dillon really punished and the first time they'd seen him back up against an opponent. It was only Dillon's furious rally in the final round that turned a certain loss into a possible draw.[115]

The *New York Times* gave the verdict to Billy, albeit by the slightest margin. Although their reporter felt Dillon tried his best, he felt Billy's height and reach put Jack at a disadvantage, and Billy's cleverness, and the fact he had landed the cleaner and more effective punches throughout the fight, earned him the victory.[116]

As the year came to a close, Billy's star shone bright as evidenced by the following newspaper quote on December 31:

> From the collection of scrappers who crowded into the spotlights of fame during the closing days of 1916 none stands out more

---

113 *Indianapolis Star*, Billy Miske Twice Puts Williams To The Floor. November 28, 1916.
114 *Minneapolis Tribune*, New Matchmaker Would Sign Billy Miske for Three Bouts, December 13, 1916.
115 *Fort Wayne News*, Make Room for Mr. Miske. December 30, 1916.
116 *New York Times*. Miske Just Beats Dillon, December 20, 1916.

prominently or holds greater promise for the future than Billy Miske. Miske became a fistic celebrity as the result of four notable battles, two with the highly touted "Battling" Levinsky, the third against Bob Moha, and the fourth against Dillon and in each encounter the St. Paul boxer was universally accorded the popular verdict.[117]

Yes, still only 22 years old, the future looked extremely promising for Billy Miske and his young wife, Marie, who was over eight months pregnant with the couple's first child.

---

117 *Lincoln Daily Star,* Boxing Bouts This Week. December 31, 1916.

CHAPTER 4

Injured Left Hand

Billy's first real health issues began to appear as early as 1915 or 1916. At various times in those years, he suffered from inflammation and stiffness in his hips, and it seemed as though the attacks would occur at the most inopportune time. He had blamed it on rheumatism,[118] a common problem and a catch-all term of the day used to describe any disorder or stiffness of the connective tissue structures of the body, especially those in the back or the extremities. But the attacks eventually stopped and he showed what he could do when he was in good health.

When the year 1917 rolled in, Billy was riding high, anticipating another big year professionally and anxiously awaiting the birth of the couple's first child. He was really making a name for himself in his hometown, money was plentiful, and he and Marie were enjoying a wonderful life together that was the envy of much of St. Paul.[119]

Wasting little time getting back into action, Billy climbed through the ropes on New Year's Day to face a familiar foe, George "Knockout" Brown. Brown won the first two rounds, but Billy gave him a beating over the remainder of the fight and easily captured the decision in the view of the ringside fight reporters.[120] It hadn't been as easy as it may have looked though. Brown gave Billy all he could handle early on and had him beat over the first five rounds of the fight. The tide finally turned in Billy's favor once he caught Brown flush on the jaw with a big right. He was disappointed Brown didn't go down and had only been staggered and dazed, but glad he was able to even things up and take the lead from then on.[121] "He was one of the toughest men I ever tackled," said Billy.

Les Darcy, Australia's great middleweight champion had been on hand to witness his first ring contest in America and came away impressed. "Miske is a good, lively scrapper," he said. "He's fast and snappy and uses both hands well. He's in and out, you know what I mean. He fights well both at a distance and in close quarters. I know something of the tough job he had facing Brown for I've fought him twice." Darcy also commented on some differences between the two countries, noting smoking and coaching from the corners was prohibited in Australia, but allowed in the States, and

---

118 *Des Moines Register,* Miske Unable to Box For Few Weeks. February 11, 1917.
119 January 10, 2010 phone interview with Billy Miske's grandson, Robert Booth.
120 *Des Moines Register,* Darcy Sees Miske Wallop K.O. Brown. January 2, 1917.
121 *Lincoln Daily Star,* Feather Champion Proves His Nerve. February 4, 1917.

32

was sure the men in the ring must be weakened by inhaling such a smoke laden atmosphere.[122]

There was talk of the possibility of a match between Billy and the young Australian. John Reisler, a.k.a. "John the Barber," had reportedly offered Darcy $30,000 to take on either Billy or Charley Weinert.[123]

"Knockout" Brown had fought both Billy and Darcy, going twenty rounds on two separate occasions with the latter. He offered his opinion on the possible matchup, saying Billy was the harder hitter, and if they ever met in a ten-round bout he'd bet all he had Billy would outpoint him.[124]

In the meantime, Billy tackled heavyweight Charley Weinert on January 12 at the Harlem Sporting Club in New York. After ten rounds of non-stop action on Billy's part, he earned another decisive newspaper decision, and was lauded for his stamina. Weinert, referred to as the "Jersey Adonis," gave all he had, but had been clearly beaten.[125] Although Weinert enjoyed advantages in height, reach, and weight, the latter by 9 pounds, Billy's aggressive work on the inside was too much for him to contend with. Billy won all but the second, sixth, and ninth rounds, and was the fresher of the two men at the final bell.[126]

The win over Weinert prompted talk of a match against heavyweight Fred Fulton. Although Fulton was much taller and heavier than Billy, the way he'd handled Weinert convinced promoters the match would be competitive.[127]

Four days later, on January 16, Billy met Jack Dillon for a fourth time. They fought a ten-rounder at the Broadway Sporting Club in Brooklyn. Dillon was reportedly in much better shape than he was when the pair had met the previous month. It didn't help though, as Billy outfought Dillon, winning every round except for the seventh, in which Dillon held him even, according to one source.[128]

The *New York Times* gave Billy the edge in the second, fifth, ninth, and tenth rounds, Dillon the first and seventh rounds, and scored the remaining four rounds even. Billy's ability to keep Dillon at a distance, where he continually landed left hand hooks and jabs, and right crosses to Dillon's head, was the key to his victory. The *Times* went on to call Billy the "foremost boxer" of the light-heavyweight division.[129] Billy weighed 175 ½ pounds and Dillon 172. The win proved costly for Billy, though, as he injured his left hand.[130] It troubled him for a number of months afterward.

---

122 *New Castle News*, Darcy Has Praise for Billy Miske. January 2, 1917.
123 *Fort Wayne News*, Les Darcy May Accept Offer. January 4, 1917.
124 *Warren Evening News*, Sport of All Sort. January 9, 1917
125 *New Castle News*, Miske Gets Win From C. Weinert. January 13, 1917.
126 *New York Times*, Miske Wins Fast Bout From Weinert, January 13, 1917.
127 *Portsmouth Daily Times*, Miske Will Meet Fulton. January 15, 1917.
128 *Lowell Sun*, Sporting News. January 19, 1917.
129 *New York Times*. Miske Again Has Better of Dillon, January 17, 1917.
130 *Fort Wayne Journal-Gazette*, Billy Miske Wins From Jack Dillon. January 17, 1917.

The bout was marred by the poor handling of the crowd both outside and inside the club. Demand for ticket reservations far exceeded supply, and many of those who did get past the ticket takers had to scramble to get seats. Many ticket holders were barred from entry and there was so much disorder outside the club that police had to wield clubs to try and maintain order.[131]

Billy's trainer for the Dillon fight, a fellow named Jim Johnson, played an important role in the contest. Billy had suffered a cut above one of his eyes in his previous fight with Weinert and four days between the two fights didn't provide enough time for it to heal. They were sure Dillon would target the cut. So, Johnson purchased tubes of paint and covered the cut so the skin looked good as new. He then painted a fake cut over the other eye and covered with some court plaster. It worked like a charm. Dillon repeatedly knocked the plaster off the fake cut and couldn't understand why he couldn't open the wound. Not until the fight was over did he learn he'd been fooled.[132]

A special correspondent out of New York reported the contest as a draw to the *Minneapolis Tribune* who wrote had the fight gone further Miske might have won decisively, though he looked like a beaten fighter early on. Continued their report:

> The slim St. Paul boy demonstrated that he has as stout a heart as ever pumped steadily through a hard ring battle. Dillon showed the outward marks of the battle. His nose was flattened and there was a deep cut over his left eye. Miske started this with a right in the second round. The eye bothered Dillon more and more as the bout went on.
>
> (Miske) started like a worn out athlete, on the verge of a knockout. But he finished like a whirlwind. The pain of the body blows which were raised on him must have been terrible. Miske's pale face would distort for an instant when the solid blows sank into his vitals. But, immediately, his thin lips would tighten and he would fight back.
>
> He always fought back, sometimes weakly, then vigorously, as his vitality would resume. There was a red spot under his heart at the end.

The Associated Press report out of New York said Billy outfought Dillon and had the better of every round except the seventh, which they said was even. They said Dillon started the fight with a rush, but Billy was too fast for him and frequently beat him to the punch, and proved the better of the two at infighting. They also indicated Billy injured his left hand

---

131 *Evening Telegram*, Miske Again Defeats Jack Dillon In Bout, June 3, 2010.
132 *Lowell Sun*, Sporting News. January 19, 1917.

during the bout and speculated it might cause him to cancel any match he had arranged in the near future. [133]

The *Brooklyn Daily Eagle* reported Billy as the winner and said that in their opinion he defeated Dillon more decisively than he had in their previous contest. He did so because of a big edge in the fifth round and the numerous big right hand blows he landed in the ninth and tenth sessions. He also landed the larger number of clean, calculated punches throughout the contest.

However, the *Eagle* also said Dillon got the better of the infighting and Billy didn't appear as strong as he had against Weinert four days earlier. While praising Billy as one of the most intelligent boxers in the heavier weight classes, they expressed an opinion he looked over-trained and in need of some rest. Their reporter expressed his regret Billy was not large enough to be considered a logical contender for Jess Willard's heavyweight crown.[134]

Billy and his wife had cause for celebration on January 20, 1917, when their first child, William Miske, Jr., was born in a St. Paul hospital. Billy's hand injury and the child's birth prompted Billy to take a long, overdue rest from the ring, and it was reported he wouldn't fight again until the latter part of February. It was a happy time for the family, with Billy finally getting some time to relax. He and his young wife were able to settle in at home with their newborn son.

While Billy enjoyed his brief vacation, longtime New York fight announcer and current matchmaker and general manager of Brooklyn's Broadway Sporting Club, John P. Dunn, sang his praises - calling Billy a second Joe Choynski. Choynski was an outstanding light-heavyweight at the turn of the previous century, and was famous for his battles against the likes of James J. Corbett, Bob Fitzsimmons, James Jeffries and Jack Johnson. He knocked out the latter in 1901, seven years before Johnson became heavyweight champion. Dunn said Billy was built like Joe, had a splendid left hand, good footwork and his right cross followed his jab like a flash. He was also impressed with Billy's willingness to mix it up with his opponent, and the way he fought back when stung. He liked the fact Billy hadn't developed a swollen head as a result of his successes. He felt that once Billy settled down, and learned to fight at intervals he would be the toughest boxer of his weight in the business.[135]

Billy Madden, onetime manager of heavyweight champion John L. Sullivan, piped in as well voicing his opinion Billy was big enough to whip any professional fighter in the world.

---

133 *Minneapolis Tribune*, Miske-Dillon Fight Reports Do Not Agree, January 17, 1917.
134 *Brooklyn Daily Eagle*, Billy Miske's Versatility Is His Strongest Point. January 17, 1917.
135 *New Castle News*, Billy Miske Real Comer. January 30, 1917.

That youngster is one of the best fighters I ever saw and I've seen the best in the game for the last forty-five years, and as for size and weight, Miske is big enough for all purposes. It isn't necessary for a man to weigh more than 175 or 180 pounds in order to whip the best man in the world. These giants like Willard, Fulton and Carl Morris are too big to be first class fighters. Men of that size are naturally slow and get lost against the fast, quick-hitting men of normal size. Miske is very fast and shifty and he delivers his blows with both hands in rapid-fire fashion. He is an ideally built fighting man, and I might say the best I've ever seen.

Madden went on to say that he'd wager on Miske against Willard with all the confidence in the world. "John L. Sullivan, when he was at his best, weighed about 180 pounds. Jim Corbett, when he beat Sullivan at New Orleans weighed exactly 178," said Madden, "and Jack Johnson never was as formidable as when he weighed 185 pounds."[136]

Billy's successes in the ring brought him more attention from the local press as well. The *Minneapolis Tribune* ran a story claiming Billy liked to fight, and his tag, "Fighting Billy Miske," fit him perfectly. According to their story, a certain business manager of a St. Paul newspaper claimed when Billy worked there he supplied him with sparring partners who tested his fighting skill throughout his newspaper career.

According to the newspaperman, though he knew nothing of the art of science of boxing at the time, Billy was said to be a "bear with his dukes" and the newsroom often forced to run one man short for a day or two after these skirmishes as a result of various hurts and bruises suffered at the hands of young Miske. After this had happened more times than the circulations manager cared, he reportedly tried to find a fellow who could lick Billy. But Billy whipped them one by one. The boss didn't want to fire Billy because he was a good worker and he admired his fighting qualities.

He said Billy eventually found work in the railroad shops alongside Mike Gibbons. Hearing of the money Mike was making in "sneak" fights around the Twin Cities Billy decided to try his hand at the game as well. He used to try and attend every fight he could that Mike participated in and as much as possible he tried to emulate Mike's style.[137]

On February 9, Billy and "Battling" Levinsky were matched for a contest to take place in St. Paul on February 27. Both men came into the fight over the light-heavyweight limit, Billy weighing 182 ½ pounds, and Levinsky 188 ½. The two men promised a fight from the opening bell. While Billy forced the fighting most of the time, Levinsky's feigned punches

---

136 *The Telegram*, Medium-Sized Men Are Best Fighters. January 28, 1917.
137 *Minneapolis Tribune*, Here's Boxer Who Enjoys Being in Fight; Billy Miske Just Loves to Be Scrapping, February 11, 1917.

drew him into costly leads. As a result, newspapermen at ringside agreed Levinsky earned a decisive victory.[138]

Once again, the *Minneapolis Tribune* said Billy had produced a disappointing performance. "That he should be a champion in New York and as ordinary a scrapper in his hometown doesn't seem reasonable," wrote Fred Coburn. Though Billy's effort fell short of expectations, Coburn felt Levinsky demonstrated considerable cleverness and proved himself a far better boxer than Billy. The receipts for the contests amounted to slightly over $7,000 and Billy and Levinsky split $4,000 between them.[139]

Local fight fans couldn't help but wonder why Billy had tried to outbox Levinsky. Manager Pearl Smith urged him throughout the contest to fight, not box, but Billy failed to do so until the tenth round. By then Levinsky's lead was too great to overcome.[140] Billy would have been well advised to avoid fighting Levinsky until his injured left hand had fully healed. The damage done to Billy's hand in this fight lead to the cancellation of a planned fight with Gus Christie in March, and prompted Billy to return home to rest for another month while the hand healed.

In late April, Billy traveled east to finish training for another match with Levinsky on May 1, and made a side trip to a hospital to have his hand examined. The doctor took an x-ray of the injured appendage and said, "It's badly broken," as he shared the result with Billy. Crestfallen, Billy had no choice but to return to St. Paul and give the hand time to heal. He figured the injury ended up costing him as much as $15,000 in lost wages.[141] While recovering, Billy and his family spent the next couple of months thawing out from another Minnesota winter in their two-story cottage that sat on a steep slope along the shore of Lake Johanna.

It was during this period of time that any hope of a lucrative match with Les Darcy vanished. Tragically, the 21-year-old from Australia passed away on May 24, 1917. Officially, the cause of death was listed as pneumonia, but some said it was really from a broken heart over the treatment he received from the press back home.

After all his success in Australia, the young man had come to America in search of a world championship, but the circumstances surrounding his departure from Australia led to a failure to obtain a single match in America. Australia was at war and in 1916, when Darcy was becoming famous for his work as a boxer the war in Europe was raging. There was tremendous pressure put upon young Australian men to enlist.

At the same time, Darcy was receiving offers of big money to fight in America. Jack Kearns, who became Jack Dempsey's manager, tried to

---

138 *Des Moines Register*, Battling Levinsky Beats Billy Miske. February 28, 1917.
139 *Minneapolis Tribune*, Kilbane and Brock May Fight on Next Card of St. Paul Boxing Club, March 1, 1917.
140 *St. Paul Pioneer Press*, Levinsky Defeats St. Paul Boxer. February 28, 1917.
141 *Milwaukee Free Press*, Miske Breaks Hand. May 1, 1917.

convince Darcy to come and fight in America under his guidance in 1915. Darcy became confused: urged by some to enlist in the army, by others not to enlist; by some to go to America, by others not to go to America.[142]

He was supporting his mother and other family members and, in October of 1916, made the decision to stow away on a vessel bound for America. He decided he would make a tour of America to make a pile of money before either volunteering, or being drafted, for military service. He turned 21 the day after the ship sailed. Back home, he was branded a slacker. While there was a lot of excitement in America over his arrival that December, and talk of numerous lucrative matches over the ensuing months, political forces conspired to prevent him from fighting in the country. This was despite Darcy's contention he planned to participate in three or four fights and then enlist.

When a number of bouts in various states fell through, Darcy made plans to become an American citizen. He traveled to Memphis, Tennessee, where he signed with a promoter named Billy Hack for a fight with Len Rowlands of Milwaukee on May 7, and then immediately went to an aviation school in Memphis and enlisted. After a routine training run on April 27, he collapsed and was taken to St. Joseph Hospital. There it was learned his tonsils had a streptococcus infection. That caused blood poisoning and inflammation of the heart, ultimately leading to pneumonia, and tragically his death.[143]

Billy returned to action on July 24 with a second round technical knockout victory over Denver heavyweight Joe Bonds at the Broadway Club in Brooklyn. He followed that performance with a ten-round fight in the same club on September 18, in which he tamed "Wild Bert" Kenny. The best of four professional boxing brothers, the others were named Frank, Roy and Billy, Canadian born and bred William was tagged "Wild Bert" for his whirlwind fighting style. Kenny had battled in the professional ranks since 1908 and had faced a number of first rate fighters including Kid Norfolk, Tommy Gibbons, Willie Meehan, Leo Houck and Jack Dempsey. While he typically came out on the short end of these contests, he was a hit with the fans for his willingness to fight every moment.[144] In one of his biographies, Dempsey said of the fight with Kenny:

> We earned our money that night at Gibson's. I dropped him in the second. He bounced me off the floor a couple of times in the third. By then we had learned each other's strong points and weaknesses, and for the next seven rounds I fought one of the most brutal fights of my life. Every newspaperman at the ringside gave me the decision. (Billy) Gibson gave me thirty dollars; two dollars for the towel man,

---

142 Swanwick, Raymond. *Les Darcy, Australia's Golden Boy of Boxing*. Ure Smith, Sydney, Australia, 1965.
143 Swanwick, Raymond. *Les Darcy, Australia's Golden Boy of Boxing*. Ure Smith, Sydney, Australia, 1965.
144 *Lowell Sun*, Looks Like a Good Bout at the Armory A.A. October 29, 1917.

and fourteen each for Price and me. I could have sold the blood for fourteen dollars.[145]

Billy weighed 177 pounds and looked slow and out of condition when he met Kenny according to at least one newspaper report, but he still had his way with him for the most part.[146] He dropped Kenny for a nine count in the second round with a right to the jaw. Three rounds later, Kenny was saved by the bell and then floored three more times in the ninth round. "Wild Bert" was all but out on his feet when the bell rang to end the tenth and final round. According to the *National Police Gazette*, Wild Bert was "decidedly tame after he had been pounded and hammered for ten rounds by Billy." They reported, that with the exception of the first round, when Bert landed a wild swing and bloodied Billy's nose, he served as a punching bag, and the only question was whether or not Bert would be able to avoid a knockout.[147]

Anxious to make up for lost revenues and to return to the level of performance he exhibited the previous year, Billy fought again ten days later, on September 28, 1917, and earned a decisive newspaper decision over Oklahoma's huge heavyweight, Carl Morris, at the Harlem Sporting Club. One of the original white hopes when promoters were searching for possible men to dethrone Jack Johnson in 1913, the thirty-year-old Morris stood 6'4" and weighed 228 pounds to Billy's 178 pounds. Morris, it was suggested by at least one source, would have become a champion had he fought back in the days under the old London prize ring rules that combined wrestling with boxing.

With his great bulk, strength and endurance, it was thought that Morris had the ability to withstand more rough play than any other heavyweight in the ring and, in a go-as-you-please fight, would wear down Willard or any other opponent.[148] He'd been disqualified in a bout held against Fred Fulton in Canton, Ohio on September 3 for butting with his head and hitting when the referee broke the men from a clinch. Still, before the disqualification, it was reported that Fulton became so discouraged by the rough tactics of Morris that he attempted to leave the ring upon the conclusion of the fifth round, before being stopped by one of his seconds.[149] Fulton later refuted that he tried to quit and claimed that he had only started to depart the ring because he thought Morris had been disqualified by the referee for a foul.

Morris wasn't as successful against Billy, who had too much speed for the bigger man during their ten-round bout according to the *National Police Gazette*. The *Gazette's* report credited Billy with a cagey, heady fight, and said

---

145 Dempsey, Jack. *Dempsey.* Simon and Schuster, Inc., New York, N.Y. 1960.
146 *Trenton Evening Times,* News of the Boxers. September 19, 1917.
147 *National Police Gazette,* Miske Tames Wild Bert Kenny, October 6, 1917.
148 *National Police Gazette,* Willard and Fulton Bout, January 26, 1918.
149 *National Police Gazette,* Fred Fulton Wins on Foul, September 15, 1917.

that he used his speed of foot and fist to pop Morris on the head or body before Morris could "set" himself to throw a punch. Then after leading, Billy would start to work at close quarters and punish his bigger foe about the body.

While Billy didn't appear to hurt Morris, he landed the cleaner and greater number of punches. Morris's right eye was closed at the end of the bout. The result convinced that periodicals reporter that Billy, despite his comparatively small size, was a worthy opponent for all the heavyweights around there, including Jim Coffey, Frank Moran, Bill Brennan and the rest.[150] The *New York Times* said Billy carried the fighting to Morris throughout the contest and shook the bigger man several times with heavy blows to the jaw.[151]

Prior to the loss to Billy, Morris was hoping to gain an opportunity to fight Jess Willard. The loss to Billy, as well as a subsequent defeat he suffered against Jack Dempsey in December of 1918, again as a result of a disqualification for fouling, effectively ended the heavyweight title aspirations of Carl Morris. He became a steam shovel operator later in life and passed away in Pasadena, California on July 11, 1951 as a result of cancer at the age of 64.

Only four days after his contest with Carl Morris, on October 2, Billy tackled heavyweight Charley Weinert for a second time and carried the fight to the heavier men throughout in route to an easy ten-round decision victory at Brooklyn's Broadway club. Billy almost knocked Weinert out in the second round when he landed a heavy left hand blow to the stomach that caused Weinert to momentarily lower his hands. Quick as a flash, Billy followed up with a right to the jaw and another left to the chin. Weinert's knees buckled and he bent forward and rushed into a clinch. Billy pushed him off and landed a number of blows to the body. Weinert was about to fall when the bell rang to bring an end to the round.

Weinert came out for the third round and hung on to Billy for all he was worth as he attempted to recover from the beating he'd received in the second round. In the fourth round, Charley tried to box Billy but stopped once he found himself continually on the end of Billy's left hand jabs.

Charley pulled out all the stops in the tenth and final session in a valiant attempt to overcome a huge deficit. He landed a two-punch combination high on Billy's head, and another blow to the stomach, but Billy countered with a right that sent Charley spinning. Billy forced Charley to a corner where he whaled away at his head and body until Charley sought refuge by way of another clinch.

---

150 *National Police Gazette*, Billy Miske Easily Defeats Carl Morris and Weinert, October 20, 1917.
151 *New York Times*. Miske Gains The Verdict, September 29, 1917.

The fight ended with Billy pounding away at Charley, while the latter covered up and waited for the welcome sound of the final bell.[152] Billy weighed 176 ¾ pounds for the fight to Weinert's 184.[153]

Billy's successes against Morris and Weinert prompted more talk of a possible matchup against big Fred Fulton. But, while Billy was being considered as a serious candidate to face Fulton, most believed the reigning heavyweight champion, Jess Willard, would be much too big for him.[154]

A bigger question on the minds of many fight fans was whether or not the champion would ever fight anyone. Earlier that year, Jess had become the sole owner of a circus that he'd been appearing in. Some interpreted this, along with the fact that he terminated his managers Jack Curley and Tom Jones in July, as a sign he was finished with boxing. Willard, who had been extremely inactive inside the ring since winning the title against Jack Johnson, wasn't a particularly popular champion. Unlike past champions like John L. Sulllivan, for example, who would provide exhibitions from time to time to contribute toward a worthy cause, Willard insisted upon a fee for his services, and was viewed as a money-grabbing mercenary. The amount of money that it appeared it would take to lure the champion into the ring again made it difficult for any promoter to make a match. None would produce a large enough gate to ensure a profitable return.

On October 16, Billy suffered a setback when he tackled Kid Norfolk in a 12-round contest in Boston. Norfolk, born William Ward in Virginia on July 10, 1893, stood approximately 5'9" and was a quick, stocky fighter, considered by some to be the best new black fighter to enter the game in some time. He started fighting as a number of young black fighters did in those days, by participating in what they called Battle Royals. It was a practice where a number of young boys would be put in the ring to face off against one another at the same time for the entertainment of the patrons, the winner being the last standing.

While fighting in nearby Baltimore, Norfolk was "discovered" by a big time engineer named V.A. Mason. Mason was doing a lot of work on the Panama Canal project and was a huge fan of boxing. While stationed in Panama, he witnessed the popularity of the sport there and realized a man could make a lot of money representing a stable of fighters there. He returned to Baltimore looking for young fighters and a number of the local experts recommended Norfolk. When the Kid arrived in Panama he was only 19 years old.

As it turned out, the Panama Canal project consumed so much of Mason's time he wasn't able to devote any attention to Norfolk and boxing. When he and Norfolk had a falling out over a request to run out and purchase Mason some cigars, Mason ended up selling his contract to a local

---

152 *National Police Gazette*, Billy Miske Easily Defeats Carl Morris and Weinert, October 20, 1917.
153 *Minneapolis Tribune*, Billy Miske Gives Weinert Bad Beating, October 3, 1917.
154 *Des Moines Daily News*, Miske May Tackle The Big Men, October 14, 1917.

sporting man named H.R Cambridge. Cambridge didn't think the Kid looked like much of a fighter but he complied with his request to get him some fights.

The next thing he knew, Norfolk had knocked out twenty men in 1913, most of them inexperienced laborers. Eventually he passed a much stiffer test, knocking out an American heavyweight named Bill "Steamboat" Scott in three rounds, and the locals really began to take notice of the young fighter.

He suffered his first setback against another import from the United States, an experienced heavyweight named Jeff Clarke, a.k.a. "The Joplin Ghost." But he learned from the loss and rebounded with wins over "Rough House" Ware and Bill Tate, before avenging the loss to Clarke in a second hard fought twenty rounder. Subsequent performances against heavyweights Sam McVea and Arthur Pelkey only enhanced his reputation and caught the attention of Leo Flynn in New York, who purchased his contract.

Flynn brought him to New York and the Kid continued his winning ways, defeating established professionals such as Tom Cowler, Gus Christie and "Gunboat" Smith.[155] By October of 1917, a number of fighters, including the likes of Carl Morris, seemed to be doing their best to avoid him, and as it turned out it would have been wise for Billy to do so as well.

Norfolk was awarded the referee's decision. Billy looked like a sure winner in the opening session and, for the first five rounds, overall the fighting was generally even. Norfolk gradually took command and, by the end, he was clearly the victor. Norfolk's blows to the body were his most effective. Billy tried to score with his right hand repeatedly but Norfolk was too elusive for him. Most of Billy's blows were blocked and those which landed didn't appear to have much effect.[156] Billy claimed he had injured his hand again during the fight.[157]

The *Boston Daily Globe* gave the weight of each fighters weight as 175 pounds and also reported Norfolk as the clear winner in an action packed fight. They lauded Norfolk for his cleverness and said he tied Billy up so well in clinches that Billy was unable to do much infighting. Norfolk, himself, was able to land to Billy's body freely with both hands.[158]

Then, for the second time in 1917, Billy fought "Wild" Bert Kenny, this time on October 30 in Boston. The fight was awarded to Billy in the fifth round when the referee had to stop it to save Kenny from further punishment. Billy hit Bert repeatedly to the body and head. He put Bert down for a count of eight in the second round and Bert was essentially helpless thereafter, floundering about the ring and clinching at every

---

155 Smith, Kevin, *The Sundowners, The History of the Black Prizefighter 1870-1930* CCK Publications, 2006.
156 *Evening Times*, Norfolk Wins From Miske. October 17, 1917.
157 *Lowell Sun*, Looks Like Good Bout At The Armory A.A. October 29, 1917.
158 *Boston Daily Globe*, Miske Favorite, Loses to Norfolk. October 17, 1917.

opportunity in an attempt to avoid punishment. He was in sad shape when the referee stopped the contest.[159]

Billy concluded 1917 with a fifth and final meeting against Jack Dillon on November 12 at Brooklyn's Broadway club. Once again he proved Dillon's master over ten rounds, winning every round but the fourth.[160]

Dillon demonstrated a flash of his former greatness in the second round when he caught Billy with a right hook to the jaw, knocking him into the ropes. But, over the second half of the fight, it was really only a matter of whether Dillon would go the distance. In the seventh, eighth and ninth rounds, Billy hit Dillon with all manners of blows and everyone wondered what was holding Dillon up.

Finally, Billy sent him to the canvas with a vicious left hook to the jaw. But he was up before the referee could begin counting.[161] He staggered blindly to his corner at the conclusion of the ninth round as Billy appealed to the referee to stop the bout, but Dillon wouldn't have it, and continued on, exhibiting one of the gamest exhibitions ever witnessed in the club.[162]

By the end of the fight, Dillon's face was a mass of cuts and bumps, his eyes almost closed and he was covered in blood. As he made his exit from the ring, he muttered with some consolation, "He couldn't knock me out, anyway."[163] Billy weighed 176 ½ pounds to Dillon's 167.[164]

The beating Dillon suffered against Billy effectively eliminated him in the view of most in the consideration for light-heavyweight supremacy. "Battling" Levinsky, Tommy Gibbons, and Billy were then considered the best of the weight class.[165]

Dillon continued to fight on until February of 1921. He made one final forgettable appearance in January of 1923, before hanging his gloves up for good. He ultimately retired to Florida where he owned and operated a restaurant next to his home in Chattahoochee, Florida. He died August 7, 1942 at age 51.

In December of 1917, Fred Fulton's manager, Mike Collins, laid claim to the heavyweight title for his man on the grounds that Willard had refused to defend it.[166] He wasn't going to earn the title that way, but Collins was doing his best to goad the champion into a fight. Pearl Smith joined in and said Fulton wouldn't be the holder of the title for long. He was certain Billy could defeat Fulton.[167]

---

159 *National Police Gazette*, Miske Stops Wild Bert, November 10, 1917.
160 *Milwaukee Free Press*, Miske Whales Dillon. November 14, 1917.
161 *New Castle News*, Jack Dillon Falls Before Bill Miske. November 14, 1917.
162 *New York Times*, Miske Batters Dillon In Fast 10 Round Bout. November 14, 1917.
163 *New Castle News*, Jack Dillon Falls Before Billy Miske. November 14, 1917.
164 *New York Times*, Miske Batters Dillon in Fast 10 Round Bout. November 14, 1917.
165 *Warren Evening Mirror*, Levinsky Miske and Gibbons Are Light-Heavyweight Kings. December 7, 1917.
166 *Milwaukee Free Press*. Miske Would Battle Fulton Winner Take All. December 11, 1917.
167 *Racine Journal*, Miske Demands a Bout With Fulton. December 12, 1917.

Collins responded to Smith's challenge and said Fulton would knock Billy out within five rounds. Still, he added if Billy could assure them of a good crowd, they would take Billy on for a little practice for Fred.[168]

Three days later, it was announced Fulton and Billy would fight at the St. Paul Auditorium on January 18. Although he was generally reported to be 6'4" tall, Fulton always claimed he was really closer to 6'7." Fulton would outweigh Billy by 50 pounds, 230 to 180.[169] It was agreed Fulton would receive 45% of the gate receipts, while Billy would receive 20% of the gross. It was estimated the receipts would total $12,000.[170]

After hearing of the possible matchup, Sam Austin of the *National Police Gazette* informed his readers that Billy had his eye on the heavyweight championship and figured that Jess Willard was through. The only real obstacle in Billy's path was Fulton. While acknowledging that Billy had whipped the much larger Carl Morris, Austin claimed that, unlike Morris, Fulton had some boxing ability, and might be able to successfully stand Billy off with his cleverness, and ultimately knock him out. Still, he thought the match would draw a nice sized crowd.[171]

As for the champion, Jess Willard, and his heavyweight title, Billy said that when he met Fred Fulton, he would prove to the public's satisfaction that he wasn't too small for the task of dethroning Willard. He pointed to his convincing victory over Carl Morris as evidence that a great disadvantage in size could be overcome. He left no doubt as to his own heavyweight championship aspirations when he said, "Before Jess Willard won the championship he was defeated by smaller men than I am, and now that he has gone back there is no reason why I am not big enough to do the trick."

As the year came to a close, Billy's future continued to look very bright.

---

168 *Racine Journal*, Collins to Give Jess One Chance. December 13, 1917.
169 *Milwaukee Free Press*, Fulton vs. Miske. December 16, 1917.
170 *Racine Journal*, Odds and Ends. December 27, 1917.
171 *National Police Gazette*, Sam Austin's Fistic News and Pugilistic Gossip, December 29, 1917.

CHAPTER 5

Fulton, Dempsey & "Gunboat" Smith

In 1918, Billy fought some of the biggest names in boxing. His opponents during the year included Fred Fulton, "Gunboat" Smith, and future legends Jack Dempsey and Harry Greb, among others.

Fred Fulton, a.k.a. "The Rochester Plasterer", like Billy, was born in Minnesota, and was in his prime in 1918 at age 26. When the year began, he was considered the leading contender for Jess Willard's heavyweight title.

But that didn't faze Billy. After all, he'd proven too fast for big Carl Morris and defeated him with ease, and he knew he would have the same advantage against Fulton.

Furthermore, if one examined Mr. Fulton's career, they would find that there were a number of questions concerning the big man's fighting heart. For example, in his last bout of 1917, on Christmas Day in Little Rock, Arkansas against little known Harry "Texas" Tate, he was accused of finding the going too rough for his liking and taking the easy way out by intentionally fouling Tate and being disqualified by Referee Billy Haack.

According to the *National Police Gazette*, to those seated at ringside, it appeared "as if Fulton found the going so steep in the first minute that he was unwilling to take the chance of being beaten with Jess Willard looking up with a half-hearted promise for a bout. So he preferred to lose on a foul." According to their report of the fight, Tate had the better of the few exchanges and landed two or three blows with such power and drive that Fulton looked and acted in distress. After receiving a hard right to the jaw, Fulton sent Tate to the canvas with a blow so low that the referee offered to give the fight to Tate. But, Tate's manager, Billy McCarney, refused the offer and after a sufficient time to recover, action was reconvened.

Tate rushed Fulton around the ring with a shower of blows to the head and body. When the pair fell into a clinch, Fulton fairly picked Tate up and threw him through the ropes. The referee immediately disqualified him for the action. The crowd cheered the decision and booed Fulton.

While Fulton redeemed himself with a dominating second round stoppage of Tate only sixteen days later, it wasn't the only time that Fulton's fighting heart was called into question, or he'd been accused of quitting. In one of their articles published in June of 1917 the *National Police Gazette* wrote that while Fulton had many advantages in his favor, he was only a good boxer as long as his nerve was not shaken and that, when called upon to fight an uphill battle, he forgets everything he has learned.172

As the fight drew near, it generated great interest among the local fight fans. Fulton, at a height reported anywhere from 6'4 ½" to 6'7" tall would tower over Billy and he was considered the harder hitter of the two. Those facts, along with the huge advantage he would have in both, reach and weight, contributed to make him the betting favorite at odds of two to one. It was pointed out that one thing in Billy's favor was he would bore in on the bigger man, while Fulton preferred to stand off and box at long range.173 Billy was confident he could defeat him.

On January 13, Fred Coburn, of the *Minneapolis Tribune*, gave his readers his prediction of the outcome of the fight writing Billy could not hope to win against Fulton on anything but a fluke. "It is an uneven match on the face of it," said Coburn, "almost every writer of pugilistic affairs in the country regards it as a foregone conclusion Miske will be unable to go the full ten rounds. His chances seem to depend upon a fluke, a foul or a flivver."174

To help prepare for the bout with the taller man, Billy's manager, Pearl Smith, secured the services of three large sparring partners, including black heavyweight Bob Armstrong. Five days before the fight, Fulton's manager, Mike Collins, advised Fred was in the best condition he had ever been in, and should put up the battle of his life against Billy. Fulton, while not discounting Billy's ability, said "they all look alike to me – even Jess Willard."175

On January 16, 1918, the *Minneapolis Tribune* reported Billy planned to win a guarantee of $500 that Fulton's manager, Mike Collins, had offered to any man Fulton couldn't knock out within the first five rounds. While Collins and Fulton had been trying to lure the reigning heavyweight champion, Jess Willard, into a fight, Collins distributed thousands of fliers claiming the championship for Fred. The flier guaranteed the $500 to any man Fulton couldn't knock out within five rounds. Billy saw the flier and said he could use the $500 as well as anybody else, so he decided to remind them of their offer.

When Collins was informed of this, he replied:

> Miske doesn't need to worry about the $500. If he wins it, he'll get it. He'd better go ahead and get in shape, and not think too much about staying five rounds. Fred likes $500 pretty well himself and he'll knock Miske out fast in order to keep the money in his pocket.176

---

172 *National Police Gazette*, Wallops and Courage Win Championship Titles, June 16, 1917.
173 *Racine Journal*,"Fulton Will Meet Miske At St. Paul." January 14, 1918.
174 *Minneapolis Tribune*, Fulton-Miske Contest a Bad Match on Face of It, January 13, 1918.
175 *Minneapolis Tribune*. Fulton Arrives At Last; Starts Training Today, January 14, 1918.
176 *Minneapolis Tribune*. St. Paul Men Offer Purse to Willard, January 16, 1918.

Most "fight experts" believed Fulton would prove too big for Billy. Boxing writers Billy Rocap, Ed Smith, Tom Andrews and Otto Floto, among others, each expressed the opinion. However, one knowledgeable reporter, a New York writer named Hype Igoe, offered a different viewpoint:

> Billy Miske will surprise them and Fulton, if he hasn't fallen off from lack of work. He will make Fulton go lickity split to win. We thought here it was a shame to put poor William against Carl Morris a few months back, but Willie went about the business of giving Carl a bumping in such a startling way that we vowed then and there that they'd never come too large for the St. Paul perpetual motion machine. You folks haven't seen Billy at his best, and his best has been of the niftiest sort around New York.[177]

Billy expressed his confidence in the task before him, saying:

> I boxed Fulton once in a gymnasium workout and he wasn't hard to hit. If I can hit him, I can beat him. I have a defense for his long left hand and I will make Fred know he has been in a battle no matter what the result may be. I'm pretty sure I can pile up enough points to get a decision and I am sure that Fred cannot knock me out.[178]

The fight, which took place on January 18, 1918, attracted approximately 8,000 fans. It was the largest gathering seen at the St. Paul Auditorium since boxing was legalized in Minnesota, and the hometown crowd was strongly in favor of their smaller boy.[179]

There were no knockdowns scored, and when the bell rang to end the 10-round fight Billy was standing toe-to-toe and matching Fulton blow for blow. Every newspaper critic at ringside gave Billy a draw or better.[180]

Billy was the clearly the aggressor of the pair in the early rounds of the contest, carrying the fighting to Fulton and continually boring in, despite the fact Fred landed a number of hard rights.

In the second round, Billy hammered Fulton with combinations to the body and the bigger man wore a worried expression. It could be seen Billy's blows were having an impact on Fulton by the fact he winced time and again when they landed. It was clear to those present that Billy's attack to the body was causing Fulton a lot of discomfort and prompted him to cover up in attempt to avoid the punishment.

Although Fulton was much taller and heavier, Billy was the much faster and shiftier of the two, and repeatedly frustrated Fred by getting inside his long left jab and beating him to the punch. Fulton did manage to do some

---

177 *Minneapolis Tribune*. Champs Says Collins Can Sight Him Up, January 17, 1918.
178 *Minneapolis Tribune*. Fred Fulton and Billy Miske Will Battle In The Ring Tonight, January 18, 1918.
179 *Beloit Daily News*, Billy Miske Gets Draw With Fulton. January 19, 1918.
180 *Ogden Standard*, Miske Shows Up Fulton In Bout. January 19, 1918.

damage of his own though as the fight progressed with his left uppercut and hard right crosses.

Fulton demonstrated the superior boxing skills and was at his best when able to use his long left jab to keep Billy at a distance.181 *The National Police Gazette* praised Billy's performance and expressed admiration for his ability to overcome Fulton's physical advantages.

>Miske showed the fans he wasn't afraid of Fulton. He resorted to no tactics of trying to keep away from him. He bored in from the start and more than once compelled Fulton to resort to clinching. He also took some of Fulton's stiffest jabs without wincing, and time and time again stood toe to toe and slugged with the plasterer.182

Local newspaper results varied. The *St. Paul Daily News* named Billy the winner, while the *St. Paul Pioneer Press*, *St. Paul Dispatch* and *Minneapolis Daily News* all called it a draw, and the *Minneapolis Journal* and *Minneapolis Tribune* each said Fulton won by a shade.

The *Tribune* said Billy was "on his feet and strong and coming at the finish." Their reporter, Fred Coburn, wrote Billy's objective was to stay ten rounds, and he attained the goal without being in distress more than once during the bout. Still, Coburn felt the only rounds Billy won were the sixth and the ninth. They reported Billy's weight as 186 pounds, to Fulton's 218 pounds.183

Fulton claimed he was handicapped by a broken bone in his left hand, and a local physician backed him up, claiming he gave Fred a shot of cocaine to ease the pain in the hand prior to the bout. Fred claimed the drug prevented him from doing his best. The *National Police Gazette* said while this may be true, it all seemed like an eleventh hour attempt to hide the fact Fulton's poor showing proved he wasn't a fighter of championship quality, and was in no way qualified to challenge Jess Willard for the heavyweight title.184

Fulton's failure to stop Billy cost him dearly in his campaign to obtain a match with Jess Willard, while it only enhanced Billy's stock. Fulton never received a chance to fight for the heavyweight title, and suffered a first-round knockout six months later to future champion Jack Dempsey. Fulton later claimed he'd expected Dempsey to go along with him for a fast eight-round exhibition, and that he'd followed his managers instructions to give a good exhibition, and the pair would have a real fight at a later date, but Dempsey double crossed him, and knocked him out in the first round.185

A week after Billy's fight with Fulton the *Minneapolis Tribune's*

---

181 *National Police Gazette*, Willard Need Not Fear Fred Fulton As A Rival, February 9, 1918.
182 *National Police Gazette*, Light-Heavyweight Miske Surprises Giant Fulton, February 9, 1918.
183 *Minneapolis Tribune*, Fulton Gains Shade Over Miske, January 19, 1918.
184 *National Police Gazette*, Willard Need Not Fear Fred Fulton As A Rival, February 9, 1918.
185 *National Police Gazette*, Sensational Story of Fred Fulton's Confession, March 8, 1919.

sportswriter, Fred Coburn, wrote in his column that he'd learned Billy was about to claim the heavyweight title because of his good showing against Fred and the fact that the champion, Jess Willard, wasn't willing to defend his title. Coburn pointed out that Billy had recently lost a decision to Kid Norfolk, and that John Espin, a former Fulton sparring partner, had won a decision over Norfolk, and jokingly suggested that Espin claim the championship.[186]

Billy defeated Gus Christie on February 27 in a close contest he pulled out with a big final round during which he knocked Christie all over the ring.[187]

On March 2, the *National Police Gazette* suggested that Fred Fulton and Billy still stood head and shoulders above every other heavyweight in the ring except Jess Willard. While Jack Dempsey was held up as a comer as a result of his victory on a foul over Carl Morris, the *Gazette* thought he needed to defeat someone of higher esteem before he would be taken more seriously. They suggested that a fight with Billy, who "fights first, last and all the time, and has never been involved in anything shady," would put Dempsey to the proper test.[188] Still, many others were now viewing Dempsey as a leading contender for the title, so it seemed only natural to make a match between him and Billy especially when Dempsey added Bill Brennan to his growing list of victims.

Eleven days later, on March 13, fight fans in Minnesota were surprised to learn Billy and his manager, Pearl Smith, had parted company. Since Billy's match with Fulton there had been a lot of discussion about possible matches between the champion, Willard, and Fred Fulton, or rising heavyweight phenomenon Jack Dempsey. By all accounts, despite his recent successes, Billy was suddenly on the outside looking in. Smith had been trying without success to make a match with Dempsey.[189] Dissatisfied with his manager's efforts to secure a match with any of these men, and believing he'd do better under new management, Billy severed the relationship.[190]

Two days later, St. Paul promoter and matchmaker, Jack Reddy, was in Chicago trying to close arrangements for a Dempsey–Miske fight. On March 19, it was announced that Reddy, an experienced handler of boxers in addition to his matchmaking duties, and a long-time friend of Billy's, had become his new manager.[191] The match between Billy and Jack Dempsey was subsequently clinched for May 3 at the St. Paul Auditorium.

Milwaukee-based fight promoter and newspaper scribe, Tom Andrews, also tried to make a play to take over the management of Billy's career, but

---

186 *Minneapolis Tribune*, Coburn's Column, January 26, 1918.
187 *Milwaukee Free Press*, Christie Gives Miske An Interesting Time. February 28, 1918.
188 *National Police Gazette*, Dempsey and Fulton to Fight for Willard's Favor, March 3, 1918.
189 *Beloit Daily News*, Miske Demands To Know Where He's To Get Off. March 13, 1918.
190 *Milwaukee Free Press*, Billy Miske to Change Bosses. March 14, 1918.
191 *Milwaukee Free Press*, Billy Miske Signs Up J. Reddy As Manager. March 19, 1918.

by the time he arrived in Minneapolis on March 16, Billy had already reached an agreement with Reddy.192

While awaiting the opportunity to fight Dempsey, Billy was matched to face a 26-year old British heavyweight named Tom Cowler on April 8 before another Minnesota crowd. Cowler, a.k.a. "The Cumberland Giant" after his homeland, stood in the range of 6'2" to 6'3" tall and typically weighed anywhere from 205 to 220 pounds over the course of his career.

Cowler was a powerful fighter and had defeated a number of good men, including "Gunboat" Smith, Bill Brennan, and Tom "Bearcat" McMahon, but had been knocked out in his most recent fight with Fred Fulton. Up until the time he found himself on the wrong end of a terrific right hand swing and was knocked out in the fifth round, Cowler had given a very good account of himself against Fulton, punching him all around the ring and sending him to the canvas twice.

On no less than three occasions, Fulton seemed on the verge of suffering a knockout, but it was one of those times when he came to fight. The third and fourth rounds were fiercely contested with the advantage shifting back and forth between the two men. The end came in the fifth round when Fulton landed a hard left that sent Cowler crashing to the canvas. Cowler then made the fatal mistake of rising too soon and not taking advantage of a few seconds to regain his senses. As soon as he rose, Fulton moved in and landed another heavy blow which sent him to the mat again. Cowler revisited the canvas two more times before he was finally unable to rise.193

St. Paul fans who watched Cowler prepare for the match were impressed with his boxing and hitting abilities, and those assets combined with the advantages he would enjoy in height, reach and weight, led many to believe he would be able to defeat the local favorite.

Still, it was noted Cowler also possessed a "fragile jaw" and Billy's friends believed he would be able to take advantage of the fact.194 As it turned out, Billy's friends were right. He battered Cowler around the ring until the referee stepped in to save him from further punishment in the seventh round after Billy put him down with a hard left to the stomach and a right to the jaw.195 Cowler, who weighed 210 pounds to Billy's 175, appeared bewildered by Billy's aggressiveness.196

The *National Police Gazette* reported that Billy outclassed the heavier man, taking every round except the third, which was even. Billy repeatedly landed a left hook to the face followed by a right hook to the body, and dominated the battle during the clinches and infighting as well. The writer expressed

---

192 *Minneapolis Tribune*, Rumors Over Big Ring Go Fill the Air, March 17, 1918.
193 *National Police Gazette*, Cowler Scores Knockout Over Giant Fred Fulton, March 30, 1918.
194 *Minneapolis Tribune*, St. Paul Fans Take a Liking to Tom Cowler, April 3, 1918.
195 *Milwaukee Free Press*, Miske Hangs K.O. on Tom Cowler. April 9, 1918.
196 *Racine Journal*, Billy Miske Wins a Technical K.O. April 9, 1918.

the opinion it was unfortunate Billy was too light at 175 pounds to take on Jess Willard, although he acknowledged it hadn't prevented him from decisively defeating big Carl Morris.[197]

Billy added long-time heavyweight contender "Gunboat" Smith to his growing list of victims next with a ten-round decision victory in Atlanta, Georgia. Smith and his longtime manager, Jim Buckley, had parted ways approximately five months earlier over money matters. Smith charged Buckley with unfair tactics. Buckley, in turn, declared that Smith failed to keep himself in condition and was on the downward grade.[198] The bout was fought for the benefit of the Camp Gordon athletic fund. Like Cowler, Smith was troubled by Billy's aggressiveness and continually clinched to avoid punishment.[199] Only once did Smith come out of his shell. It happened in the seventh round when he finally attempted to initiate the action and did enough to earn a shade over his lighter opponent.

But, overall, the contest was a relatively tame affair because Smith spent the majority of the time covering up, and Billy was forced to be content with out-boxing his opponent, sending in heavy blows whenever the opportunity presented itself.[200] Jack Dempsey awaited his own turn with Billy.

Local Minnesota sportswriter, George Barton, first met Jack Dempsey on February 25, 1918 in Milwaukee, Wisconsin, where Dempsey was matched with Bill Brennan. The 22-year old was drawing a lot of attention for his recent wins over "Gunboat" Smith, Carl Morris, and "Fireman" Jim Flynn. He was under the guidance of Jack "Doc" Kearns who was telling anyone and everyone he was managing the future heavyweight champion of the world. Kearns had written Jack Reddy suggesting a match between Miske and Dempsey in St. Paul.

Reddy decided to travel to Milwaukee to take his own look at Dempsey and invited Barton to tag along. They visited Dempsey and his manager in their hotel on the morning of the fight with Brennan. Barton met a man who stood 6'1" tall, weighed about 180 pounds, and was powerfully built with unusually thick wrists and large hands. Barton was impressed with Dempsey's enthusiastic, yet modest manner and the way he broke in on the buildup Kearns was delivering to tell him not to get too carried away with all his praise.

Later that day, Barton was further impressed to witness a fighter who was amazingly fast on his feet, very graceful and who delivered punches with "the split-second speed and accuracy of a rattlesnake."[201] Dempsey gave Brennan a fearful beating in the bout, before hitting him so hard with

---

[197] *National Police Gazette*, Miske Scores Knockout, April 27, 1918.
[198] *National Police Gazette*, Shutters Go Up On Public Boxing in New York State, December 1, 1917.
[199] *Warren Evening Mirror*, Billy Miske Adds Gunboat Smith To List of Victims. April 13, 1918.
[200] *Minneapolis Tribune*, St. Paul Boy Easy Winner in 10 Rounds, April 13, 1918.
[201] Barton, George, *My Lifetime In Sports*. The Olympic Press, Minneapolis, MN 1957.

a left hook in the sixth round that caused him to fall so awkwardly he broke his ankle.

Afterward, Reddy asked Barton what he thought of a possible Dempsey–Miske match. George, a former fighter who had once defeated the great Terry McGovern, told him that if he wanted to see Miske beaten, he'd found the right man to do it. Reddy didn't agree, believing Dempsey's style was made to order for Billy, but the two would make for a good match.202

With the May 3 fight rapidly approaching, both men worked out before Minneapolis and St. Paul crowds which were much larger than those normally experienced in the local gymnasiums. On April 28, more than 300 viewed Billy in action at the Potts gym, while nearly twice as many watched Dempsey go through his paces. Miske boxed several rounds with his new sparring partners, Hughie Walker of Kansas City and "Big Boy" Butler of Los Angeles, while Dempsey put in four fast rounds with Jock Malone, in addition to working with his usual heavyweight sparring partners. This concluded the heavier training sessions for both men. They would both take it easy from then on out until the day of their contest.203

The fight generated national interest. Tex Rickard, the game's leading promoter, had indicated the winner would receive serious consideration for a match with the champion, Jess Willard. Many of the top boxing writers in the country were seated at ringside.

Dempsey was extremely confident and felt the fight wouldn't last more than two or three rounds. He didn't think Billy looked nearly as formidable as either Carl Morris or Bill Brennan, two heavyweights he had defeated earlier in the year. But, Billy's toughness came as a big surprise to Jack.204

As it turned out, Barton, a licensed official in the state of Minnesota, was named to work the bout. He remembered Dempsey weighing 181 pounds and Billy 183. Other reports said 182 for Billy and 187 for Dempsey, and still another, 185 pounds for each man. Barton said the two men were as fast as middleweights and as game as English pit bulls. In his view, it added up to a thrilling contest during which both men demonstrated equal courage in their delivery and acceptance of punishment.

Billy was aggressive and "swarmed over him like a flock of bees in the early rounds," according to Dempsey.205

Dempsey landed a hard left hook in the sixth round and sent Billy reeling into the ropes. Rather than seeking a clinch to clear his head, Billy ripped into Dempsey and the two men stood trading blows for the last minute of the round.206

---

202 Barton, George, *My Lifetime In Sports*. The Olympic Press, Minneapolis, MN 1957.
203 *Minneapolis Tribune*, Fans Crowd Gyms to See Miske and Dempsey in Stunts, April 29, 1918.
204 Dempsey, Jack, *Round by Round*. Whittlesey House, New York, N.Y. 1940.
205 *Evening State Journal*. Champions and Chance, February 19, 1924.
206 Barton, George, *My Lifetime In Sports*. The Olympic Press, Minneapolis, MN 1957.

By the end of the sixth round, Miske had landed more telling blows than Dempsey, and he suddenly came at him with a volley of blows that nearly put Dempsey out. Dempsey was groggy and floundering around. It was all he could do to keep from going down. He clinched whenever he could. When the bell finally ended the round, Dempsey was all in. He knew Billy was way ahead on points, and would almost certainly get the decision."207

Throughout the fight, Billy had landed more blows than Dempsey did, and he seemed to be really piling up points. Both men were tired, and even though Dempsey was able to drive in a few, Billy covered up well.208

In the seventh round, Dempsey went after Billy with everything he had. Billy was tired, too. He couldn't keep Dempsey off as successfully as he had during the first rounds, when he danced around without letting him land a single hard blow.

Ultimately, Dempsey was able to drive a good left to Billy's stomach and follow it with a stiff right to the head. If Dempsey had been fresher and able to put more steam behind the punch, it would have ended the fight. As it was, he had him in serious trouble. He tried to finish him. But, Billy covered up and clinched, as Dempsey had during the preceding round, and managed to last through to the bell.

After that, both men were both too tired to do much more than stumble around and fall into clinches. Without the desperate rally in the seventh round, there was no question in Dempsey's mind the decision would have gone to Billy, but that round earned him a draw."209

The *Minneapolis Tribune* gave Dempsey the shade in the fight on the strength of his big seventh round. While noting that Billy was groggy, weak and glassy-eyed at the end of the round, they credited him for coming back with everything he had in the eighth round when Dempsey tried to bring an end to the fight. The writer, Fred Coburn, reported Billy's best asset was his courage under fire and felt that he appeared the stronger and better man when the final bell rang.210

The fight went the full ten rounds. There were no knockdowns. Barton said he felt Dempsey won it, and the next day predicted Jack would become the next heavyweight champion of the world.211

Dempsey didn't seem to share Barton's view, at least so far as having won the fight, again writing in a 1940 autobiography:

> At the start of the fight, and I think in most of the rounds, Miske out-boxed me. Again and again, I tried the shift that had proved effective against (Bill) Brennan – a sudden step forward and a hard

---

207 Dempsey, Jack, *Round by Round*. Whittlesley House, New York, N.Y. 1940.
208 Dempsey, Jack, *Dempsey*. Harper & Row, New York, N.Y. 1977.
209 Dempsey, Jack, *Round by Round*. Whittlesley House, New York, N.Y. 1940.
210 *Minneapolis Tribune*. Dempsey Gains Shade Verdict Over Billy Miske, May 4, 1918.
211 Barton, George, *My Lifetime In Sports*. The Olympic Press, Minneapolis, MN 1957.

blow accompanying it - but each time Miske was watching for it and stepped out of harm's way.[212]

The Ring magazine founder and editor, Nat Fleischer, also said Miske out-boxed Dempsey most of the fight with the exception of the seventh round, and added "Miske smothered Dempsey's best blows, and in the main, gave as good as he was sent."[213]

Otto Floto, a longtime sportswriter for the *Denver Post*, witnessed the fight and later said, of all the slashing, cutting, fast bouts he had ever watched, this was one of the best. He said it was a give and take affair, with both men standing toe to toe, sending the best they had and taking all the other man sent their way. Otto felt Dempsey had earned the shade by the end of the bout, but not by so much as to be able to brag about it.

Afterward, Otto accompanied Dempsey, his manager "Doc" Kearns, and another fighter named Spider Kelly, aboard a train for Chicago and said he would never forget Dempsey's comment upon entering the sleeper car that night: "If I ever have to fight another tough guy like that I don't want the championship. The premium they ask is too much effort," said Jack. [214]

The popular view of the result of the fight was the first, fifth, and ninth rounds were even, while Dempsey won the second, third, seventh, eighth, and tenth rounds, and Billy won the fourth and sixth rounds.[215] Some newspapers reported Billy as the winner. The *Sheboygan Journal* reported Billy out-boxed Dempsey most of the fight with the exception of the seventh round.[216] The *St. Paul Pioneer Press* called it a draw, reporting Billy out-boxed his rival, while Dempsey evened things up with his aggressiveness and harder punching.[217] The contest drew a gate of approximately $25,000, Billy receiving 25% of the gross, and Dempsey 33 1/3%.[218]

Recalling the fight in 1952, Jack Dempsey said from the moment the fight began Billy and he were slugging away for keeps, a possible match with the heavyweight champion on their minds. In the fourth round, Dempsey landed a hard right low, but Billy didn't complain. "For the last two rounds it was hard to fend off Miske," said Jack, "he was hitting from all sides. I was hitting harder, but he was landing so often my punches were weakened. Newspapermen there, from all over the country, gave me the unofficial decision, but it was easy to see Miske had won a popular 'victory' by not getting knocked out and by keeping me off balance."[219]

---

212 Dempsey, Jack, *Round by Round*. Whittlesey House, New York, N.Y. 1940.
213 Fleischer, Nat, '*Jack Dempsey. The Idol of Fistiana*. The Ring, New York, N.Y. 1929.
214 *Denver Post*, Miske Meets Burke On Great Ring Card At Stadium Monday, July 9, 1922.
215 *Star*, Dempsey Winner By Newspaper Decision. May 4, 1918.
216 *Sheboygan Journal*, Salt Lake Mauler Baffled By Miske. May 4, 1918.
217 *St. Paul Pioneer Press*, Miske and Dempsey Box 10 Round Draw. May 4, 1918.
218 *Racine Journal*, Miske-Dempsey Would be Winner. March 30, 1918.
219 Billy Miske's Last Christmas, *Men Magazine*. September 1952.

CHAPTER 6

Work or Fight

In May of 1918, Major General Enoch H. Crowder's 'Work or Fight Order' was sending shockwaves through the sporting world. The United States had entered World War I in 1917 and, by 1918, was sending thousands of soldiers to France every day. On May 23, Crowder and U.S. Secretary of War, Newton D. Baker, announced baseball, a.k.a. "The National Pastime," was a "nonessential occupation." All players would have to enlist in the military or work in a shipyard or defense plant by July 1, or they would be automatically inducted into the armed forces.[220] Obviously, if baseball players weren't exempt from the draft, boxers wouldn't be either.

Crowder's 'Work or Fight Order' stated that all men of draft age, regardless of their classification, must engage in employment held to be productive or join the army. Specifically mentioned among the examples of nonproductive employment were persons engaged in games of sport. This meant men such as Billy could potentially be drafted for service and sent overseas.[221]

Billy didn't waste much time getting back into action after the Dempsey fight, traveling to San Francisco in late May to face three men within the span of 15 days. Henry Hendricks was first, and Billy punched him at will on May 31 before the referee stopped the contest 50 seconds into the second round. The proceeds of the event were donated to benefit American soldiers. Billy knocked Hendricks down twice in the first round with rights to the jaw. The *San Francisco Chronicle*'s fight reporter, Harry Smith, said Hendricks looked as though he was scared stiff by Miske. Offering his assessment of Billy as a fighter, Smith wrote, "If there is any criticism of Miske, it is that he works too fast, doesn't set himself and, consequently, cannot land as hard a punch as he ought." But, Smith allowed that might have had something to do with his opposition for this fight.[222]

Seven days later, on June 7, Billy fought Willie Meehan in a four-round contest to fund the purchase of athletic equipment for the sailors. The referee declared the fight a draw, but newspaper men said Meehan had the advantage.[223] Meehan was a short 5'9" tall, fat fellow, with an awkward fighting style, and didn't look like much of a fighter, but he enjoyed a

---

[220] Lynch Jr., Michael, *Harry Frazee, Ban Johnson and the Fued That Nearly Destroyed the American League*, McFarland Publishing 2008.
[221] *Gettysburg Compiler*, Work Or Fight Order, June 29, 1918.
[222] *San Francisco Chronicle*, Miske Stops Hendricks in Second Round, June 1, 1918.
[223] *Ogden Examiner*, Miske and Meehan in Benefit Bout. June 8, 1918.

55

surprising amount of success over a 17-year long professional career. He was born in San Francisco on Christmas Day in 1893. His many nicknames included "Battling Willie," "Wee Willy" and "Fat William." By the time he finally retired in late 1926, his resume included wins over a number of great fighters including Jack Dempsey, Sam Langford and Jack Dillon.[224] Willie fought Jack Dempsey five times in the years 1917 and 1918. The contests were only of four-round duration, the maximum allowed in California at the time, but Willie gave a good account of himself against Dempsey, winning twice, and drawing on another occasion.

Dempsey referred to Willie as a "fat little clown with a wonderful sense of humor," but also gave him his due, saying he "could box very well," and acknowledged Meehan had made him look bad in San Francisco.[225] Willie had a way of getting his opponent's goat and his awkward fighting style could make him a difficult man to figure out, especially in a short bout. In his initial contest with Billy, Meehan had him bleeding badly from the nose and mouth from the first round on, and it was generally conceded he'd come out on top at the end of the fourth and final round.[226]

Jack Reddy blamed Billy's loss to Meehan on a lack of training. Once the pair arrived in Northern California, where Billy would fight next, Jack said too much entertaining in Southern California was Billy's undoing. "They were all the time inviting Miske on automobile trips," Jack said. "The consequence was he didn't have a chance to do any training and when it came to boxing a tough boy like Willie Meehan, it was a hard proposition. Now, for Kruvosky we're not going to make any mistake. Billy is going to train and train hard."

Billy fought Edward "K.O." Kruvosky in San Francisco on June 14, 1918. Kruvosky had a win over Willie Meehan on his resume, and since Billy had just suffered a loss to Meehan, the locals felt Kruvosky might be able to duplicate the trick. It wasn't one of Billy's more impressive outings, but he floored Kruvosky three times on his way to a four round decision.[227] The *San Francisco Chronicle*'s reporter was unimpressed with Billy. He felt that while Billy won all the way, he should have been able to knock Kruvosky out. He said Billy looked slow, much slower than he had against Hendricks, and he didn't seem to have the same force behind his punches.[228]

Just 11 days later, on June 25, it was reported Billy was now a farmer at Small Lake, in Ramsey County in Minnesota, and when not tilling the soil, he would continue to appear in boxing matches.[229] Four days later, the same newspaper expanded on the news, writing Billy was now ready to face

---

224 Phillips, John, *The Story of Willie Meehan*, Privately published, Kathleen, GA 2009.
225 Dempsey, Jack, *Dempsey*, Simon and Schuster, New York, N.Y. 1960.
226 *San Francisco Chronicle*, Meehan Shades Miske in Southern Benefit, June 8, 1918.
227 *Oakland Tribune*, Billy Miske Lacks Speed in Ring Work. June 15, 1918.
228 *San Francisco Chronicle*, Miske Wins From Kayo But Can't Knock Him Out, June 15, 1918.
229 *Capital Times*, Unknown article title, June 25, 1918.

General Crowder's "work or fight" order as he had purchased an eighty acre farm near Snail Lake in Ramsey County, and planned to take an extensive course in farming during the summer. But, once again, they pointed out he had no intention of retiring as a boxer.[230] A few months later, it was pointed out one of the primary reasons he was staying in condition was so he could appear in Red Cross benefit shows.[231]

Interestingly, in mid-September of 1918, Fred Fulton also decided the life of a farmer might suit him well, and it was reported he was through with the boxing game and had purchased a farm where he expected to work until the end of the war. "Just what he will do after that isn't known," the article said.[232] Clearly, Jack Dempsey, who suffered a lot of criticism and was charged with being a "slacker" for not participating in World War I, wasn't the only professional fighter who didn't want to serve overseas. But, in their defense, it can be said many of these men boxed in a number of shows in which they donated their purses toward the war effort during this period of time.

Nine months after the war ended on November 11, 1918, General Crowder submitted his *Final Report* on the operations of the Selective Service System from 1917 to 1919. He pointed out that it was primarily unmarried men whose occupations they deemed inessential to the material needs of a nation during wartime who had been drafted. So, in all likelihood Billy would not have been drafted as a married man.[233]

In mid-July of 1918, Billy fought three matches within four days on the East Coast. His first opponent was "Gunboat" Smith at the Baseball Park in Jersey City, New Jersey, on July 12. Billy earned an eight-round newspaper decision over Smith.[234] The *New York Times* noted Billy had Smith on the defensive throughout the contest and had an easy time outpointing the veteran heavyweight.[235] Billy weighed 178 pounds for the fight to Smith's 179.[236]

He followed up with another eight-round newspaper decision over Bartley Madden in the same venue three days later.[237] He carried the fight to Madden in every round, landing right hooks to the head and body. Billy was hit low twice in the fourth round, but didn't complain.[238] He participated in an exhibition against George Ashe in New York's Madison Square Garden the very next day to help raise $20,000 for the War Department's Training

---

230 *Capital Times*, Unknown article title, June 29, 1918.
231 *Fresno Bee*, Billy Miske Boxer Now a General Farmer, September 18, 1918.
232 *Fort Wayne News and Sentinel*, Fulton's Career is Over, September 21, 1918.
233 Shenk, Gerald E., *Work Or Fight!*, Palgrave Macmillan, New York 2005.
234 *Milwaukee Free Press*, Miske Outpoints Smith. July 13, 1918.
235 *New York Times*. Miske Batters Opponent, July 13, 1918.
236 *San Francisco Chronicle*, Billy Miske Beats Old Gunboat Smith, July 13, 1918.
237 *Racine Journal*, Billy Miske Winner Over Bartley Madden. July 16, 1918.
238 *San Francisco Chronicle*, Miske Wins; Boxes Dempsey Tonight, July 15, 1918.

Camp Activities Fund. Ashe substituted for Jack Dempsey, who had suffered a badly sprained ankle early in the afternoon.[239]

After that flurry of ring activity, Billy returned home for a well-earned rest with his family. It was hard for Billy to be away from home for so long and he always enjoyed the time they spent together relaxing at their property along Lake Johanna.

Billy eased back into action on September 14 and knocked Billy Hart out with the only punch he landed in the first round of their contest in the St. Paul Auditorium.[240] It set up a second meeting with middleweight Harry Greb in Pittsburgh, Pennsylvania.

The two men met before 2,000 fans at Forbes Field on September 21 and Billy was 15 pounds heavier (174 – 159 lbs.) than Harry for this meeting. Interestingly, although the hometown papers reported Greb the winner of the greater number of rounds, they were mixed in their views of the winner of the fight. A number of them, including James Long of the *Pittsburgh Sun*, Richard Guy of the *Gazette-Times*, George McCoy Jr. of the *Pittsburgh Leader* and Jim Jab of the *Pittsburgh Press*, took the stance that although Harry clearly won more of the rounds, Billy's advantage over the last two rounds was so great it was enough to overcome Greb's large early lead.

It wasn't until the sixth round, when Billy started to land punishing blows to the body and right hands to the chin that he began to have anything resembling success against Greb. The ninth round was the real key for Billy, though, when he backed Greb into a corner and managed to land a hard right and reopened a cut Harry had suffered during a sparring session ten days earlier. The blood immediately began to pour down the side of Greb's face and clearly bothered him. Billy wasted no time taking advantage of the situation and launched an attack that left Harry badly beaten upon the round's conclusion.[241]

Greb recovered during the break and came out strong in the tenth and final round, but he was too weak to maintain his earlier pace. Billy landed a heavy right that caused his opponents knees to buckle, and for a moment it appeared as if he might go down, but he managed to stay on his feet. Greb fought back but he was badly hurt again before the fight's conclusion.

Contrary to a number of their counterparts, Florent Gibson and Harry Keck of the *Pittsburgh Post* agreed Greb was the winner by virtue of the simple fact he had won a greater number of the rounds.[242]

The *St. Paul Pioneer Press* had the first two rounds even, with Greb getting the better of rounds three through five. They had Billy taking the

---

239 *Nevada State Journal*, Unknown article title July 16, 1918.
240 *St. Paul Pioneer Press*. Miske, Malone, Ertle Victors, September 15, 1918.
241 *Pittsburgh Daily Dispatch*, Greb is Outpointed in Furious Encounter by St. Paul Scrapper, September 22, 1918.
242 *Pittsburgh Post*, Round by Round Story of The Greb-Miske Fight, September 22, 1918.

sixth and seventh rounds, with the eighth even, and Billy capturing the final two rounds.[243]

The event proved a flop for the promoters who staged it. They had expected much better attendance, but the cold weather for the outdoor match reduced the turnout. As a result, the gate receipts were much smaller than expected. Greb only received $600 while Billy made $1,000 because he held out for that amount before he would agree to enter the ring.[244] Both men had originally been guaranteed $2,500 apiece. Billy returned home to Minnesota disappointed the purse had been less than promised.

On October 6, Jack Reddy announced if he could sign West Coast heavyweight Willie Meehan to head a boxing card with Billy Miske, he would stage the event at the Minneapolis Auditorium later that month for the benefit of the wounded soldier' and sailors' fund.

Meehan was in the area performing exhibitions with Kid McCoy, and while expressing a willingness to meet Miske, he let it be known he could not do so without the permission of the naval authorities from San Pedro, California. Reddy was said to be seeking their permission.

It was reported that Billy had helped raise somewhere in the neighborhood of about $60,000 over the past six months by way of exhibitions held to benefit various armed services funds.[245]

While Reddy continued his efforts to put together the November benefit, he arranged a much smaller event for the St. Paul Athletic club members. The event took place October 21. The evening's entertainment was provided by local boxing amateurs, and included a professional three-round exhibition between Miske and a tough local light-heavyweight named Billy Ehmke.

Speculation was Billy might not come back east until after the war had ended, but he returned to Pittsburgh and earned a newspaper decision over Tom "Bearcat" McMahon on November 18. The event raised $4,000 for the soldiers' fund.[246]

Then, it was on to Philadelphia for a second meeting with Jack Dempsey. Dempsey had continued his destruction of the heavyweight division since his first fight with Billy, knocking out 10 of 11 opponents, seven of them, including Fred Fulton, in the first round.

The two were matched to fight on Thanksgiving Day afternoon, November 28, for a percentage of the gross gate receipts, expected to exceed $9,000. Dempsey would receive 40% and Billy 30%.[247]

Dempsey won a clear cut six-round newspaper decision over Billy in a somewhat dull affair that failed to live up to expectations. He focused his

---

243 *St. Paul Pioneer Press*. Miske All But Knocks Out Greb In Ten Round Go at Pittsburgh, September 22, 1918.
244 *Warren Evening Mirror*. Sport Salad. October 2, 1918.
245 *St. Paul Pioneer Press*. Hot After Meehan, October 6, 1918.
246 *New Castle News*. Local Boxers Reap Results. November 21, 1918.
247 *Milwaukee Free Press*. Dempsey vs. Miske. November 27, 1918.

attack in the early rounds to Billy's body, Billy taking care to protect his jaw, and returning light punches to Dempsey's head. Billy landed a hard uppercut to Dempsey's jaw in the third.

Billy displayed signs of tiring in the fifth session and Dempsey shifted his attack to the head. Billy was on the receiving end of a number of hard hooks to the jaw, but skillfully rolled away from the blows to diminish the impact. Billy was forced to clinch frequently to save himself, especially after receiving a hard right to the jaw, followed by a left hook to the stomach. At the conclusion of the round, he fended Dempsey off with stiff left jabs.

The sixth and final round belonged entirely to Dempsey. Billy was game to the end, increasing his pace whenever Dempsey let up, but Dempsey gave him a beating and left little doubt concerning his superiority.

Afterward, Billy had no hesitancy in naming Dempsey the greatest fighter in the country, saying, "I've fought them all except Willard, but Dempsey is by long odds the best. He hit me flush any number of times and nearly all of his blows hurt. I am happy however, I was able to go the full route."[248]

So dominant had young Jack Dempsey become, even Billy seemed to be content to stay the limit with him, while so many others were being disposed of within one to two rounds.

Reflecting on this fight a number of years later, Dempsey said, "Miske spent six rounds trying to hang on. He hampered every attack by grabbing at my neck and waist and arms. Finally, the bout was halted. Miske seemed exhausted and Referee Lew Grimson stopped the match.[249]

Billy concluded the year with fights against "Fireman" Jim Flynn and Gus Christie. Flynn's real name was Andrew Chiariglione and he was born in Hoboken, New Jersey on Christmas Eve of 1879.[250] His family moved to Pueblo, Colorado and it was there he obtained a job as a fireman for a railroad as a young boy, keeping the locomotive fired up and operating smoothly for the engineer, thus the nickname "Fireman". Eventually, the stocky 5'9" young man took up boxing and participated in his first professional contest in December of 1899, just a few days shy of his twentieth birthday. Despite suffering a loss in his debut, Flynn went on to enjoy a relatively successful career over the next 25 years, fighting many of the greatest fighters of his era, and getting a chance to fight for the heavyweight title twice, first against Tommy Burns in 1906, and then a second time against Jack Johnson in 1912.

The fight against Burns in Los Angeles, California on October 12, 1906 occurred eight months after Tommy had defeated Marvin Hart for the world championship. Flynn wasn't expected to present much of a challenge for Burns, but the young man surprised the champion, pushing him to the

---

248 *Bridgeport Telegram*. Dempsey Best Boxer I've Met. November 30, 1918.
249 Billy Miske's Last Christmas. *Men's Magazine*, September 1952.
250 *Salt Lake City Tribune*, Only Man With Knockout Over Dempsey Passes, April 13, 1935.

limit, until Burns was finally able to deliver the finishing blow in the fifteenth round. Flynn's second shot at the title came against Johnson in Las Vegas on July 4, 1912. It was the second time he'd faced Johnson, losing by way of an eleventh round knockout in November of 1907. He was disqualified in the 1912 title bout against Johnson in the ninth round, when a local legal authority finally stepped in and called a halt to the contest after Flynn had failed to heed to continual warnings from the referee for attempting to head butt the champion.

But, Flynn fought many other greats and leading contenders of his era over the course of his career, including the likes of Billy Papke, "Battling" Levinsky, Jack Dillon, Sam Langford and Jack Dempsey. On February 8, 1910 Sam Langford took him too lightly, showed up out of shape, and suffered a rare loss. Langford avenged the defeat five weeks later with an eighth round knockout. Ultimately, he defeated Flynn three more times when both men were in the twilight of their careers.

Flynn's other claim to fame was the fact he is the only man to ever knockout Jack Dempsey. Dempsey incurred a first round knockout loss to Flynn in Murray, Utah on February 13, 1917. Jack was really just beginning his climb up the heavyweight ranks and Flynn, although past his prime at 38 years old, was a seasoned veteran. The outcome of the fight has been debated for many years. Some claim the fight was fixed. To support this, boxing historian, Monte Cox, points to a series of articles the *Chicago Tribune* published concerning Dempsey from February 15, 1920 to March 8, 1920, and an article titled "The Fight at Murray," in which the event's promoter and Dempsey's manager, Al Auerbach, were interviewed. Auerbach maintained the fight was fixed in exchange for a $500 payout. Cox points out that Dempsey was blackballed in the area thereafter, and although nearby Salt Lake City was a big fight town during that period of time, and Dempsey was essentially an area native, he never fought in the area again.[251] In a biography written about Dempsey by Roger Kahn, the author says Dempsey claims to have hurt his right hand a few days prior to the fight while working as a pin boy in a bowling alley, while his first wife, Maxine Cates, said the truth was Dempsey threw the fight because he was offered more money to lose than to win.[252]

Interviewed at the time Flynn passed away, Dempsey said at the time he lost to Flynn he was just a kid, 22, and had just got back from New York, on the brake rods of a freight train, after suffering a couple of broken ribs against John Lester Johnson, just when he thought he was ready to set the world on fire. Dempsey said,

---

251 http://coxcorner.tripod.com/dempsey_dive.html, accessed October 15, 2010.
252 Kahn, Roger, *A Flame of Pure Fire, Jack Dempsey And The Roaring '20s*, Harcourt Brace, New York, 1999.

I was broke and having plenty of family trouble. I got back from Salt Lake, and Flynn was a big shot. They were looking for someone to 'feed' him. I was in no shape. But they offered me $200 and that looked like all the money in the world. I grabbed it.

That night, as we shook hands, he crossed a terrific right to my chin before I got my hands up. They tell me I went down face first. I never knew what hit me. Everything went black. I got up two or three times and he put me right back down again. Halfway through the first round my older brother, Bernie, who was seconding me, tossed in the towel. I guess I couldn't have gotten up anyway.

Getting knocked out wasn't so bad at that stage of the game, but it finished me on top of the Lester Johnson flop. I walked out that night and was certain I'd never fight again. I was going back to mining. I don't think I ever would have fought again, except that Flynn kept telling everybody he could do the same thing to me any time. He kept talking that way. I got so mad I forgot about mining. All I wanted was revenge.

I left Salt Lake and my luck in the ring turned right away. I started to nail 'em. They began to go down and stay down.[253]

Dempsey avenged the defeat, almost a year later to the date, when he returned the favor and knocked Flynn out in the first round of their second fight, which took place on February 14, 1918 in Fort Sheridan, Illinois.

In Dempsey's first autobiography, *Round by Round*, he makes no mention of getting hit by Flynn right after shaking hands at the outset of the fight, and instead waded in, punching with everything he had in the first round, indifferent to what might happen to himself, and got caught "cold" by Flynn before the round was a minute old, and sent to the canvas by a right to the jaw. He says he got back up and was knocked down three more times before his brother, Bernie, threw the towel in from the corner.[254]

In another biography, as told to Bob Considine and Bill Slocum, Dempsey says of the fight with Flynn that in the first minute of the fight (Flynn) hit him with a right that put him on the deck, and again that he was subsequently dropped three more times in the round before his brother threw the towel in from the corner.[255]

And finally, in yet another biography written by Dempsey with his daughter Barbara, in 1977, Dempsey again say's he failed to properly warm up prior to the fight and was caught "cold" early in the fight, and floored a

---

[253] *Steubenville Herald Star*, Dempsey Tells Story of How Jim Flynn Made Him Mad, Later Causing Him to Be Successful Boxer, April 13, 1935.
[254] Dempsey, Jack, '*Round by Round*, Whittlesey House, New York, 1940.
[255] Dempsey, Jack, '*Dempsey, by The Man Himself as Told to Bob Considine and Bill Slocum*', Simon and Schuster, New York, 1960.

few times, before his brother threw the towel in to bring an end to the fight.[256]

But as Cox and others have surmised it is possible Dempsey would have been concerned that admitting to participating in a fixed fight would be much more damaging to his reputation than a knockout suffered early in his career, and chosen to deny it as a result. If nothing else, it's interesting Dempsey would tell one version of the fight at the time of Flynn's death in 1935, about getting hit before he could get his hands back up after touching gloves at the outset of the fight, but then tell an entirely different version of the fight in his three autobiographies.

Billy faced Flynn on December 16, 1918 in Tulsa, Oklahoma, and knocked him down twice, the bell saving Flynn from a knockout at the end of the first round, before then extinguishing the "Fireman" with a knockout blow in the second frame.[257] Flynn continued fighting for many years, and at the ripe old age of 44, defeated future middleweight champion, Tiger Flowers, by way of a technical knockout. He finally hung up the gloves in 1925, a couple months shy of his 46th birthday. In the final months of his life, he operated a bar in Los Angeles, before suffering a fatal heart attack on April 12, 1935 at age 55.

Billy's last fight in 1918 was a ten round victory over Gus Christie on December 27. The *National Police Gazette* reported Billy outslugged and out-boxed Gus in every round of the no-decision bout, and although he did not succeed in putting him out, had Gus groggy in nearly every round, and only Christie's stamina enabled him to go the full route.[258] The loss convinced Christie to bring an end to his long career. He retired from the ring and ended up spending 25 years as an athletic director for the Milwaukee Athletic Club.[259] Overall, 1918 proved a pretty successful year for Billy.

---

256 Dempsey, Jack, '*Dempsey*', Harper & Row, New York, 1977.
257 *Galveston Daily News*, Billy Miske Knocks Out Jim Flynn Twice Before Count, December 17, 1918.
258 *National Police Gazette*, Miske Nearly Puts Christie Out, January 18, 1919.
259 *Milwaukee Journal*, Gus Christie's Quarter Century of Service Recognized by Club, February 20, 1944.

CHAPTER 7

Billy Learns His Fate

When the year 1919 arrived, Billy and Marie were looking forward to another exciting year. They were expecting the birth of their second child in March, and despite the recent setback against Jack Dempsey, Billy was still a rising star with the potential to earn a lot more money inside the ring. In fact, as the year began, there was talk of the possibility of a third fight with Dempsey, this time over 20 rounds, in New Orleans.[260] But, Dempsey and his manager really had their sights set on Jess Willard and his heavyweight crown. So another meeting seemed unlikely for the time being.

Billy was matched, instead, to fight Tom Cowler, an English heavyweight who had been after a match with Dempsey. The pair met on January 11 at the National Athletic Club in Philadelphia. Cowler was the bigger of the two, and if he could get by Billy, there was reason to believe he might get a shot at Dempsey next.

Billy put an end to Cowler's ambitions with a convincing six-round newspaper decision over the Englishman. He was the aggressor throughout the contest and dropped Cowler for a count of either seven or nine, depending on the source, in the first round with a right to the jaw. Cowler recovered a bit during the rest at the end of the round, but fought on the defensive for the remainder of the contest.[261] The best that could be said of Tom's performance was he took all of the punishment that came his way.[262]

Later that month, Billy suffered an injury to his right hand in training, and a January 27 bout with Hugh Walker of Kansas City had to be called off.[263]

Meanwhile, Dempsey was touring the country, offering $1,000 to anybody who could stay three rounds with him, and there was more talk of a possible match between Billy and Jack to take place in New Orleans on March 4. That Billy was anxious to face Dempsey a third time is clear from the following quotes which appeared in the *National Police Gazette* in early February:

> It might seem strange to some to hear me say that I am happy over the prospects of meeting the Salt Lake City sensation over the twenty round route. I met Dempsey in St. Paul for ten rounds and believe I

---

260 *Bridgeport Standard Telegram*, Billy Miske May Mix with Dempsey Over Long Route. January 6, 1919.
261 *National Police Gazette*, Miske Beats Cowler, February 1, 1919.
262 *Philadelphia Evening Bulletin*. Miske Defeats Cowler. January 13, 1919.
263 *Galveston Daily News*. Miske-Walker Bout at Joplin is Called Off. January 28, 1919.

64

defeated him. Again, we clashed for six rounds in Philadelphia and I experienced no trouble with him although I was not as fit for that fight as I would have liked to have been. I am making no alibis but it frequently happens that a boxer is not in the best physical and mental condition when he engages in a battle. My stomach went back on me two days before our last fight.

I realize what an aggressive boy Dempsey is; I know he can punch for I have had ample opportunity in our sixteen rounds of milling to test his ability along that line. Over the twenty-round course I feel that my showing will not be disappointing. I know Dempsey will rip into me for the first ten rounds, and I certainly intend to do the same thing to him, so there can be no soreness on his part when he ascertains early in the battle that my intentions are to stop him with the first punch just as he stopped Fulton if the chance presents itself.

I shall certainly train for this battle; it means everything to me as well as it means everything to Dempsey. It should be a bear of a fight, for Dempsey only knows one way of fighting and that is to settle things as quickly as he knows how. As this is my style, things should hum. I figure that I have more on Dempsey in the way of experience, speed and fully as much stamina. If he shows any leg or arm weariness after the tenth round, he will find it pretty tough going from then to the finish if the fight lasts the twenty rounds.

In making the match my manager, Jack Reddy, certainly grabbed the best battle of my career. We will go to New Orleans and do our work there in preparation for the fight. When we enter the ring I want my friends to know that I am there to do my best, and everyone who has ever seen me battle knows what that is. May the best man win, with a very strong wish that the best man will be myself.[264]

It turned out the announcement of the signing for the fight had been a bit premature, and in February, the talk of another match between Billy and Dempsey in New Orleans effectively came to an end as it became clear the fighter's managers and the promoter weren't going to be able to come to an agreement upon the terms for the meeting.

A March issue of the *National Police Gazette* suggested Billy was deserving of a shot at the title against Willard. As far as the *Gazette* was concerned, the fact Billy had met all of the best in his class, never been downed, and had practically put Jack Dillon out of business in their last fight, earned him the right. They praised him as a class act, and said what a strong family man he was, refusing to fight on holiday's so he might spend time with his wife and

---

264 *National Police Gazette*, Dempsey and Miske Sign for Twenty Round Battle, February 8, 1919.

children. "The holidays belong to my family. I want to stay home with the wife and the boys," said Billy.[265]

While Billy's hand healed he helped prepare a young middleweight training partner for an upcoming fight. On March 16, Jack Reddy announced that Billy's hand was fully healed and he was ready to resume hard training. The layoff had cost him thousands of dollars as he had to cancel many fights lined up before the injury.[266] He was then matched to meet Tom Cowler again on March 28 at the Albaugh Theater in Baltimore, Maryland.

Billy made quick work of Tom Cowler, knocking him out in the fourth round with a left to the stomach. Cowler appeared helpless against Billy[267] and had been floored twice previously with rights to the jaw.[268] The win proved costly though, for Billy reinjured his right hand in the second round with a blow that landed on the top of Cowler's head. He was unable to use the hand as effectively in succeeding rounds.[269]

The next day, on March 29, an article about Billy's manager, Jack Reddy, appeared in the paper in which Reddy attributed Billy's success in the ring to his living and training outdoors so much. Reddy said Billy had developed from a 158-pound fighter only three years earlier, to a heavyweight of 190 pounds. He claimed outdoor training more than anything was the key factor in Billy's "remarkable" physical transformation. He added that he kept Billy in the open whenever weather permitted, and since he lived at one of the nearby lakes in the summer he devoted much of his time to rowing, swimming and running. Once the weather turned cold, Reddy said he insisted that Billy incorporate long walks, skating, skiing, tobogganing and jumping into his training routine.[270]

Billy's next fight, only three days after his knockout of Cowler, took place on March 31 at the Duquesne Gardens in Pittsburgh against the incomparable Harry Greb. Shortly before climbing through the ropes, Billy was informed of the birth of his second child, a boy he and Marie named Douglas, after Billy's friend and admirer, the enormously popular actor, Douglas Fairbanks, Sr. Fairbanks was a boxing fan and went on to star in a number of successful adventure films in the 1920s, including The Mark of Zorro, Robin Hood, The Black Pirate, The Thief of Bagdad and The Three Musketeers. Billy and the actor first became friends while working together at a benefit for the Red Cross in Los Angeles, California.

---

265 *National Police Gazette*, Miske Deserves Fight With Champion Willard, March 15, 1919.
266 *Minneapolis Tribune*, Miske to Resume Work After Enforced Layoff, March 16, 1919.
267 *Fort Wayne News*. Takes the Count Early. Marcy 29, 1919.
268 *Sandusky Register*. Miske Gives Cowler K.O. Blow in Fourth. March 29, 1919.
269 *Evening Telegram*. Cowler Proved Game in Late Bout. April 9, 1919.
270 *Bridgeport Standard Telegram*. Outdoor Life Has Done Wonders for Billy Miske. March 29, 1919.

During the fight, Greb proved too fast for Billy, winning eight of the ten rounds, the final round viewed as even, Billy winning the seventh round as a result of his vicious infighting.[271]

Afterward, Jack Dillon, who officiated the match, claimed the fight wasn't on the level. Prior to making any public statements, Dillon gave an official report to local Sheriff William Haddock, and Superintendent of Police Robert Alderice. The statement from Dillon, himself a deputy sheriff and former member of the city detective force included the following excerpts:

> The bout between Miske and Greb last Monday night looked to be 'crooked' as far as Miske was concerned. It certainly looked to me as though he pulled his punches. Both men hit low and I was so disgusted that I thought it best to report it to you (the sheriff) and then give the facts out to the public.
>
> From the outset, I was satisfied that Miske was "pulling" and in the clinches he would play a light tattoo on Greb's stomach. He hit him low in the third round, but this didn't hurt much.
>
> Greb tired in the last round mostly on account of being mauled and pulled around in the clinches, where Miske's weight advantage came into play. Had I stopped the bout, the people who fought their way in and paid to see the exhibition would have suffered. I continually called on Miske to fight.
>
> To my mind, the only remedy is to have clubs make the boxers sign an agreement that if there is any intentional foul or stalling on their part they forfeit their portion of the receipts. Several bouts where champions and near champions have appeared here, to my mind, haven't given the public a run for the money and unless the clubs make some arrangements to better protect the public from possible stalling I will refuse to referee any more bouts.[272]

However, another article in the same paper revealed Billy may have hurt his right hand against Tom Cowler three days earlier and was incapable of using it effectively against Greb as a result. But, Sheriff Haddock, who attended the fight, was convinced Billy had "stalled" and "faked" and he called in officials from the club who promoted the bout and advised them Billy would not be permitted to fight in the city again. The sheriff exonerated Greb because he was convinced had done his best.[273]

Billy's manager offered a different opinion on the issue. To Reddy's way of thinking, the only thing queer about the match was the work of the

---

[271] *Pittsburgh Post*. Unknown article title, April 1, 1919.
[272] *Cumberland Evening Times*. Miske – Greb Bout Crooked Writes Referee Jack Dillon. April 5, 1919.
[273] *Cumberland Evening Times*. Billy Miske is Barred in Pittsburg Ring. April 5, 1919.

referee. Said Reddy, "In the third round, after about a minute had elapsed, Miske hit Greb with a left hook to the stomach, and Greb went to his knees right in his own corner. He crawled over to his chair and sat down. The referee made no attempt to count, but waved Bill to his corner. I asked him what had happened. He said Miske had fouled Greb. But, he did not have him examined, nor did he award him the fight. He merely stood there while Greb rested until the end of the round, and during the minute intermission, and after that ordered them back into the ring. It was a horrible piece of work and the only crooked thing about that fight that I saw."

Continuing, Reddy said, "I am not making any alibi for Miske. He did not show the best fight in the world, but I thought he won by a fair margin and so did a few of the writers. Most of them, however, gave the battle to Greb, who seldom loses there. The crooked talk, to my mind, is just a lot of bunk. Dillon knows nothing about the ring game, and I accepted him as referee solely because "Red" Mason, Greb's manager, told me he was competent, capable and experienced. He's not one of the three." The fight drew a total gate of $9,800.[274]

Three days after Billy's loss to Greb, Jack Dempsey was asked to comment on the idea there were no formidable foes for him to face should he defeat Willard in July. Dempsey said those who said that, "probably forgot Billy Miske. There's a tough one. He's game, he's fast, clever and he can hit. I fought him twice and I haven't stopped him yet. That certainly entitles Billy to another crack at me and as soon as I get through with the Willard fight. Billy can try it again with me, whether I'm champion or not."[275]

Billy was back in action again on April 28 in Tulsa, Oklahoma where he faced heavyweight contender Bill Brennan. Brennan, who stood 6'1" tall, weighed between 185 and 200 pounds and had been fighting professionally since 1913. Born William Shanks in Louisville, Kentucky in 1893, Bill was of German descent. Early in his career he adopted the name Brennan and made up a story about his family migrating from Ireland in order to distance himself from his German heritage when World War I broke out.[276]

Although Brennan had suffered a technical knockout against Jack Dempsey the previous year, and was coming off a second consecutive loss to Harry Greb that year, he was still considered a dangerous proposition. He and Billy went the distance, Billy pulling out the decision on the strength of a big fourteenth round that left Brennan staggering upon its conclusion.[277]

On June 1, Billy was asked for his pick of a winner in the upcoming heavyweight title fight between Jess Willard and Jack Dempsey. Billy picked

---

274 *Minneapolis Tribune*, Miske-Greb Bout Fake, Assertion of Referee, April 4, 1919.
275 *Fort Wayne News and Sentinel.* James J. Corbett syndicated column. April 3, 1919.
276 Kahn, Roger, *A Flame of Pure Fire.* Harcourt Brace & Company, New York, N.Y. 1999.
277 *Beloit Daily News.* Miske Takes Bout From Billy Brennan. April 29, 1919.

Dempsey to stop Willard inside of six rounds, adding: "I never boxed Willard, but saw him in action. I've boxed Dempsey twice and know he's the hardest hitting heavyweight that I've ever met."[278]

Meanwhile, Billy's next opponent was Willie Meehan, a man he'd fought over four rounds in California a year earlier. This time, however, the fight took place on June 6 in Billy's home town, St. Paul, over a greater distance of ten rounds.

Billy emerged from the battle with Meehan with a decisive newspaper decision, and came close to finishing the flabby, but clever fighter. Billy sent Meehan to the canvas in the ninth round with a left to the jaw. Meehan came back quickly, but in the tenth round he was all but helpless. Billy won nearly every round.[279]

Only three days later, Billy was in Forbes Field in Pittsburgh, Pennsylvania, where his ban had been lifted. He faced Kid Norfolk for the second time in his career. Anxious to reverse his loss on points to Norfolk in 1917, Billy entered the ring weighing 180 pounds to Norfolk's 182. But, once again, Norfolk proved the better man. He was the aggressor throughout, and earned the newspaper decision by a wide margin.[280]

Billy never had a chance. Norfolk was too fast for him. At a distance, the well-built fighter peppered Billy with lefts and rights whenever he desired, and whenever he moved inside, he roughed him up. In the fifth round, Norfolk landed a big right hand that appeared as though it may have broken Billy's nose. In the first half of the seventh round, he hammered Billy so frequently it looked as though Billy might not last the round. But, Billy bounced back, tearing into Norfolk and forcing him to let up.

In the eighth round, Billy landed a hook to the jaw and forced Norfolk to clinch, but by the end of the round the latter was back in charge. The ninth round was Billy's worst. On two separate occasions, he suffered numerous blows to the head and only brought an end to the attacks by holding onto his opponent until the referee managed to pry them apart.

Billy made a gallant last ditch effort in the final session, rushing Norfolk, and fighting toe to toe during the greater part of the round. But, at the bell, there was no doubt it was Norfolk's fight by a mile.[281]

The *Minneapolis Tribune* reported Billy was off form as a result of continuous traveling, and speculated the combination of the fight only three days earlier and the long train trip to Pittsburgh had taken it out of him.[282]

Sheriff Haddock, at ringside, to ensure Billy gave his best, said afterward he thought Billy had tried harder against Norfolk than against Greb but he now believed Billy had been overrated in Pittsburgh in the past.

---

278 *Syracuse Herald*. What Prominent Boxers Think of Big Bout. June 1, 1919.
279 *Reno Evening Gazette*. Miske Defeats Meehan. June 7, 1919.
280 *Cumberland Evening Times*. Forbes Field Contest Last Night Draws Big Crowd to See Heavyweights in Ten Rounds. June 10, 1919.
281 *Pittsburgh Gazette Times*. Norfolk Easy Winner Over Miske at Forbes Field. June 10, 1919.
282 *Minneapolis Tribune*. Miske Bit Off Form. June 9, 1919.

Harry Keck of the *Pittsburgh Gazette Times* echoed the same sentiment adding:

> "The performance of Miske last night bears out the writer's contention all along since the last Greb fight that Miske is overrated here and that there is a very closely drawn limit to his ability. He's all right against a big, slow-moving fighter like himself, but against a fast man he's all at sea. In the writer's opinion, Miske, while beaten last night, vindicated himself on the charges that he did not try against Greb. In the bout with Greb, he tried just as much as he tried last night, but his best then, as against Norfolk, was far from enough to keep him in the running.[283]

Despite a number of victories over the likes of men such as Bill Tate, Jeff Clarke, "Gunboat" Smith, "Battling" Jim Johnson, John Lester Johnson, "Tiger" Flowers, and "Battling" Siki, in addition to Billy, during his 12 year ring career, Norfolk never did get a chance to fight for a world championship. A technical knockout loss suffered against Tommy Gibbons in December of 1924 essentially put an end to any remaining ideas the Kid may have had about achieving the goal.

Billy's hectic schedule didn't offer any relief as he was scheduled to face Tommy Gibbons at Nicollet Park in Minneapolis on June 19. It was viewed as a sign that Tommy's manager, Eddie Kane, wasn't taking the fight with Miske lightly when it was reported that he'd engaged the services of the great black heavyweight, Sam Langford, to come to St. Paul and work with his man. Tommy was expected to try and take off an extra five pounds, to come in at 165 pounds for the fight with Billy, in order to make even greater use of the advantage he would have in speed between the pair.[284]

A week before the contest, Billy became ill and was ordered to bed by his doctor. To make matters worse, he was also afflicted with a number of boils, a painful skin disease resulting in the accumulation of pus and dead tissue. Four days before the fight, his manager informed the promoter, Mike Collins, it would be impossible to go through with the fight. Collins asked local sportswriter and referee, George Barton, to accompany him on a visit to Billy's home on June 15.

According to Barton, Collins told Billy there were already $18,000 in advance ticket sales and he was sure the figure would climb to $30,000. He was worried that with the local baseball team coming to town for a three-week home stand any postponement of the fight would cause a loss of interest. He told Billy it meant a big payday for all concerned, and urged him to try and go through with the fight.

---

283 *Pittsburgh Gazette Times.* Norfolk Easy Winner Over Miske at Forbes Field. June 10, 1919.
284 *Minneapolis Tribune*, Sam Langford Comes to Aid T. Gibbons. June 10, 1919.

Miske, still in bed and running a fever, told Collins, "I'll get up tomorrow. If I can walk around the block without falling down, I'll fight Gibbons for you Friday night."[285]

The word in St. Paul was Tommy planned to enter the ring weighing no more than 165 pounds to be as fast as possible against Billy.[286] In addition to the upcoming Gibbons fight, Billy was also scheduled to face Bill Brennan again on June 25 in St. Louis, Missouri, followed by "Battling" Levinsky in Toledo, Ohio on July 3.

Twin Cities fight fans eagerly anticipated the Miske-Gibbons fight. The expectation was that Gibbons would earn a victory via a decision if he chose to box rather than mix it up.

True to his word, Billy kept his June 19 date with Tommy Gibbons before the largest crowd ever to attend a fight in Minnesota up to that time. There were approximately 9,000 fans on-hand to witness the contest, with another 1,500 estimated watching from neighboring rooftops. The total gate for the event was $17,000, with the two fighters earning a share of $4,500 apiece.

Billy ended up earning a draw with Gibbons in the view of *Minneapolis Tribune* writer Fred Coburn. "The fight was a draw and nothing else," said Coburn. "Miske was the better man on aggressiveness and Gibbons landed the cleaner punches and did the snappier work. Yet, Gibbons showed no desire to stand and mix things with his bulkier opponent. Miske fought a tear-in fight, but he experienced much difficulty in locating the elusive Tommy, who danced, dodged and side-stepped his way all over the squared circle, occasionally stopping long enough to shoot in lefts or rights that frequently stung but never did any material damage," continued Coburn.

Coburn felt Gibbons work gave him a shade in the earlier rounds, but Billy's "great showing of willingness and aggressiveness evened things up for him in the closing sessions." It was noted the two men warmly congratulated each other upon the conclusion of the fight. The announced weights were 167 for Tommy, and 177 for Billy, who looked considerably stronger. Each man earned $3,500 for their work.[287]

Looking back on the fight over a year later, Billy said:

> I was covered with boils the day of the bout and had nine of them lanced. I had a fever but got it down and got by the medical examination. My back ached, my legs were numb. I had dark specs in front of my eyes. I said my prayers, gritted my teeth, and said, "I'm going to go those ten rounds." I know it wasn't a good fight, but

---

285 Barton, George, *My Lifetime in Sports*. The Olympic Press, Minneapolis, MN 1957.
286 *Minneapolis Tribune*. Sam Langford Comes to Aid T. Gibbons. June 10, 1919.
287 *Minneapolis Tribune*. Miske and Gibbons. June 20, 1919.

those who saw it know that I kept after Gibbons all the way, even though I don't know how I did it.[288]

Barton, who refereed the match, recalled that as weak as Billy was from his illness, he fought furiously for ten rounds and extended Gibbons to the limit.[289]

Six days later, and still suffering from boils on his neck, Billy fought an eight round draw in St. Louis with Bill Brennan. Two days afterward, he cancelled plans to go to Toledo, Ohio to assist Jack Dempsey in preparations for his title fight with Jess Willard so he might instead focus on his health.[290]

Once Billy was well enough to travel, he made his way to Toledo to put in some last minute training for his upcoming match with "Battling" Levinsky. On the afternoon of July 2, he put in a long workout at the Edward Ford Plate Glass club in Rossford, Ohio. Rossford is located just across the river from Toledo. The promoters of the Miske–Levinsky bout were anticipating gate receipts of as much as $15,000 despite the fact the Willard – Dempsey title fight would take place only a day later in neighboring Toledo.[291]

Billy and "Battling" Levinsky met in Rossford on July 3 in a 12-round event promoter Jimmy Shea billed as being for the light-heavyweight championship of the world. Shea thought so many fans would be in nearby Toledo for the heavyweight championship between Willard and Dempsey a day later, he might be able to draw a good many of them to Rossford the day before to witness a match between Levinsky and Miske.

The bout was characterized as a slow 12-round draw.[292] The *Toledo Blade* reported Levinsky shaded Billy in "an uninteresting 12-round clinching match". Billy forced the fight, but was unable to escape Levinsky's counter left and right hand jabs to the face throughout the contest. The crowd was plainly dissatisfied with the performance of the fighters, and let the fighters know about it.[293] The two men earned $1,900 each for their work.[294] A total of 10,000 fans were reported as having attended.[295]

On July 4, Billy was at ringside to witness Jack Dempsey take on heavyweight champion Jess Willard. Sportswriter George Barton said during more than a half century of association with boxing, he never saw a boxer train harder and under more unfavorable weather conditions than Dempsey did in preparation for this fight. Despite the intense heat in Toledo, Dempsey ran eight to ten miles every morning, and spent the greater part of

---

288 *Fort Wayne Journal-Gazette.* Billy Miske Tells How He Hopes to Beat Jack Dempsey, August 29, 1920.
289 Barton, George. *My Lifetime in Sports*, The Olympic Press, Minneapolis, MN 1957.
290 *Evening Gazette.* A Tale of Two Fists. June 28, 1919.
291 *Minneapolis Tribune*, Arena Dust, July 3, 1919.
292 *Minneapolis Tribune.* 10,000 Persons See Prelude to Heavyweight Championship Today. July 4, 1919.
293 *Toledo Blade.* Miske Shaded by Levinsky, July 4, 1919.
294 *San Antonio Evening News.* Levinsky and Miske Copped $1,900 Each. July 16, 1919.
295 *San Francisco Chronicle*, Billy Miske and Levinsky Box Draw, July 5, 1919.

two hours sparring under the hot afternoon sun each day. By the time of the fight, he was a mean, lean, and hungry fighter.

The 38-year-old Willard, on the other hand, loafed through his training sessions in a ring covered by a canopy and appeared anything but well trained by the time of the fight. The 6'6" champion, known as the "Pottawatomie Giant", looked fat and slow, and was thought to scale over 250 pounds. When Barton mentioned to him beforehand he had a tough fight on his hands and should have trained harder, Jess replied: "Don't be silly. A little fellow like Dempsey can't lick one side of me. I'll knock him out when I get ready – maybe in two rounds and three at the most."[296]

Unlike Dempsey, who seemed to love to fight, Willard never really liked it. He became a national hero when he defeated the unpopular Jack Johnson in Havana, Cuba in April of 1915 for the world heavyweight championship. "I never had a glove on until I was 28," Jess once said. "I never liked it. In fact, I hated it but there was money in it. Harming the other fellow seemed to be cruel."

The temperature read 118 degrees at ringside by the time of the fight. Dempsey absolutely destroyed Willard in three rounds, flooring the champion six times in the first round, and beating him so badly that by the end of the third session, Willard's face was swollen to twice its normal size. There was a deep cut on his right cheek, his right eye was completely closed, his left partially closed and blood was flowing freely from both his nose and cheek. Barton had never seen a fighter subjected to such a beating. Willard's chief second threw in the towel before the fourth round, finally bringing the slaughter to an end.

Afterward, it was learned Willard's right cheekbone was fractured, his nose broken and he'd suffered the loss of six teeth.[297] The Dempsey championship reign had officially begun.

Many people believed Dempsey's first title defense would come against Billy, although Dempscy and his manager had their sights set on a French sensation named Georges Carpentier. They believed Billy's performance against Levinsky would diminish interest in another match between him and Dempsey.

In July of 1919, Billy made the decision to see a specialist. He hadn't been feeling well for some time, and the pains through his back and hip persisted.[298] He was first diagnosed with what was called a "nephritic condition" or the early stages of Bright's Disease. The disease was named after Dr. Richard Bright, who described the condition in the early nineteenth century. Lack of understanding of kidney function at the time meant several different conditions could be considered Bright's Disease. These included inflammation of the kidney, commonly called nephritis.

---

296 Barton, George. My Lifetime in Sports. The Olympic Press, Minneapolis, MN 1957.
297 Barton, George. My Lifetime in Sports. The Olympic Press. Minneapolis, MN 1957.
298 *Lima News*. Billy Miske Can't Meet Anybody For a Long Time. July 22, 1919.

The symptoms most commonly associated with Bright's Disease were intense pain on either or both sides of the lower back. Billy had been experiencing this pain for some time. Fever might be present and intense edema, or retention of fluids, might cause the extremities to appear extremely swollen. Breath could be labored and difficult, particularly if kidney failure caused fluid to accumulate in the lungs. Those affected might also find eating difficult, or might have periods of nausea or vomiting. All of the symptoms indicated a very serious disease, which was usually not treatable at the time. Two specialists had already given Billy this diagnosis that summer and he awaited the verdict from the third.

He must have struggled to maintain a positive outlook as he awaited the doctor's diagnosis. Undoubtedly, he feared the worst based on the previous feedback. He probably wondered how he would break the news to Marie if the doctor confirmed the previous opinions.

When the third and final specialist walked in to deliver his findings, the news wasn't any better. It couldn't have been easy telling a remarkably fit looking athlete his diagnosis was the same as the previous specialists, and there was little that could be done. In all likelihood, the 25-year-old had less than five years to live.

Surely, Billy would have been somewhat prepared for the news, but receiving this confirmation must have been a severe blow. There was no getting around the fact he was a dying man, with a young wife and two small boys under the age of three. Any number of men might have chosen to accept their fate and ask what they could do to make themselves as comfortable as possible during the time they had left and try and take it easy. But, Billy was a fighter. He wanted to know what steps he could take to try and beat the disease, so he asked the doctor what he should do. Then, he went home and broke the news to Marie.

Just how much he shared with Marie is unknown. Billy may not have let her know just how serious his condition was, because years later she revealed she was always convinced her big strong healthy looking husband wasn't really that sick and would overcome the odds.

By July 10, the news was public, Billy had been ordered by physicians to rest in bed, undisturbed, in a quiet darkened room for at least a month on a milk diet. Bed rest was a common prescription for the disease at the time. Additionally, one's diet was considered to be of great importance. Meat and eggs were to be avoided. Fresh fruit juices, selected fruits, and grains in the form of toasted preparations, nut foods and vegetables were all considered good options. Any food or liquids which might irritate an already inflamed kidney were to be avoided at all costs. At the same time, cleansing of the bowels with a daily hot enema was also typically prescribed.[299]

---

[299] Rossiter, Frederick, B.S. M.D. *The Practical Guide to Health*, Pacific Press Publishing Association, Mountain View, California, 1908.

Billy was told he was to do no boxing for several months, if ever. Tentative matches with a number of fighters were immediately cancelled.[300] This didn't prevent his manager from working the media concerning the possibility of a future match between Billy and the new heavyweight champion. While acknowledging that Billy was on a vegetable diet for a spinal ailment, Reddy insisted he would be fine in another month and could then start training if Dempsey would accept his challenge.[301]

When Reddy visited Milwaukee and continued his crusade, at least one writer questioned the merits of their challenge. Quoting Walter Heisnor, the referee of Billy's fight the previous month against Bill Brennan:

> Billy Miske didn't show very much in his bout with Knockout Brennan. He's one of the kind that thinks fighting consists in preventing the other fellow from doing any. His contest with Brennan was extremely disappointing to those who had heard of his reputation. He's hard to knock out, but he doesn't deserve many decisions if he contents himself with leading and following it into a clinch right after.[302]

But, just what kind of physical condition had Billy been in for his contest against Brennan, or many of the other men he fought that year or the most recent years for that matter? One thing was clear, the recent descriptions of Billy's fighting, filled with comments about the frequent clinching, and lack of aggressiveness, were far from those of the man who was characterized as extremely aggressive and unrelenting a few short years ago.

Writer Jack Keene offered his own view in mid-August in his column titled "Sport Snap-Shots:"

> Billy Miske is out of the ring for a time. He's suffering from a spine and hip ailment, believed to have originated from a sprained hip two years ago. His kidneys also have been affected.
>
> Despite the sufferings he has gone on and boxed with the sturdiest men in his division. He has never been knocked out, nor has he been badly beaten, even by the champion, Jack Dempsey, who twice met Miske.
>
> Within the past five weeks he has boxed five tough opponents, including Norfolk, Brennan, Tom Gibbons, and Levinskly, but on his return from Toledo immediately placed himself in the hands of three prominent diagnosticians for a verdict.

---

300 *La Crosse Tribune and Leader-Press*. Physicians Order a Rest for Miske. July 10, 1919.
301 *Beloit Daily News*. Billy Miske May Challenge Dempsey. July 26, 1919.
302 *New Castle News*. Billy Miske Receives Raz. July 29, 1919.

His manager, J.E. Reddy, announced the results of those consultations. According to Reddy, the physicians stated Miske being able to fight at all, let alone meeting the best men in the world and invariably making a good showing, approximated the eighth wonder of the world. They said he had the injury for about three years in their opinion and must have suffered intense pain during a great many of his ring battles.[303]

The biggest fight of Billy's young life was at hand, and he was determined to take whatever actions he could to give himself every advantage in the battle ahead.

---

[303] *Janesville Daily Gazette*. Sport Snap-Shots. August 16, 1919.

CHAPTER 8

The Elgin Six

Billy spent the rest of the summer of 1919 with his young family at their cottage on the shore of Lake Johanna. The lake, despite its relatively small size of approximately 211 acres, was good for fishing. And fishing, along with hunting, was one of Billy's favorite pastimes.

His doctor prescribed rest and relaxation, along with specific dietary instructions and Billy did his best to comply. It must have been very difficult for a man used to being as active as Billy. Under different conditions, the property on the lake would have been an ideal place to spend the summer months relaxing with Marie and his two boys. But, thoughts of providing for his family surely must have weighed heavily on his mind during this difficult time.

Ironically, in late September, Dempsey's manager, Jack Kearns, said there were two American heavyweights he felt were qualified for a shot at Dempsey's title. One of those was Bill Brennan and the other was Billy. Kearns said:

> Dempsey never has been able to knock out Miske. In their fights, Dempsey has outpointed Miske by a mile, but there is something baffling about this style – and Dempsey has not been able to solve it. I have had several offers for a battle between Dempsey and Miske and there is a likelihood right now that I will accept for a bout to be put on in New Orleans during Mardis Gras week.[304]

But, the chances of Billy fighting for Dempsey's title seemed very slim at the time. In fact, in the latter part of October, it was reported Billy was in the hospital suffering from a spinal ailment and would not be in condition to box again for six months, if ever. But, his manager, Jack Reddy, continued to maintain Billy would return to the ring, although it would be another three months before he could even consider training.[305]

As it turned out, the rest and dietary changes seemed to work wonders for Billy. By November, he resumed light activity and Reddy was telling everyone Billy's "old-time vigor" had returned. Billy agreed, saying he was as healthy as ever.[306]

On November 30, 1919, it was announced Billy would head a boxing card staged the following week by St. Paul's Ace of Clubs. Billy's return to

---

304 *Syracuse Herald.* Jim Corbett's column, September 26, 1919.
305 *Waterloo Evening Courier.* Miske Still Crippled, October 20, 1919.
306 *St. Paul Pioneer Press.* Miske to Come Back, November 1919.

the ring occurred on December 5 in a four-round contest against a journeyman heavyweight who went by the name of "Farmer" Lodge.

All four of the bouts on the club's card were fiercely contested. Lodge, a popular local draw, produced one of the better efforts of his career. Though he was clearly outpointed by Billy, Lodge hurt him with a couple of heavy blows, and was still fighting hard at the conclusion of the fourth and final round.[307] It wasn't one of Billy's better outings, but it gave him an opportunity to gauge his health, and all things considered, he viewed it as a success.

Later that month, it was announced that Billy had entered the automobile business, sinking the better part of his ring savings into an Elgin automobile dealership in St. Paul with an associate named A. H. Badnals. The dealership, named Miske Auto Co. Distributors and Dealers, was located at 200 West Fourth Street in an area known as "auto row."

It was a decision Billy had given a lot of thought to. He wasn't sure if he would be able to return to the ring, and the doctors had told him it would be unwise to do so. The dealership looked like a good business opportunity to him.

The Elgin Motor Car Corporation (1916 – 1924) was run by the same executives who ran the Elgin watch company. They purchased the New Era Motor Car Company of Joliet, Illinois and moved it to a 210,000 square foot factory housed on 13 acres of land in Argo, Illinois, a suburb of Chicago. Their motto was "Built like a Watch" and, in keeping with the theme of the timepieces they were better known for producing, they referred to their automobile as "The Car of the Hour."

Although Chicago never really rivaled Detroit as the premier auto manufacturing capital in the country, during the first decade of the twentieth century there were 28 companies there producing a total of 68 different models of automobiles.

The Elgin was a conventional car which had performed remarkably well in Midwest endurance contests staged in Illinois. Auto manufacturing had begun to decline in the area by World War I, and The Elgin Motor Car Company was the last Chicago automobile manufacturer of significance. They built over 16,000 cars in their Argo plant between 1916 and their ultimate bankruptcy in 1924.[308]

At the time Billy bought his dealership, Elgin was championing its six-cylinder engine, graceful design and dependability and obtainable price. The company boasted of the roominess and comfortable ride of its automobiles, and stressed a noticeable economy of both tires and fuel. The smooth ride was attributed to a rear spring suspension perfected by Elgin engineers. The ad accompanying the announcement of Billy's new dealership offered consumers their choice of a five-passenger touring car ($1,485), sports

---

307 *St. Paul Pioneer Press*. Ace of Clubs Has Real Boxing Show, December 6, 1919.
308 Fink, James J., *America Adopts the Automobile*. Harvard University Press, Cambridge, MA 1970.

model ($1,585) or sedan ($2,450). Business was strong for the Elgin Motor Car Company and undoubtedly seemed like a wise investment at the time.

The announcement of the opening of the dealership made it clear Billy hadn't officially retired as a boxer, but an article a week later, reiterated that only a few months earlier his doctor had said it would be at least a year before he could be in fighting condition.[309] Of course, there really was no way of knowing if Billy would be able to continue to fight. Either way, it was clear the bulk of Billy's time during the beginning of 1920 would be spent trying to sell automobiles.

A few months later, Billy had to be questioning his purchase of the dealership. He really didn't have a business or sales background. He must have felt like a fish out of water while he was trying to learn all the nuances of operating an automobile dealership. The year, 1920, was the Elgin Motor Car Company's strongest, but good sales were short lived as the post war recession set in and Billy's dealership suffered. All the money he had invested in the dealership, along with the day-to-day cost of operation, and no more income from boxing, combined to drain the bulk of his savings.

By the spring of 1920, there were renewed discussions of a possible match with heavyweight champion, Jack Dempsey. Dempsey hadn't fought since lifting the title from Jess Willard the previous July, and while he was picking up easy money in Los Angeles making movies, he was anxious to get back into action. Floyd Fitzsimmons, a boxing promoter in Benton Harbor, Michigan, had just returned from Los Angeles, and claimed Dempsey would make his first title defense in his hometown on July 5 against the best heavyweight he could. Billy was one of five possible opponents mentioned, including Fred Fulton, Willie Meehan, Tony Melchoir, and Bill Brennan. Fitzsimmons, a native son, had been staging boxing shows there for the past ten years.[310]

Billy responded to the talk, claiming he had undergone a "rigid medical examination" and the specialist's verdict was so favorable he planned to start training right away. "I believe I shall soon be as good as I ever was. I intend to try myself out with one or two bouts soon, and by July I shall be ready to meet Dempsey. Jack stopped Levinsky, Brennan and Fulton, but he could not knock me off my feet in two bouts. I am the logical challenger."[311]

With the automobile dealership losing so much money, it became clear to Billy he had little choice but to return to the ring. Within five months, he had lost $55,000 in his new business, and he needed additional money to carry on.[312] He accepted a tune-up bout against a mediocre St. Louis heavyweight named Jack Moran to take place on June 11 at the Armory in

---

309 *Des Moines Capital*. Miske Sells Autos, January 4, 1920.
310 *New Castle News*. Dempsey Fights on July Fifth, April 8, 1920.
311 *Perry Daily Chief*. Miske Wants Chance, April 26, 1920.
312 Barton, George, *My Lifetime in Sports*. The Olympic Press, Minneapolis, MN 1957.

Minneapolis. To prepare himself physically, Billy spent several weeks training in a rough northern Minnesota lumber camp.[313]

As expected, Billy made short work of Moran, knocking him out in the second round of the scheduled ten-round event. He knocked Moran down three times in the first round and four times in the second round, before Moran was finally counted out.[314] Eight days later representatives of Billy and Jack Dempsey met in Chicago to discuss the details of a title fight between the two men, to take place on Labor Day, instead of July 5.[315] It would take some time to come together, but by July 17, it was beginning to appear the fight would take place, especially if the boxing commission of Michigan would sanction a decision at the end of ten rounds.

"I have battled Dempsey twice and got nothing for it. I want to win the title and think I can, that's why I insist on a decision," said Billy.[316] Decisions were possible in the state of Michigan under the law, their boxing commission having the right to allow a verdict if they saw fit.

On July 27, it became official. Dempsey was matched to meet Billy in a 10-round heavyweight championship fight to a decision in an open-air arena at Benton Harbor on Labor Day. Dempsey was guaranteed $50,000 and the privilege of accepting a percentage of the receipts, while Billy was guaranteed his largest payday ever, a flat fee of $25,000.[317] Lightweight champion, Benny Leonard, had successfully defended his title against Charlie White in the same arena earlier that month.

Jack Reddy said when he phoned Billy long distance to tell him he had been matched with Dempsey, Billy smiled so loud he actually heard it on the other end of the line.[318]

Looking back at the events leading up to the signing for the fight 32 years later, Dempsey said:

> Miske's manager, Jack Reddy, asked Kearns for another bout. It seemed useless to ask. Miske was through as a serious contender. He was not nearly as fast as he'd been just two years before, and his tricky defense and hard offense were gone, too.
>
> Reddy asked again and again. He begged and pleaded. I knew full well that Billy Miske would give me no real fight, but I'd been hearing stores from other fighters that he was broke and needed the money badly. Miske was a favorite among boxers. He was kind and

---

313 Blair, George, *Billy Miske, The St. Paul Thunderbolt*, Self-published, 1988.
314 *San Francisco Chronicle*, Miske Knocks Out Moran of St. Louis, June 12, 1920.
315 *Billings Gazette*. $50,000 Offered for Dempsey-Miske Bout, June 20, 1920.
316 *St. Paul Pioneer Press*. Miske and Dempsey May Meet for Bout in Benton Harbor, July 17, 1920.
317 *North Adams Transcript*. Jack Dempsey to Meet Miske, July 28, 1920.
318 *Fort Wayne Journal-Gazette*. Fans Given Chance to Judge Boxer's Merits, August 31, 1920.

generous. The least I could do was help him out of a little financial jam. So, I asked Kearns for the fight.[319]

But there was another reason to accept the match according to Kearns:

I owed Fitzsimmons a favor. Back when we arrived in Chicago, in January 1918, hungrily looking for a bout, it was Floyd who gave us our big break. He was managing Homer Smith, who had title aspirations of his own, but Floyd got us that shot at Racine in which Dempsey knocked out Smith in the first round and started us on our way.[320]

Fitzsimmons also told Kearns that Billy was suffering from a kidney disease, had lost his life savings of $45,000 on his automobile investment and was drowning in bills. "But he's back up to 190 pounds and looking for a big payday. It'll be a big favor if you'll give us the shot," said Fitzsimmons. Since Kearns felt he owed Fitzsimmons, and Dempsey liked Billy and wanted to help him, they agreed to the match.[321]

Benton Harbor is located along the southeastern shore of Lake Michigan, approximately 100 miles northeast of Chicago, and 186 miles west of Detroit. It was originally named Brunson Harbor after Sterne Brunson, one of the first founders of the area. It was renamed Benton Harbor in 1865, in honor of Thomas Benton, a Missouri senator who assisted Michigan's efforts to become a state.

Shortly after articles for the fight were signed, it was announced Billy and his manager would depart St. Paul for Chicago in mid-August, where he planned to train for a week before continuing on to Benton Harbor. It was expected hundreds of Twin-Cities fans would travel to Benton Harbor to witness the fight. Arrangements for special trains to carry the spectators over the 500 mile trip from St. Paul and Minneapolis were already underway.[322]

As formidable as the champion was, a number of St. Paul's leading fighters believed Billy was up to the job. Mike Gibbons, perhaps not as knowledgeable about Billy's health issues as one might expect, was one of those men. He felt Billy had a good chance of lifting the heavyweight title from Dempsey and said:

I don't know what has kept Miske out of the ring for nearly a year, but I do know that I have never seen him looking better or boxing better than he is right now. Billy tells me he's stronger than ever before and he surely looks it, and he certainly is putting more snap

---

319 Billy Miske's Last Christmas. *Men Magazine*, September 1952.
320 Kearns, Jack, *The Million Dollar Gate*. The MacMillan Company, New York, N.Y. 1966.
321 Kearns, Jack, *The Million Dollar Gate*. The MacMillan Company, New York, N.Y. 1966.
322 *St. Paul Pioneer Press*. Unknown article title, August 1, 1920.

into his punches than I can ever recollect seeing, and I have seen a lot of him.

It would be hard to imagine anyone better qualified to judge Billy's abilities than Mike Gibbons. He'd worked with him on a number of occasions in the gym in the past, and he'd also witnessed many of his fights.

> Miske, I think, is better than he has ever been before and I don't think Dempsey is. Champions seldom improve during the first year after they win the title, especially if they do no fighting in that year. Miske is a better boxer than Jack, though of course, he cannot hit as hard. Now that he's stronger and is punching better than ever before, I figure he's going to give Jack Dempsey a lot of trouble. Personally, I believe he will not only go the distance but I think he will also outbox the champion and possibly hold him even in fighting.

Billy expressed his confidence in the upcoming battle against Dempsey and provided the following statement:

> I have twice met Dempsey, and don't figure that he had anything on me in either of our bouts. I have not done much battling for a year, but the champion has done none at all. I know I am stronger and that I hit harder than ever before. I also am boxing better than ever before. If I was good enough to hold Jack even two years ago, and I have greatly improved since then, why shouldn't I beat him. Jack has spent a lot of time in the film world since he won the title, and the moving picture business does not tend to improve a boxer's condition. I am going to knock out Dempsey if I can. I am not going in there to stay ten rounds. I am going to be there to beat Jack and lift the heavyweight crown.

Billy was subjected to a thorough physical examination by Carl Rothfuss, former physical director of the St. Paul Y.M.C.A, and an acknowledged physical culture expert. Rothfuss said he didn't believe Billy ever had Bright's Disease. He examined Billy two hours after a six mile run and said:

> I have seldom seen anyone in better physical condition. Whatever he may have suffered from in the past year, he's surely rid of it now. Miske is a fine physical specimen of a young athlete in the prime of his career. He's one of the strongest men I have ever examined of his size and weight, and his reactions to every test show he's in superb health.[323]

Despite the sunny observation, a prognosis of Bright's Disease was considered grave. However, if the patient conformed to a proper diet, it was

---

[323] *St. Paul Pioneer Press*. Mike Gibbons, Other Experts Give Billy Miske Good Chance to Win Title, August 8, 1920.

believed they could live for a number of years, enjoying periods of remission, demonstrating every appearance of health.

On the night of August 15, St. Paul's mayor and a number of other citizens and friends accompanied Billy and his manager to the local train depot to express their well wishes. Billy and Reddy were leaving for Milwaukee, where he would train for a few days before continuing on to Chicago to train for the remainder of the week. Afterward, his entourage would continue on to Benton Harbor where they would set up training camp and make their final preparations for the bout.

Many of those who witnessed Billy's last workout in St. Paul earlier in the day were amazed at his condition. Mike Collins, a local promoter and manager of Fred Fulton, said he thought Billy hit harder than he ever did, and accused Reddy of keeping Billy's wonderful condition under wraps while his efforts to secure the fight with Dempsey were underway.[324]

Expectations were high as the two men departed St. Paul and began their trip east.

---

324 *St. Paul Pioneer Press*. Miske Starts on Trip for Title, August 15, 1920.

Billy's father Herman Miske.
Courtesy of grandson Bill Miske.

Mike Gibbons
Courtesy of John Ochs.

"Pearl" Smith & Billy Miske. Courtesy
of Don Scott, Boxing Collectors News.

"Spike" Kelly
Courtesy of Lawrence Davies.

George Ashe. Courtesy of Tony Triem.

Jack McCarron. Courtesy of Tony Triem.

Billy Miske. Author's collection.

George "K.O." Brown. Author's collection.

Harry Greb. Author's collection.

"Pearl" Smith & Billy Miske. Courtesy of John Ochs.

Jock Malone & Billy Miske. Courtesy of Bill Miske.

Tommy Gibbons. Courtesy of John Ochs.

Jack Lester
Courtesy of Lawrence Davies.

Terry Kellar
Courtesy of Lawrence Davies.

Billy Miske. Courtesy of Bill Miske.

Marie Miske. Courtesy of Bill Miske.

Marie and Billy Miske's wedding day October 15, 1915. Courtesy of Bill Miske.

Packey McFarland, unknown & Billy Miske. Courtesy of Bill Miske.

Unknown & Billy Miske. Courtesy of Bill Miske.

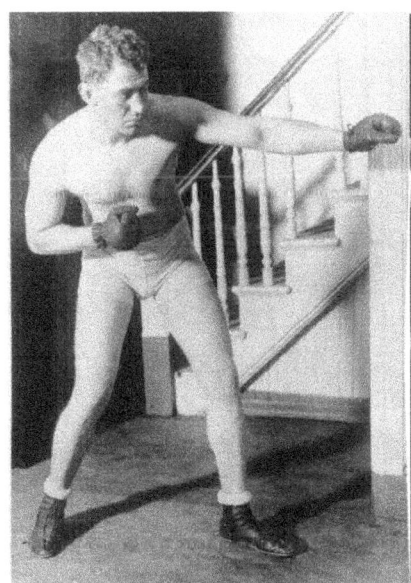

"Battling" Levinsky
Courtesy of John Ochs.

"Wild" Bert Kenny
Courtesy of Tracy Callis.

Billy Miske faces off with "Battling" Levinsky. Courtesy of Bill Miske.

Billy Miske. Courtesy of Bill Miske.

Manager Jack Reddy & Billy Miske. Courtesy of Bill Miske.

Clay Turner & Billy Miske. Courtesy of Bill Miske.

Unkown & Billy Miske. Courtesy of Bill Miske.   Billy Miske. Author's collection.

Jack Dillon. Courtesy of John Ochs.

Fred Fulton. Courtesy of John Ochs.

Willie Meehan. Courtesy of John Ochs.

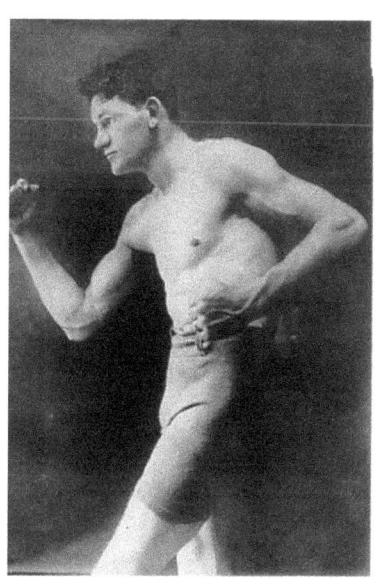
"Gunboat" Smith. Courtesy of John Ochs.

Billy Miske. Courtesy of David Bergin, Pugilistica.com.

Jack Dempsey. Author's collection.

Jack Dempsey vs. Billy Miske, St. Paul Auditorium, May 3, 1918. Referee, George Barton, pictured between the fighters. Courtesy of Bill Miske.

Billy Miske. Courtesy of Bill Miske.

Billy Miske & unknown. Courtesy of Bill Miske.

Billy Miske & unknown. Courtesy of Bill Miske.

Billy Miske. Courtesy of Bill Miske.

Billy Miske & 3 unknowns. Courtesy of Bill Miske.

Billy Miske. Courtesy of Bill Miske.

Billy Miske. Courtesy of Bill Miske.

Billy Miske. Courtesy of Bill Miske.

Jess Willard versus Jack Dempsey, July 4, 1919, Toledo, Ohio. Author's collection.

Billy Miske with two unknowns. Courtesy of Bill Miske.

Advertisement for the Elgin automobile. Courtesy of Jay Wolf.

Billy Miske. Courtesy of Bill Miske.

Bartley Madden. Author's collection.

Carpentier vs. Levinsky, October 12, 1920, Jersey City, New Jersey. Courtesy of John Ochs.

Billy Miske vs. Tommy Gibbons, October 13, 1922, Madison Square Garden. Courtesy of John Ochs.

Billy Miske. Courtesy of Bill Miske.

Billy Miske. Courtesy of Bill Miske.

Billy Miske with his three children; Douglas, Donna and Billy Jr.
Courtesy of Bill Miske.

Billy Miske & son Billy Jr. Billy Miske Jr. Author's Collection.
Courtesy of Bill Miske.

Billy Miske May 17, 1921. Courtesy of Don Scott, Boxing Collectors News.

Jack Dempsey vs. Tommy Gibbons, July 4, 1923, Shelby, MT. Courtesy of John Ochs.

Billy Miske with wife Marie and children Billy Jr., Donna and Douglas at the Mountain Valley bathing pool near Hot Springs, Arkansas in 1923. Courtesy of grandson Robert Booth.

Gene Tunney vs. Jack Dempsey, September 22, 1927, Soldiers Field. Author's collection.

Billy Miske. Courtesy of Bill Miske.

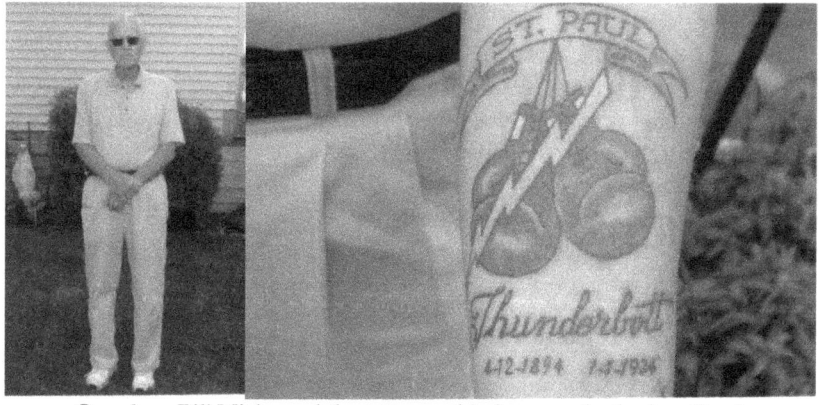

Grandson Bill Miske and the tattoo on his forearm. Author's collection.

CHAPTER 9

Training for the Title Fight

On August 19, 1920, word came from Chicago that fans who witnessed Miske's daily training were surprised he appeared in such good condition. All that anyone who followed the sport had been reading was how ill Billy was, but the fighter they saw in training looked fit as a fiddle.

Billy was now reported to weigh 192 pounds.[325] A day later, his manager, Jack Reddy, proclaimed Billy a "new man," saying he had rid himself of the curvature of the spine through chiropractic care, a condition he had suffered from since he was 16. Reddy proudly proclaimed Billy's one inch height increase and weight gain of fifteen pounds had resulted from the near miraculous treatments.[326]

The champion, Dempsey, had already been in Benton Harbor for a week and had increased his training program to include five miles of running, bag punching, rope skipping, shadow boxing and other exercises. He was working hard to make up for the many months he had spent performing for theater audiences since winning the championship. His sparring partners were beginning to file into camp.[327]

On August 22, it was reported Billy would extend his stay in Chicago for a few days at the request of the fight's promoter. Fitzsimmons wanted to assure the fight fans in Chicago that Billy was fit to face the champion.[328] But, Billy was anxious to get to Benton Harbor and begin serious training. He unexpectedly arrived in the city on the 22nd and immediately went to work with three of his sparring partners.[329]

Billy's camp was located about a mile south of Dempsey's quarters. It was the same camp that lightweight champion Benny Leonard had used for his title fight with Charlie White two months earlier. The ring was staked off beneath the shade of thickly foliaged trees. The house was a roomy, two-story structure set up for training purposes. Ike Bernstein was in charge of Billy's training and sparring sessions which were scheduled to take place at 2:30 in the afternoon.

Dempsey's training camp was located in a big old fashioned farm house on the outskirts of Benton Harbor, within a block of the arena where the two men would fight on Labor Day. Dempsey's sparring sessions took

---

325 *Beloit Daily News*. Miske Trains for Dempsey Battle, August 19, 1920.
326 *Beloit Daily News*. Miske Cured; To Give Jack Hard Battle, August 20, 1920.
327 *North Adams Transcript*. Dempsey Lengthens Training Program, August 20, 1920.
328 *St. Paul Pioneer Press*. Miske in Chicago Until Wednesday, August 22, 1920.
329 *St. Paul Pioneer Press*. Miske and Dempsey in Fast Workouts, August 23, 1920.

place in the arena and were scheduled to begin an hour later than Billy's so crowds would have an opportunity to witness both men in action.[330]

On August 23, sportswriter Robert Edgren, of the *New York Evening World*, produced a story in which he called the upcoming fight a mismatch. Edgren called Billy a "splendid" boxer, and a well-built fighter who was lion-hearted as far as any other heavyweight was concerned, but he claimed to know for a fact that Billy was afraid of Dempsey.

Explaining, Edgren said he had matched the two men for the main event at an army athletic fund show in Madison Square Garden in July of 1918, but Billy came to his office on the afternoon of the show and begged to be unmatched.

According to Edgren, Billy said he knew he'd come under a lot of criticism, but he preferred that to being knocked out, and he was sure Dempsey would knock him out. "You have no idea how hard that fellow hits. He's matched with Fulton now, and he's going to knock out every man he meets. He'll knock out Fulton in a round or two and then he'll get Willard and knock him out the same way. Nobody can stand up against Dempsey. I'm winning fights and going along pretty well, and if Dempsey knocks me out it'll spoil it all for me," he quoted Billy.

Edgren said he did everything in his power to convince Billy to go on, ultimately suggesting he announce from the ring it was purely an exhibition. But, he said Billy told him Dempsey would knock him out just the same and he couldn't trust him not to. "You have no idea how strong that fellow is and how hard he hits," he quoted Billy.

Dempsey wasn't known for being able to pull his punches and ease up on a man. He had a well-earned reputation of beating up his sparring partners and anyone else foolish enough to get in a ring with him. The famous vaudeville singer, Al Jolson, once sparred with him for publicity purposes and came away with a broken nose for his trouble. "That guy couldn't pull a punch to save himself – or me," said Jolson.[331]

Per Edgren:

> Usually, Billy is the gamest of the game. But, he's afraid of Dempsey. He was two years ago, and there's nothing in Billy Miske's record to suggest that he will be any more able to ace the champion today than he was then. The night before Dempsey knocked out Willard in Toledo a year ago July 4, Miske boxed a slow, disappointing bout with Levinsky in a nearby town. Miske at that time was said to be losing his fighting form. Now we are supposed to believe that he's better than ever, heavier, stronger, more clever and fit to give

---

[330] *Titusville Herald.* Dempsey Is Training On Farm Near Scene Of Labor Day Fight, September 2, 1920.
[331] *The Bee.* Dempsey Notorious For Things Like, August 4, 1920.

Dempsey a fight. I find it hard to picture him standing up to Jack and giving him a real battle.

Edgren went on to say Billy told him he didn't know how he managed to last 10 rounds with Dempsey two months beforehand, and Jack had hit him with a blow in the fourth round that put him on queer street for the next four rounds.[332]

It seems hard to believe Billy was afraid of Dempsey. He fought him a second time only four months after the event Edgren describes. It seems more likely that if there was any truth to the article, it was in what Edgren said about how much it was to expect of Billy to go on and meet a man of Dempsey's caliber without receiving any compensation, for the sake of a benefit.

Dempsey had his own charges of fear to respond to concerning a refusal to fight Joe Jeannette in late 1918. According to a book by Tom Meany titled '*Collier's Greatest Sports Stories*', Dempsey had agreed to an exhibition in New York's Madison Square Garden in November of 1918 against a second rater named Joe Bonds in benefit of the United War Work Fund. But, when Bonds was unable, or declined, to keep the commitment, an aging black heavyweight named Joe Jeannette showed up in his place and Dempsey's manager Jack Kearns refused to let his fighter go on.

To be fair, Dempsey had stipulated beforehand that his opponent be a white fighter, but many in the crowd were unhappy he and his manager refused to go on with a black fighter just shy of 40 years old who was eager to take him on.

The incident is well documented by New York newspapers of that period of time. It was understood Dempsey and his manager had no intention of fighting a black man, but it had to have been a humiliating experience for Dempsey to be guided away from the ring while the crowd hissed and booed him and Jeannette stood with arms folded inside the ring.[333]

In response to Edgren's article, Billy didn't deny begging out of the event, but responded:

> I was sick at the time, and knew that Dempsey would certainly knock me out. It would have hurt my entire career as a boxer and I felt that I was justified in not going with him at that time. It's different now. I didn't come to Benton Harbor to get licked.[334]

Work on the arena in Benton Harbor was underway to add three tiers of seats, 3,000 in total, to increase seating capacity to 20,000. A heavyweight championship fight was assured of drawing a much larger crowd than the

---

332 *San Antonio Evening News*. Dempsey-Miske An Uneven Match, August 23, 1920.
333 Meany, Tom, '*Collier's Greatest Sports Stories*', A.S. Barnes and Company, New York, N.Y. 1955.
334 *Fort Wayne Journal-Gazette*. Fans Given Chance to Judge Boxer's Merits, August 31, 1920.

lightweight championship had a couple of months earlier. Ringside seats were priced at $30, while other tickets were made available at $25, $10, and $5, plus an applicable war tax.[335]

On August 25, it was reported Billy was in need of more sparring mates. He floored a Chicago heavyweight named Jack Heinen several times and only boxed a total of four rounds.[336] Meanwhile, Dempsey spent six rounds working on body blows against his more impressive sparring partners, Panama Joe Gans and Bill Tate.[337]

Billy limited his sparring to four rounds on August 26 because of the condition of his sparring partners. Reddy took exception to criticism Billy's workout partners were subpar, and claimed they were every bit as good as those Dempsey was using.[338]

Jack Dempsey, responding to questions about Billy, said both he and his manager, Kearns, had a lot of respect for Miske. Jack said he thought Billy was a better fighter than Willard, was a stiffer puncher and much faster. "He can stand up under severe punishment. I even failed to knock him down, although I put every ounce of strength behind my punches," added Jack.[339]

On August 26, it was reported that Reddy had exhausted all sources in search of more sparring partners for Billy. Supposedly, the three they had were so battered up that they were not providing Miske with sufficient work. Billy had once again dropped the Chicago heavyweight Jack Heinen in their workout. Heinen had worked with both Jack Johnson and Jess Willard when they were champions. Comparing Billy to those two, Heinen said: "I worked with both Johnson and Willard when they were champions and stopped some of their best punches too. Never before however, have I been hit any harder than Miske hit me."[340] On August 27, a speedy welterweight named Johnny Tillman was added to Billy's stable of sparring mates.

The next day writer Frank Menke reported Billy was working hard to transform himself from a boxer to a knockout artist:

> Miske certainly is attempting the rather dangerous experiment of converting himself into a gentleman who bowls over foeman. He figures jabbing won't whip Dempsey – that a pile driver wallop, or several of them, rightly placed, can do the trick, so he aspires to create just such a punch. But, the trouble is that Miske is extremely awkward when assuming the haymaker attitude. He telegraphs every

---

335 *Waterloo Times-Tribune*. Arena To Seat 20,000 People, August 25, 1920.
336 *St. Paul Pioneer Press*. Miske Has Easy Day, August 25, 1920.
337 *Beloit Daily News*. Miske Needs More Slugging Fodder, August 24, 1920.
338 *St. Paul Pioneer Press*. Dempsey Reportedly Seriously Hurt But He Takes Strenuous Workout, August 26, 1920.
339 *North Adams Transcript*. Jack Dempsey Has Respect For Miske, August 26, 1920.
340 *Waterloo Times Tribune*. Billy Miske May Spring Surprise, August 27, 1920.

time he's ready to unlimber the right for the jaw. No man ever telegraphed Jack Dempsey who wasn't prone upon the canvas almost before the last word of the message had been flashed.[341]

On August 29, nine days from the fight, Billy explained why he was confident of beating Dempsey:

> I've met him twice before, doing what no other fighter did, going ten and six rounds. I never was off my feet. I guess that everyone who saw us fight at the St. Paul Auditorium will say that I fought him. I did not run for cover. I fought him. He shook me up in the second round with a fearful left, yet I fought him off his feet and drove him into the corner before that same round ended.
>
> He cracked me another big punch in the seventh round and I shook it off and came back and made him break ground, before the gong rang. I was not well when I fought him in St. Paul and was very ill when we boxed the second time in Philadelphia. Now I am well, am bigger, heavier, and much stronger than ever before in my life. My chances of beating him are much better.
>
> Until six months ago I've not been well for several years. I've had trouble with my hip which caused a pressure on the nerves in my back and as a result my back was weak. I suffered pains similar to those of neuritis. I could not train properly, was unable to do road work, as my legs and back would ache. I was getting worse and when I met Dempsey the last time I should not have been in the ring. When I met Tom Gibbons a year ago last June, I should have been in bed, the same the last time I boxed Bat Levinsky.
>
> Now, if in that condition I could give Dempsey the kind of argument I did twice in 1918, why should I not feel confident of beating him when I meet him for the third time? I am stronger than before. I am heavier by about 15 pounds than when I quit boxing. Each pound has brought increased strength. I am faster, my eyes are better, clear, not blurred. I am punching harder, as Dempsey will find out. I am a new Miske.
>
> Dempsey is heralded as a "superman" as the greatest fighter of all time. As I sat in the arena on July 4, 1919 and saw Dempsey better the great big Jess Willard, I marveled. If I hadn't met Dempsey twice previous to that bout I might really wonder now if I could take any of Dempsey's punches and stand up. But I know I can, as I've taken them in two fights and was never off my feet.

---

341 *San Antonio Evening News*. Miske Works To Develop Kayo Punch, August 28, 1920.

Billy then went on to explain why he would fare better against Dempsey than Willard had, saying he would fight Dempsey differently than most of those fellows. He claimed he wouldn't let Dempsey back him around, landing his terrible hooks. He planned to box Dempsey at all times, blocking some of the hooks and bobbing down, and then if any of Dempsey's punches shot over him, come in close and batter him to the body. Billy said:

> It worked before, [and] now that I am punching better I expect to shake him up when I hit him. When I boxed him last I had no punch, yet I out-boxed him. What will I do when I'm heavier and stronger and meet him again? If you stand still with Dempsey and lead at him he counters with hooks. He hurts when he lands, he's bound to land some, but this time I am also going to land. I shall try to win the world's title on Labor Day and come back home to St. Paul to my friends as champion.[342]

George Wilson and Jake Wagner, two more heavyweights from Chicago, joined Billy's camp on the 29th. Wilson opened a cut over Billy's eye when he accidentally butted him with his head, but it didn't prove to be much of a concern.[343] Neither Billy nor Dempsey did any boxing on August 30, backing off their training for a day to avoid going stale.

As the final week of training began, Michigan's best heavyweight, Homer Smith, joined Billy's training camp. The record of the 25-year-old heavyweight from Kalamazoo, Michigan included wins over respected men such as Terry Kellar, Andre Anderson, Sandy Ferguson, and Bill Scott, but he wasn't good enough to defeat the heavyweights found in the top tier of the division.

Both men were back in action on August 31, and for the first time Dempsey knocked out one of his sparring partners, Soldier Jack Riley. Billy wore felt headgear to protect his ears and the cut over his left eye during his own sessions with Wilson, Wagner, and Homer Smith.[344]

On September 1, Dempsey was established as a 10 to 6 betting favorite. He told reporters he weighed 189 ½ pounds and he looked every bit as good, if not better, than he had at Toledo for his fight with Jess Willard the previous year. Billy weighed 192 and planned to drop five more pounds by the date of the fight.[345]

Dempsey put in one of his hardest days of training yet on September 2 and afterward declared himself thoroughly satisfied with his condition. He said he felt better than he did when he faced Jess Willard. "I know I am

---

342 *Fort Wayne Journal-Gazette*. Billy Miske Tells How He Hopes to Beat Jack Dempsey, August 29, 1920.
343 *St. Paul Pioneer Press*. Rain Spoils Miske, Dempsey Workouts, August 30, 1920.
344 *St. Paul Pioneer Press*. Dempsey Kayoes Sparring Partner, September 1, 1920.
345 *Daily Capital News*. Jack Dempsey is 10 to 6 Choice to Beat Miske in the Fighting on Labor Day, September 1, 1920.

ready to step the full 10 rounds at top speed, but I don't think it will go that long," he said.[346]

One of the more interesting aspects of Dempsey's training was the fact Harry Greb had joined the camp as one of his sparring partners. Greb defeated every heavyweight he ever faced, and was the only man who ever defeated Gene Tunney, handing him the worst beating of his career. Sadly, Greb's request to face Dempsey for the title was never granted.

Dempsey sparred three rounds with Greb on September 1, and the 165-pound Greb gave him all he could handle. Greb was all over him, forcing him all around the ring. Dempsey couldn't do anything with him, while the speedier Greb seemed to be able to hit the champion at will. Time and again Greb made Dempsey miss, and countered with heavy blows about Jack's head and body.[347] Dempsey had already sparred three rounds with Bill Tate prior to sparring with Greb. But, that really shouldn't have adversely impacted his performance against Greb, given the condition Dempsey was in at that point in his training.

In Miske's camp, sparring partner Jack Heinen sang Billy's praises saying:

> I never was more confident of anything than that Billy will knock out Jack Dempsey. He has startled me by his speed, and fairly amazed me by his punching power. There's a snap to Miske's punching that (Jack) Johnson and Willard never knew. He's hitting faster than any man I ever saw in action and he's getting his 192 pounds into every drive for the jaw.

In response, Dempsey's sparring partner, Bill Tate, said:

> This boy Dempsey is ringing all them there bells he used to ring in Toledo when he hit – and a few more, too. I always thought that boy sorta reached the top of his punching power just before he fought Willard, but I made a mistake. This boy is hitting harder than he ever did. And nobody believes, who knows the game, that Miske has a ghost of a show.[348]

On September 3, Dempsey put in another hard day of sparring and once again it was Greb who extended him. Greb immediately rushed the champion and caught him by surprise. There were 2,000 fans on hand and they witnessed as much action in three rounds as you normally see during an entire contest. The crowd enthusiastically cheered the action on a number of occasions.[349] The three-round session between the two men was

---

346 *Waterloo Evening Courier.* Dempsey and Miske Taper Off Training for Monday's Bout, September 2, 1920.
347 *New York Times.* Dempsey Satisfied With His Condition, September 2, 1920.
348 *Olean Evening Herald.* Billy Miske Hasn't a Chance, September 2, 1920.
349 *New York Times.* Big Battlers Work Out At Top Speed, September 3, 1920.

described as being more in the nature of a real fight instead of training camp sparring. Greb staggered Dempsey twice with blows, and Dempsey tore into Greb with vicious shots to the body, and lifted him off the canvas with a hard right to the ribs.[350]

Twin-Cities writers voiced the opinion Miske was in even better condition than Dempsey, but noted once again he only boxed four rounds because he ran out of sparring partners. Billy was not extended in the least, toying with his partners, and not breathing hard afterward, while Dempsey was going through his much more strenuous sessions.

Billy remained confident, and said to "tell the fans of St. Paul that I am going to win the championship, not merely stay ten rounds. I've never been half as good as I am today and if I was good enough two years ago to go the full distance with Dempsey twice, I figure I am good enough now to beat him."

His trainer, Ike Bernstein, who often handled greats Benny Leonard and Packey McFarland, piped in and said he had never had a fighter in better condition than Billy. Reddy said he could hardly believe his own eyes while watching Billy work, he was so improved, and "hitting like a fiend."[351]

The general public remained unconvinced. Many thought the champion had picked out "a cripple" for his first title defense, and would knock Billy out within two rounds if he chose to."[352]

The *St. Paul Pioneer Press* reported on the "immense difference" between the sparring partners' quality in the two camps after the September 2 workouts, writing:

> Compared with Dempsey's aides, those of Miske are clowns, lacking in ability to improve his boxing as much as Greb and Farrell help train the champion's judgment of distance and at the same time give him excellent practice in blocking. Miske made his aides look like fourth raters, and it would require a charitable estimate to rate them much higher. On the other hand, Greb and Farrell made Dempsey work and word hard. Yesterday Dempsey's workout with Greb brought forth some adverse comment from critics, but today it was different. Dempsey for the first time since he started training, uncovered his real stuff and every time he did so a furious rally ended with the Pittsburgh cyclone breaking ground and covering up as he was crowded to the ropes.[353]

As one would expect, Reddy strongly disagreed with the characterization of Billy's sparring partners. He claimed Billy was so good anyone who was put in front of him immediately looked like a clown. He even went so far as

---

350 *Waterloo Times-Tribune*. Dempsey and Greb Battle, September 3, 1920.
351 *St. Paul Pioneer Press*. Miske in Better Condition Than Dempsey, September 2, 1920.
352 *North Adams Transcript*. The Minute Man's Column, September 3, 1920.
353 *St. Paul Pioneer Press*. Dempsey and Miske in Last Hard Workout Today, September 3, 1920.

to make the outlandish claim Harry Greb wouldn't be able to stand before Billy for two rounds. The fans in St. Paul hoped it was true, but it certainly appeared Billy hadn't received the same quality of training Dempsey had. Speed was supposed to be an area where Billy held the advantage, but those who had watched both men spar noted Dempsey looked to be the much faster and lighter on his feet.[354]

On September 3, Dempsey got his first glimpse of Billy since the two men had arrived in Benton Harbor. Afterward, he said he was happy Billy was going into the fight in good condition. He also noted Billy was much larger than the last time the pair met.[355]

Dempsey's comment about Billy's appearance conflicts with a comment he made concerning that period of time when he reflected upon it 32 years later. In a 1952 magazine article, Dempsey said of the fight in Benton Harbor between the two men, "Miske looked bad. He looked thin and much, much older, like a man 20 years behind his age of 26."[356] It's possible the comment Dempsey made about Billy's appearance just prior to the fight was provided with an idea of not saying anything which might hurt ticket sales, or maybe the comment Dempsey provided 32 years later was more specific to Billy's appearance in the ring just prior to the fight.

Despite the talk about the differences in the quality of the fighters' sparring partners, Billy continued to express his confidence, maintaining he was punching harder and straighter than ever before. "With the new strength I will have at my command this time, plus the experience I've gained, I'm sure that I have the stuff to bring the world's championship back to St. Paul with me," the challenger said.[357]

Others remained unconvinced. The day before the fight, one paper said Dempsey seemed to be at his best, while Billy looked a little stale. Over the past few days, Dempsey had demonstrated he hadn't lost any of his punch, and he could deliver his blows with uncanny speed and accuracy. Billy, on the other hand, they said had looked slow and awkward during his last sparring session of training.

> Time and again the slow-moving Heinen, a truck horse in comparison with the thoroughbred Dempsey, stepped out of the way (when Billy tried to deliver a big blow), and always Miske, unlike Dempsey, was in a dangerously awkward position (afterward).[358]

Billy's hometown paper, the *St. Paul Pioneer Press*, summarized the thoughts of a number of folks when they wrote Billy had a fair chance to go

---

354 *St. Paul Pioneer Press*. Fight Managers in Deadlock Over Referee, September 5, 1920.
355 *Oshkosh Daily Northwestern*. Miske Has Grown Bigger in Opinion of Jack Dempsey, September 3, 1920.
356 Billy Miske's Christmas. *Men Magazine*, September 1952.
357 *Olean Evening Herald*. Expect to Announce Referee, September 4, 1920.
358 *The North American*. Say Miske Lucky to Last Five Rounds, September 5, 1920.

the distance with Dempsey again, but the odds would decline in direct proportion to any efforts he made to slug it out with the champion.[359]

---

[359] *St. Paul Pioneer Press.* Fight Managers In Deadlock Over Referee, September 5, 1920.

CHAPTER 10

Referee Controversy

With only three days remaining before the Dempsey-Miske title fight of September 6, 1920, the issue of who would referee the contest remained unsettled. Thomas Bigger, Chairman of the Michigan State Boxing Commission, was scheduled to arrive in Benton Harbor on September 4 to help resolve the matter.

When Chairman Bigger arrived, he presented the fighters' managers with a list of eleven ring officials, from which he said a selection would be made. The list included only two officials living outside the state of Michigan, Ed Smith of Chicago and Matt Hinkel of Cleveland. All eleven men on the list were licensed to referee bouts in the state of Michigan.

Dempsey's manager, Jack Kearns, declared he wanted a man with experience in championship fights. The promoter, Floyd Fitzsimmons, suggested Ed Smith, who had refereed the Benny Leonard-Charlie White lightweight championship bout two months earlier, but Kearns objected.

Kearns wanted Jimmy Dougherty of Leiperville, Pennsylvania, a friend of his and Dempsey's, to referee the fight. Doughterty, an Irish sporting man who was later tagged the "Baron of Leiperville" by sportswriter Damon Runyan, was a part-time boxing promoter, trainer and official who owned the Colonial Hotel in Leiperville. The hotel housed a 75 foot long bar as well as a boxing ring. Dougherty's friendship with Dempsey had reportedly begun a few years earlier when he had taken the struggling fighter in and provided him with a job waiting on tables. Kearns, on the other hand, allegedly felt an obligation to Dougherty for arranging the hire of Dempsey in 1917 by the Sun Shipbuilding Company in Chester, Pennsylvania – to help keep the youngster out of the war.360

Dougherty was acceptable to Billy and manager Reddy, but Chairman Bigger said it was out of the question because Doughterty was not licensed to referee bouts in the state of Michigan and he wasn't going to issue him a license. Kearns told the chairman unless Dougherty was the referee there would be no fight.361

Billy, his manager, the promoter and Dempsey were all willing to waive the point and abide by Chairman Bigger's decision but Kearns was insistent. And, as far as Dempsey was concerned, Kearns was the boss.362

Meanwhile, fight fans continued to pour into the little resort town. There were already over 100 sportswriters on hand with more arriving on

---

360 Roberts, Randy, *Jack Dempsey, The Manassa Mauler*, Louisiana State University Press, 1979.
361 *St. Paul Pioneer Press*. Fight Managers Deadlocked Over Referee, September 5, 1920.
362 Dempsey, Jack. *Round by Round*, Whittlesey House, New York, N.Y. 1940

every train. While the majority of fans were expected to arrive on Sunday afternoon and the morning of Monday's fight, the town already seemed to be overflowing with people.

Hotels were full and hundreds of owners of private homes were realizing premium prices for spare rooms. Restaurants had long ago discarded their menus so as to increase their prices by the hour. The pickpocket business was in full swing. A report out of Chicago's Grand Central Station indicated that mobs of fans rushing to board trains for Benton Harbor had reported losses totaling $2,500.363

On September 5, the day before the fight, the issue over who would serve as the referee for the contest was finally resolved. Following his manager's lead the night before, Dempsey had told a representative of Chairman Bigger that Jimmy Dougherty was the only man they would accept as the referee for the bout. The chairman refused to give in, and named Al Day of Detroit as the referee.

At that point, Fitzsimmons, who stood to lose a lot of money if the fight was cancelled, went into action. He met with a Detroit sportswriter and asked him to intercede with the chairman, and help explain that if the fight were called off he would be financially ruined. In addition to all his promotional expenses, Fitzsimmons had also advanced Kearns $25,000 from monies received from the sale of tickets. Fitzsimmons also wanted the chairman to consider the possibility of a riot in the city if the fight was cancelled and he didn't have enough money to refund ticket holders.

The sportswriter and Fitzsimmons first met with Al Day, the man Chairman Bigger had appointed for the match, and explained the situation to him. Day then accompanied the pair to the home of E.A. McCauley, Secretary of the Commission, where Bigger was staying, and after a long discussion between the parties, Day agreed to step aside. The chairman finally consented to quickly issue Dougherty a license and let him officiate.

Reddy felt Dempsey's manager had been unreasonable but he didn't want to do anything which would prevent the fight from taking place. He felt Dougherty was a competent official and expressed the hope he would give Billy fair play.

The whole affair had left Dempsey in a nervous and irritable mood. A sportswriter from the *St. Paul Pioneer Press*, on the other hand, visited Billy afterward and found him in good spirits. He was looking forward to the fight. The story concerning the selection of the referee was the topic of conversation in local drinking establishments, and the handling of the matter by the champion and his manager was severely criticized.

The main body of fans from St. Paul, including Billy's wife Marie, and his father, Herman, were expected to arrive on the first train Monday

---

363 *St. Paul Pioneer Press*. Fight Managers Deadlocked Over Referee, September 5, 1920.

morning.364 Billy anxiously awaited their arrival and said he always fought best when his wife was seated ringside.365

As thousands of fans continued to pour into Benton Harbor and neighboring St. Joseph, they discovered few rooms were available. Even refreshments were hard to find. The little resort towns were used to handling swelling populations but nothing on the scale of what they were experiencing for this fight.

The champion was established as a 3 to 1 betting favorite, and many of the bets were more along the lines of whether or not Billy would still be on his feet at the end of the bout. They felt the only way the title could change hands was if Billy knocked the champion out. He and his manager had requested the state boxing commission make an exception to the state law and allow an official decision be rendered if there was no knockout, but the request was denied.

There were two quality six-round preliminary bouts scheduled to take place before the title contest and expected to prove very entertaining. The first of those was between Harry Greb, a.k.a. "The Pittsburgh Windmill," and Chuck Wiggins. The second was between Bill Tate and Sam Langford. Although Langford was well past his peak at this point in his career, a strong case could be made that both he and Greb were among the top five greatest pound-for-pound fighters in the history of boxing.

From a historical sporting aspect, the Dempsey-Miske fight was going to be significant regardless of the outcome because it would be the first radio broadcast of a prize fight. That August, a Detroit station named 8MK, later WWJ, had claimed to become the first radio station in the world to broadcast regularly scheduled programs. The broadcast of 20 watts, from the second floor of The Detroit News Building, was only received in an estimated 30 Detroit homes. The championship fight in September provided the first ringside radio broadcast over a year before the first broadcast of a baseball world series.

The fighters awoke on the morning of September 6 to a light drizzle, after a night of heavier rain, but the show was going to take place rain or shine. Later that morning, both men reported for the official weigh-in and their medical examinations by the Michigan State Boxing Commission. The champion weighed in at 187 pounds, while Billy tipped the scales two pounds heavier, at 189. Both men were pronounced fit by the commission and returned to card games to relax over the final hours before the fight.366

A tale of the tape between the two fighters revealed two men of nearly identical physical proportions. Dempsey was 25 years of age, Billy 26. Dempsey stood 6'1 ¼" and weighed 187 pounds, Billy 6'1" and 189 pounds. Dempsey enjoyed a reach of 78 inches, while Billy had a reach of 77 inches.

---

364 *St. Paul Pioneer Press.*. Dempsey Wins Referee Row, September 6, 1920.
365 *Beloit Daily News.* Inspiring Wife. September 2, 1920.
366 *Oakland Tribune.* Doctors O.K. Dempsey and Miske For Bout, September 6, 1920.

The size of their chests, neck, shoulders, waists, biceps, forearms, thighs, calves and ankles were all about the same or within one inch of the other man.

Many fans had stood in line all night in order to gain the best vantage point possible once the gates to the bleachers were opened. Many others had been forced to spend the night out in the elements due to a lack of accommodations for everyone in the small town. Numerous campfires blazed through the night, as those unable to find shelter sought to stay warm as well as they could. The majority of these folks dined on a breakfast of lemonade and hot dogs. But, it was a happy, jovial crowd, despite the hardships. They were eager to witness the action and it was observed as one of the most orderly crowds anyone had ever seen of its size.[367]

By the early afternoon, the sun shone brightly and the temperature was rising. Squads of uniformed soldiers, on loan from local Camp Custer, served as ushers at the arena to keep order. Barbed wire fences surrounded the ringside sections and numerous guards were on duty to prevent reoccurrence of the situation which took place in Toledo the previous year, when hundreds of fans stormed into the ringside seats and refused to be moved. As many as 200 women, an oddity in those days at such an event, were seen scattered throughout the arena. The Benton Harbor arena was almost filled a full half hour before the first preliminary contest was scheduled to begin at 3:00 p.m.[368]

The preliminaries were delayed slightly to account for the late arrival of several special trains and two steamers bringing fans from Chicago. By the time the first preliminary between Greb and Chuck Wiggins began, a group of sixty-one Miske fans from St. Paul, including Marie and his father Herman were seated ringside, immediately behind what would end up being Billy's corner.

Dempsey received a visit from a gambling friend an hour before the fight. The friend wanted to know if a bet on a knockout of Miske was a good one. "Well, this Miske is a tough bird, he's a tough fellow," said Jack. "I'm going to step right after him, but he's a TOUGH guy."[369]

In his own dressing room, Billy undoubtedly carried out his unique method of preparing his jaw before each fight. He attributed his ability to take punches without suffering a knockout to a long practice of loosening up his jaw and making it more insensitive to hard blows before each fight. He would accomplish this by smashing himself in the jaw very hard about ten times before entering the ring.[370]

In the two preliminaries, Greb completely outclassed Wiggins over six rounds in the opening contest, while Dempsey's sparring partner, Bill Tate,

---

[367] *New York Times*.. Great But Orderly Crowd Sees Fight, September 7, 1920.
[368] *Oakland Tribune*. Doctors O.K. Dempsey and Miske for Bout, September 6, 1920.
[369] *San Antonio Light*. Fights I Can't Forget by Tad, September 25, 1926.
[370] *St. Paul Pioneer Press*. Miske Toughened Jaw by Punching Self Before Bouts, January 2, 1924.

avenged a previous loss to Sam Langford by heavily using his left jab over six rounds to keep his much shorter opponent at bay.

Finally, it was time for the main event. Both Dempsey and Miske issued final statements before entering the ring, reiterating much of what they had already said.

Jack Dempsey:

> I shall try to win as quickly as possible. I have not made the mistake of believing that I am going to have a picnic. Miske is tough, can take and give punishment and is a dangerous fighter. I have fought him twice and was shaken to my heels both times. I have worked as hard for this fight as I did for Willard and will take no chances of losing the title. They tell me Miske is bigger and heavier than when we fought before. That means that he will be that much harder. They also tell me he's in shape. But, he has nothing on me in this regards.

Billy Miske:

> Dempsey couldn't knock me out in our previous engagements and I feel certain he won't be able to turn the trick today. This is the chance I have been waiting for. I am a better fighter than when I was when I met Dempsey two years ago and I'll carry the fight to him. But, I won't be careless. I am not going to predict that I am going to knock Dempsey out, but I am going to give him the greatest fight he ever had. Dempsey is a terrific hitter, but my previous engagements have convinced me that I can hit him.[371]

They were brave words, from a brave man. But, the time had arrived for Billy to face the most destructive man on the planet, the reigning heavyweight champion, Jack Dempsey, who many were now saying was simply unbeatable.

---

[371] *Evening Bulletin*. Dempsey Favored 3 to 1 Over Miske, September 6, 1920.

CHAPTER 11

Outcome of the Fight

At 4:49 p.m. on September 6th, 1920, Billy stepped between the ropes and into the ring of the Benton Harbor Arena to face Jack Dempsey for the heavyweight championship of the world. He was greeted with wild applause from the St. Paul contingency seated directly behind his corner, and a warm reception throughout the rest of the arena. He was wearing silk trunks with the initials "BM" embroidered on the left leg.

The ring was immediately swarmed with photographers, attendants and state officials. At one time, no less than eleven cameras were focused on Billy, but he remained unfazed by all the attention, smiling throughout, as the photographers scrambled for the perfect photo opportunity.

Despite the fact the fight was already an hour late, the champion kept Billy and the large crowd waiting for fifteen minutes before joining him in the ring. While he received an enthusiastic welcome, he showed no interest in returning the greeting of his many admirers. He appeared with a glum and determined expression on his unshaven face, and he was wearing the same old red sweater he wore into his battle with Jess Willard.[372]

The introductions of officials that followed Dempsey's arrival, and the accompanying commotion, seemed to irritate the champion. To those at ringside, he appeared ill at ease and anxious to get under way. On the other hand, Billy appeared completely at ease, laughing and talking with those folks who were nearby.

Once all the introductions were completed and the fighters had received their instructions, the ring was cleared. The arena buzzed with excitement as the two men waited for the bell to signal them into action. Finally, the bell rang and Billy rushed forward to meet Dempsey with a determined look on his face.[373]

It was Billy who landed the first blow of the fight, a left to the jaw, followed by a left hook to the champion's stomach. Dempsey responded with two hard left hooks of his own to the challenger's stomach. The two men measured each other with cautious left and right hand probes.

It quickly became apparent Billy had chosen a different strategy for Dempsey than he had in their first two meetings. Rather than box at long range, Billy stood flat footed and appeared as though he intended to slug it out with Dempsey. Dempsey, on the other hand, assumed the role of the

---

[372] *Evening Bulletin.* Miske Beaten By Heart Blow. September 7, 1920.
[373] *St. Paul Pioneer Press.* Dempsey Stops Miske in Third. September 7, 1920.

boxer in the opening session, and actually demonstrated the better skills of the two men in that area, either brushing away, ducking, or sidestepping the majority of Billy's attacks.[374]

Dempsey said later that he had decided beforehand he would focus on boxing during the opening round. He had his sights set on a future bout with the Frenchman, Georges Carpentier, who many believed to be the greatest boxer in the world at the time. As a result, he had devoted a fair amount of his time in training, and the first round of this fight with Billy, on improving and testing his boxing skills.[375]

That didn't mean the champion didn't land any telling blows during the opening round. At one point, Dempsey crossed a left to Billy's jaw and followed with a big right to the stomach that "fairly boomed upon impact." Billy quickly backed away and covered up.[376]

Billy fought back as hard as he could for the balance of the round, but he was plainly tiring as it ended. It was clear Dempsey was the much faster of the two, and Billy was already weakening.[377] The round came to an end as Dempsey feinted with a left to the body and landed a right to Billy's head.[378]

The bell opening the second round signaled the arrival of the Dempsey everyone had been expecting. No longer was he a boxer, the slugger had returned. For nearly ten seconds, neither man threw a punch, each searching for an opening. And then, Billy tried a left to the body. Quick as a flash, Dempsey countered with a terrific left hook to the body that shook Billy, and the latter clinched. Once separated, Dempsey resumed his body attack with such speed that Billy was unable to block the blows. They clinched.

After being separated, Dempsey rushed in and missed with a big right hand aimed for Billy's head. Billy countered with a series of blows to the body, but they had little effect.[379]

What happened next is probably explained by Dempsey as well as anyone:

> Miske is tough. Don't make any mistake about that. I fought him twice before and remembered that he could take an awful socking. So, I decided that rather than try to bring him down with one terrific blow I would just chop him down gradual. Cagey boy that he is, he never would give me a fair crack at his jaw or body until I tricked him into it.

---

374 *Evening Bulletin*. Dempsey Knocks Out Billy Miske in Third Round, September 7, 1920.
375 *Evening Bulletin*. Jack Dempsey's Own Story of How He Knocked Out Billy Miske, September 7, 1920.
376 *Eau Claire Leader*. Dempsey Knocks Out Miske, September 7, 1920.
377 *St. Paul Pioneer Press*. Dempsey Stops Miske in Third, September 7, 1920.
378 *Eau Claire Leader*. Dempsey Knocks Out Miske, September 7, 1920.
379 *St. Paul Pioneer Press*. Dempsey Stops Miske in Third, September 7, 1920.

And I did it with the old right-hand lead that went straight through. Most of the fighters leading with the right usually do it merely to whirl around to the other fellow so they can land with the real blow, a left hook. Naturally, every fighter, when he sees a right coming, turns in toward that right, not figuring the right is going through, and that is why I was so successful, because I follow through with the right. I led with the right for Billy's body in the middle of the second (round). He expected that I was going to land a left, that the right was only a bluff. But, I sent that right straight through, and Miske went down as the blow flashed under his heart. It was the same punch that I had used to start Jess Willard to defeat, and it sent Billy along the same road. That body smash I landed under his heart was about as hard a blow as I ever hit anybody.[380]

For a second, it didn't seem as though the blow had much of an impact, but, as Billy took a step, his legs collapsed beneath him and he fell to the canvas.[381] It was the first time in eight years of fighting, and more than 80 professional bouts, Billy had ever been knocked off his feet.

He propped up the upper part of his body on his straightened right arm. It looked as though he was temporarily paralyzed from the waist down, and he might take the count while conscious, but unable to rise to his feet. His face was distorted in pain.[382]

But, Billy struggled to his feet at the count of five and backed away, covering his stomach.[383] He was plainly dazed and his knees were wobbly. A less game fighter would have quit at that point. There was a large red welt under Billy's heart where the blow had landed. Dempsey, in an effort to bring an end to the fight, rushed Billy, but was wild and missed badly with two heavy swings, a right hook aimed at the jaw and a left aimed at the body.[384] Billy clinched, but Dempsey kept one arm free and landed three short blows to the chin.[385]

For the balance of the round, Billy clinched, weaved, and managed to stave off the furious efforts of Dempsey to bring the fight to a conclusion. "It was a marvelous exhibition of gameness, for he was really hurt,"[386] Dempsey would later say.

Billy looked "all in" as he staggered back to his corner at the end of the round. He was bleeding from the mouth and his face was flaming red.[387]

---

380 *Evening Bulletin*. Jack Dempsey's Own Story of How He Knocked Out Billy Miske, September 7, 1920.
381 *St. Paul Pioneer Press*. Dempsey Stops Miske in Third, September 7, 1920.
382 Fleischer, Nat, '*Jack Dempsey, Idol of Fistiana*', The Ring, Inc., New York, N.Y. 1929.
383 *Eau Claire Leader*. Dempsey Knocks Out Miske, September 7, 1920.
384 *St. Paul Pioneer Press*. Dempsey Stops Miske in Third, September 7, 1920.
385 *Eau Clair Leader. Dempsey Knocks Out Miske, September 7, 1920.*
386 Dempsey, Jack, *Round by Round*, Whittlesey House, New York, N.Y. 1940.
387 *Evening Bulletin*. Dempsey Knocks Out Billy Miske in Third Round, September 7, 1920.

Of the blow that sent him to the canvas for the first time in his professional life, Billy said, "I never was hit so hard in my life. The blow took all the steam out of me, and I hadn't recovered from its effects when the third round opened."[388]

When the third round began, Dempsey was confident one good punch would finish the job.[389] But, Billy wasn't going to go down without a fight. He desperately tore into the champion and landed two lefts to the face, followed by a right hook to the point of the jaw. If it had occurred earlier in the fight it may have done more damage than it did, but by this time Dempsey's blows had robbed Billy of his strength. Dempsey retaliated with a left to the face, and they clinched. Dempsey uppercut Billy with a right and then missed when he tried to repeat the blow.[390]

Once they were separated, Dempsey circled Billy a couple of times, and then bluffed a rush. When Billy came in, Dempsey hooked a short left into his stomach. When Billy winced, he knew he had him. He faked another punch to Billy's midsection to get him to drop his guard, and then whipped over a right hook that crashed into Billy's jaw and sent him down for the second time in the fight. Billy fell onto his right side with his left arm covering his face. Dempsey was sure Billy wouldn't be able to rise from the blow. But, somehow he did what Dempsey later said he didn't believe any fighter in America so badly hurt could, he climbed back to his feet at the count of nine.[391]

As Referee Dougherty conducted his count, one the *St. Paul Pioneer Press* observed as unusually fast,[392] Dempsey walked behind his fallen foe and stood leaning against the ropes. As Billy rose, dazed and bleary-eyed, he put his hands up thinking Dempsey was in front of him. Instead, the champion had positioned himself directly behind Billy. And the moment Billy was back on his feet, Dempsey moved a fraction to the side and delivered a brutal right hook to the jaw that sent Billy down and out, one minute and thirteen seconds into the third round. There were a few hisses from the crowd for Dempsey's action.[393]

H.C. Walker, Sporting Editor of the *Detroit Times*, was probably the most vocal in his criticism of the way Dempsey brought an end to the fight. His comments concerning the champion's lack of sportsmanship are provided below:

> Jack Dempsey is a bad sport. As a fighter, he's one of the best the pugilistic game had developed. I think Dempsey can hit harder than

---

388 *Evening Bulletin*. Miske Beaten by Heart Blow, September 7, 1920.
389 Dempsey, Jack, *Round by Round*. Whittlesey House, New York, N.Y. 1940.
390 *St. Paul Pioneer Press*. Dempsey Stops Miske in Third, September 7, 1920.
391 *Evening Bulletin*. Jack Dempsey's Own Story of How He Knocked Out Billy Miske, September 7, 1920.
392 *St. Paul Pioneer Press*. Dempsey Stops Miske in Third, September 7, 1920.
393 *San Antonio Light*. Fights I Can't Forget by Tad, September 25, 1920.

any fighter who ever got into a ring. When I say this, I remember Peter Maher, Bob Fitzsimmons and Jim Jeffries. He can hit a harder wallop than could any of these terrible punchers. But, I don't believe the man has any sand. He certainly is a bum sport. He got behind helpless Billy Miske the other day and knocked him cold when Billy wasn't looking, and, furthermore, when Dempsey didn't have the right to hit him. The knockout blow that put Billy Miske to sleep was one of the most cowardly blows I have ever seen. And, it doesn't lessen the offense that Jack Dempsey's personal referee didn't want to prevent that blow.

Dempsey sneaked up on Miske, hit him from behind and knocked him out. In the third and final round of the fight, Miske was knocked down. It appeared as if he was down for keeps, but, at the count of nine, he got up. He was helpless and a child could have licked him then. But, contrary to the rules under which that match and all others in this country are held, Dempsey did, despite the fact that he had no right to do it. The Marquis of Queensberry rules say:

If either man falls through weakness or otherwise, he must get up unassisted, ten seconds to be allowed him to do so, the other man meanwhile to return to his corner.

The idea of forcing the fighter to return to his corner while his antagonist was down came to Marquis of Queensbury in 1865 when he revised the old London Prize Ring rules to rob them of their brutality. These rules have therefore stood for 55 years. Under them, boxing has become more respectable, and less brutal. But, Dempsey violated the rules and hovered over Miske, behind the helpless fighter, and hit him as soon as both knees were off the floor. The bully needn't have done it, for he could have licked Miske squarely quite as easily. Only he didn't.[394]

It wasn't an unusual practice for Dempsey. He'd done the same thing to Jess Willard the year before, hovering over him after numerous knockdowns, so he might immediately deliver more blows the moment his opponent's knees had lifted from the canvas. The scene would repeat itself three years later in a wild heavyweight championship affair between Dempsey and Argentina's Luis Firpo before 80,000 screaming fans at New York's Polo Grounds. Dempsey knocked Firpo down seven times in the first round of the contest, there being no rule that a fight would end after three knockdowns in one round, and he was permitted to stand over the fallen fighter and immediately knock him down again the moment he rose to his feet.

---

[394] *Olean Evening Herald.* Jack Dempsey Knocked Cold by Editor, September 17, 1920.

Ultimately, this practice would come back to haunt Dempsey, in September of 1927, during an attempt to regain the heavyweight title from Gene Tunney. After four years of inactivity, Dempsey had lost his title to Tunney by unanimous decision in 1926. When a rematch was scheduled the following year, it was agreed by both parties that in the event of a knockdown, the fallen fighter would have ten seconds to rise to his feet after his opponent had moved to a neutral corner.

By the seventh round of their return match, it appeared Tunney was on his way to another decisive victory over the former champion. But then, he made a near fatal mistake. He misjudged the distance to the ropes at his back and let Dempsey trap him. A rapid succession of blows to the head sent Tunney crashing to the canvas with a glazed look in his eyes.

As he had done so many times in the past, Dempsey stood by closely, waiting to deliver the finishing blow should his opponent manage to rise to his feet. But, he forgot about the agreement for this fight, in the event of a knockdown the other fighter was to at once go to a neutral corner. As the referee began to count over Tunney, he noticed Dempsey standing nearby and ordered him to the opposite corner. Dempsey initially refused to move, only doing so once it became apparent the count would not be resumed until he did and by the time he finally did go to the opposite corner, a number of seconds had gone by and Tunney had received more time to recover.

Ultimately, Tunney would claim he would have been able to beat the count regardless, but when he got back up and won another unanimous decision there was a lot of controversy over the issue. The fight will forever be remembered as the "battle of the long count."[395]

As Referee Dougherty completed his count, Billy lay with his right arm crocked under his head and his eyes closed. He made no attempt to rise. He twitched twice, but that was all.[396] Once Dougherty had completed the count and pointed to Dempsey as the winner, the champion lifted Billy and held him until his seconds arrived to help him to his chair.[397]

While Billy's seconds administered aid, Dempsey stood by trying to help. The champion almost seemed to regret he had knocked out Billy.[398] "There wasn't any fun in knocking Billy Miske out. I loved the guy. He was a fine fellow as well as a splendid fighter," said Dempsey.[399]

Once Billy had been revived, he and Dempsey exchanged a brief handshake. Then Dempsey ran back to his corner to retrieve his old red sweater, threw it around his shoulders, and raced back to his training quarters.[400]

---

395 Dempsey, Jack, *Round by Round*, Whittlesey House, New York, N.Y. 1940.
396 *Evening Bulletin*. Miske Beaten by Heart Blow, September 7, 1920.
397 *St. Paul Pioneer Press*. Dempsey Stops Miske in Third, September 7, 1920.
398 Fleischer, Nat, *Jack Dempsey, Idol of Fistiana*, The Ring, Inc., New York, N.Y. 1929.
399 Dempsey, Jack, *Round by Round*, Whittlesey House, New York, N.Y. 1940.
400 *Evening Bulletin*. Dempsey Knocks Out Billy Miske in Third Round, September 7, 1920.

Heartbroken in defeat, there were tears in Billy's eyes as he praised his opponent. "Dempsey is a better man than I am. The punch that floored me in the second round all but caved in my ribs. I never was hit so hard in my life. I think Dempsey is unbeatable. I fought the best battle I could but was whipped before I really got started."[401] Continuing, he said, "I did my best and I am sorry that I did not make a better showing for St. Paul." Then he smiled and added, "Dempsey is a wonder. He hit me far harder that he did in either of the other fights, and there is no one in the world that has any chance at all with him."[402]

Marie held up well under the shock of seeing her husband knocked out, but Billy's father, Herman, took it very hard. It was several minutes before he could attempt to leave his seat afterward.[403]

As Billy departed the ring, there were bruises on both cheeks. It was initially thought one of Billy's ribs had been broken by the terrific blow he received from the champion in the second round but two physicians examined him and agreed there was no fracture.[404] An hour after reaching his camp, Billy was himself again.

The general consensus was Billy was badly outclassed by the champion and that there was nobody else in sight that would be able to stand up to Dempsey at the time. "Dempsey made Miske, long regarded as one of the speediest boxers in the game, look like a wooden-legged circus fat man," said the *Syracuse Herald*, while adding neither Harry Wills nor Georges Carpentier would stand a chance with the champion.[405]

Once he had a chance to clean up after the fight, Dempsey issued the following statement:

> I told my friends I would win. Miske is tough and I trained and fought him with as much caution as I would fight any heavyweight. The punch that started him on his way was a smash in the stomach in the second round. After that, I was confident I could end it whenever I wanted to but I fought carefully and took no chances.[406]

A number of years later, in his autobiography, Dempsey would comment, "During the fight, I began to feel that Billy wasn't giving me as tough a battle as I had expected. He did not seem like his old self."[407]

The champion also came away from this fight with a great amount of respect for the way Billy handled himself in defeat. A number of months later when reflecting upon the event and Billy's reaction to the loss Dempsey said: "If my turn ever comes before I am ready to retire, I hope

---

401 *Eau Claire Leader*. Dempsey Knocks Out Miske, September 7, 1920.
402 *St. Paul Pioneer Press*. Dempsey Stops Miske, September 7, 1920.
403 *St. Paul Pioneer Press*. Dempsey Stops Miske in Third, September 7, 1920.
404 *Evening Bulletin*. Miske Beaten by Heart Blow, September 7, 1920.
405 *Syracuse Herald*. Neither Carpentier Nor Wills Has Chance with Jack Dempsey, September 7, 1920.
406 *Eau Claire Leader*. Dempsey Knocks Out Miske, September 7, 1920.
407 Dempsey, Jack, *Round by Round*, Whittlesey House, New York, N.Y. 1940.

that I'll be as graceful a loser as Billy Miske."[408] To Dempsey's credit, when he finally met defeat, against Gene Tunney in 1926, he was extremely gracious toward his conqueror.

Dempsey and his party had dinner with the promoter to celebrate his victory and then spent the rest of the evening dancing at a summer pavilion in nearby St. Joseph. He and Kearns planned to depart for Chicago late Tuesday afternoon and then head east in search of the next opponent.[409]

Billy and his wife planned to return home to St. Paul where Billy would enjoy a hunting trip. While some thought his loss to Dempsey might mark the end of Billy's career, Billy told Minneapolis sports writer, Ed Walker, he intended to add a few more dollars to his bankroll before hanging up the gloves.[410]

On the afternoon of September 7, promoter Floyd Fitzsimmons and his wife accompanied Jack Dempsey and his manager, Jack Kearns, to the train depot to see them off. When Dempsey got ready to jump aboard the train, Mrs. Fitzsimmons, remembering the $13,000 automobile the champion had recently purchased and operated during his stay in Benton Harbor, said to him: "Jack, what shall we do with the car?" "Just keep it," replied Dempsey as he climbed aboard.[411] It was a hell of a gift to make at the time, but the money was rolling in for the champion, and there were much bigger paydays ahead.

---

408 *Bridgeport Telegram*, Dempsey Would Like to Greet Carpentier When He Arrives, May 14, 1921.
409 *Evening Bulletin*. Miske Beaten by Heart Blow, September 7, 1920.
410 *Daily Globe*. Defeat of Miske is Not Check on Plans, September 9, 1920.
411 *Daily Globe*. Defeat of Miske is Not Check on Plans, September 9, 1920.

CHAPTER 12

The Comeback Trail

The total gate receipts from the September heavyweight championship contest between Billy and Jack Dempsey was announced as $134,904. Once state and war taxes were taken out, the figure was reduced to $109,376. Dempsey's share came to $55,000 and Billy's end was $25,000.[412]

After paying his manager's share, Billy was left with about $18,000. Believing Billy's automobile business was doomed to failure, his wife, Reddy and closest friends had urged him to go through bankruptcy and save his money from the Dempsey fight. But, Billy was cut from a different cloth. "Not me, nobody is ever going to point a finger at Billy Miske and say I ever beat them out of a dime. I'm going to pay off even if I go broke again," he said. He put $15,000 of his earnings from the Dempsey fight back into the automobile business.[413]

Billy and Marie returned to St. Paul, where Billy enjoyed a brief hunting trip, and contemplated his future. A number of fight offers were received over the next three months, but Billy took his time deciding what to do, while he continued to oversee his automobile business. That October, Marie learned she was pregnant with their third child. In nine months, there would be another mouth to feed. Undoubtedly, the lack of success with his business and the oncoming birth of a third child led to Billy's decision to continue fighting. On December 3, he announced his intention to continue boxing. Later that month, he began working out at Del Hanlon's gym in St. Paul. His manager claimed to have several bouts lined up for him as soon as he was in shape.[414]

On January 4, 1921, promoter Floyd Fitzsimmons announced he had arranged a match between Billy and Eddie McGoorty to take place on January 13 in Grand Rapids.[415] Those plans fell through when McGoorty suffered an injury the next week.[416]

A week later, the Milwaukie, Oregon boxing commission announced it had signed three St. Paul boxers, including Billy, to box ten rounds each on February 9 against opponents to be determined. Ultimately, 31-year-old Lee Anderson became Billy's first opponent since the defeat against Jack Dempsey.

---

412 Fleischer, Nat, *Jack Dempsey, Idol of Fistiana*, The Ring, Inc., New York, N.Y. 1929.
413 Barton, George. *My Lifetime in Sports*. The Olympic Press, Minneapolis, MN 1957.
414 *Des Moines News*. News of the Boxers, December 20, 1920.
415 *Fort Wayne Journal*. Miske vs. M'Goorty, January 5, 1921.
416 *Indianapolis Star*. McGoorty – Miske Bout Off, January 14, 1921.

Anderson, a stocky, black 5'10" 183-pound heavyweight had been fighting professionally since 1914. He was coming off a draw with an aging, but still dangerous, Sam Langford, the previous month. He would go on to earn the biggest win of his career that coming May when he shocked the boxing fraternity with a ninth-round-technical-knockout victory over Kid Norfolk.

But, Anderson presented little challenge to Billy on February 9. Billy beat him to a pulp, winning every round in route to a convincing decision victory over ten rounds.[417] He was scheduled to face Walter "Farmer" Lodge the following month over ten rounds in the St. Paul Auditorium. The opportunity to face Billy was considered a step up in competition for Lodge, and if he were to win, or even make a creditable showing, it was said he would be in line for future bouts with Bob Martin, Charley Weinert, and Bill Brennan.

Lodge was expected to have a big edge in weight, but while he was very strong, he was also an awkward fighter. Billy was considered the much cleverer of the two, as well as the greater experienced man, and was the clear favorite as a result. The champion, Jack Dempsey, who was in town to fulfill a vaudeville engagement at the Pantages Theater, was signed to officiate the match.[418]

Billy met Lodge on March 7, 1921. He weighed approximately 180 pounds, against 220 pounds for Lodge, but knocked out his heavier and less experienced opponent in the fourth round.[419] Lodge appeared to have a slight edge in the first two rounds, landing several right hand swings and roughing Billy up on the inside. Billy began to land more blows in the second round and pounded the Farmer's ribs. Lodge sought refuge by clinching more frequently with Billy, and Dempsey had his hands full separating the two fighters.

In the third round, Billy took control of the fight, driving Lodge to the ropes on a number of occasions and rocking him with powerful blows to the jaw. At the beginning of the fourth round, Billy sprang from his corner and landed a heavy right on the jaw. He followed with a left to the body and Lodge clinched. Once Dempsey separated the pair, Billy rushed Lodge and landed three more punches on his jaw. Lodge came forward to clinch, but Billy stepped back and delivered a big punch to the stomach. Once again, Lodge came forward, and this time succeeded in tying Billy up. Billy, while trying to pull himself free, sent the big man flying through the ropes.

Lodge landed outside the ropes on his hands and knees, stretched out on the canvas to his full length, and moaned as Dempsey begin administering a count. Once he reached a count of ten, Dempsey and Billy lifted the big man to his feet and helped him to his corner while

---

417 *Olean Evening Times*. Miske Wants to Fight Dempsey, February 9, 1921.
418 *Minneapolis Tribune*, Farmer Lodge to Battle Billy Miske in St. Paul Show Monday, March 6, 1921.
419 *Evening Courier and Reporter*. Sports Flashes, March 8, 1921.

accompanied by a chorus from the crowd that was a mixture of cheers and cat calls.[420] Lodge later contended Billy purposely wrestled him out of the ring.[421]

To make matters worse for Lodge, it was learned afterward that $1,600 of his purse for the fight was tied up by the court. They did that as a result of garnishment proceedings brought forth by one Mark Gehan, due to a debt the Farmer owed Gehan for the purchase of a threshing machine way back in 1913, when he truly was a farmer and known as Lodge Flaskie.[422]

Billy was out of action for a bit then, until a ten-round match with an always dangerous Bill Brennan was arranged to take place in St. Paul on May 9. On May 1, Brennan was scratched as an opponent as a result of having his tonsils removed. A heavyweight out of Lewiston, Montana named Tommy McCarthy was quickly substituted for Brennan. Unfortunately, the replacement didn't prove to be much of a match for Billy, and he suffered an early second round knockout.[423]

The cancelled fight with Bill Brennan was then rescheduled to take place on June 6 in St. Paul's Lexington Park, the home of the St. Paul American Association baseball team. Unfavorable weather conditions forced a two-day postponement of the match. Brennan put the final touches on his training before a crowd of 600 fans in St. Paul's Rose Room gymnasium. He worked two rounds with Kid Norfolk, and another four with Tom McCarthy.

Confident of victory, Brennan said, "I am going to knock Miske out as soon as possible and send him back to the automobile business to stay." In response, Billy stated there was no way Brennan would knock him out, and promised to take care of him when they came together in the ring.[424]

The bout finally went off without a hitch on June 8. The event marked the third meeting between the two men. Most folks thought Brennan, who had recently gone 12 rounds with Jack Dempsey, would prove too tough a proposition for Billy this time around, but Billy surprised them and earned a ten-round newspaper victory. It was all the more surprising because Billy weighed in at only 180 pounds at 3:00 p.m. on the day of the fight, much less than what he had weighed when he fought Dempsey for the title, and eighteen pounds less than Brennan's 198.

Three of the first four rounds were even. Billy won the third round by a slim margin. Brennan won the fifth and ninth, but Billy took the sixth, seventh, and eighth, the sixth and seventh by a comfortable margin. The final round found both men fighting furiously and was judged even. It was

---

420 *Minneapolis Tribune*, Billy Miske Knocks Out Lodge in Fourth Round of St. Paul Battle, March 8, 1921.
421 *The Boxing Blade*, Minnesota Boxing News, February 25, 1922.
422 *Minneapolis Tribune*, Farmer Lodge, Pugilist Gets Two Court Knockouts, March 13, 1921.
423 *Eau Claire Leader*, Billy Miske Knocks Out Tommy McCarthy, May 10, 1921.
424 *Minneapolis Tribune*, Lexington Ring Ready for Battles Tonight With Kayos a Certainty, June 6, 1921.

a big win for Billy, and showed he was still one of the top heavyweights in the game.

The next day, June 9, a baby girl was welcomed into the Miske family. After two boys, Marion Donna Miske was added to Billy and Marie's growing family. It must have been both very exciting and yet somewhat worrisome given Billy's health and the family's financial condition.

On June 10, it was announced Billy would be matched with Canadian heavyweight, Jack Renault, to fight on the undercard of the July 2 heavyweight title fight between Jack Dempsey and Georges Carpentier in Jersey City, New Jersey. Renault, a Canadian policeman and a former sparring partner for Dempsey, was thought to be a rising contender. If he could get by Billy, he would be considered for a possible match with the champion. He was born in Quebec, Canada on January 18, 1895, and began his professional boxing career in 1918 at the age of 23.

The July 2 fight between Jack Dempsey and the Frenchman, Georges Carpentier, for the heavyweight title was billed as "The Battle of the Century." It was fought before 91,162 people, the largest crowd ever assembled for a boxing match up to that time. In contrast, the Dempsey-Willard title fight had been fought in Toledo before a crowd of only 20,000. The promoter, Tex Rickard, arranged for a huge wooden stadium to be built specifically for the Dempsey-Carpentier fight on a site known as "Boyle's Thirty Acres."

Every available seat was sold. The total receipts generated for the event were $1,626,580. The amount was almost four times as much as the greatest amount ever paid to see a boxing match. It was the first million dollar gate in history.

Carpentier was a brilliant aviator during the war and was a decorated French war hero. Born on January 12, 1894, Georges began boxing as a bantamweight when just a young boy. He kept winning fights as he grew older and progressed through the lightweight, middleweight, and finally, light-heavyweight classes. While only 19 years old, he knocked out England's "Bombardier" Billy Wells, a 6'3" 190-pound heavyweight, in a shocking upset on June 1, 1913 to capture the European heavyweight title. Proving the win was no fluke, he repeated the feat six months later. On October 12, 1920 he defeated "Battling" Levinsky and was acknowledged as the light-heavyweight champion of the world. Although only 172 pounds, he was very fast and carried a good wallop in his right hand. In addition to his prowess as a boxer, Carpentier also was an extremely handsome and charming fellow. He was enormously popular.[425]

When Dempsey arrived to his dressing room, he was met by a very excited Tex Rickard.

---

425 Dempsey, Jack, *Round by Round*, Whittlesey House, New York, N.Y. 1940.

Jack, you never 'seed' anything like it. We got a million dollars in already, and they're still coming. And the people, Jack! I never seed anything like the people we got, at a fight. High-class society folks. And dames. I mean classy dames, thousands of them.

Jack, this is the biggest day the boxing business ever had. I don't want you messing it up. This is just the beginning. We'll be drawing millions more before this is over.

Dempsey was nervous and irritable. "I ain't gonna mess nothin' up, Tex," he said. "Just tell that frog not to run, and I'll give you a good fight."

Tex got to the point. "Don't kill him, Jack," he said. "If you kill him you kill boxing. I just want you to knock him out, that's all. Not with a punch or in the first round. Give them a run for their money."

Rickard was afraid Dempsey, who outweighed Carpentier by approximately twenty pounds, would knock the Frenchman out shortly after the fight began, thereby depriving the tremendous crowd of enjoying much of a fight for their money. He also believed there was a possibility Dempsey might actually kill him.

When Rickard finished talking, Dempsey replied, "Tex, this guy is going out as soon as I can take him. I'm not carrying nobody for anybody, even for you."[426]

Despite the fact Carpentier was a foreigner, and the champion was defending the heavyweight title on his home soil, it was the Frenchman who was the overwhelming favorite of the crowd when the two men entered the ring. It was a well-known fact Carpentier was a decorated war hero, while the champion still carried the label of a "slacker" for not enlisting himself.

The champion received little applause when he was introduced, and a low murmur spread throughout the crowd. In contrast, Carpentier's introduction was accompanied with wild applause.

The first round wasn't much to speak of, each man feeling the other out. In the second, the challenger landed a big right, high on Dempsey's left cheekbone. It shook him up, and if it had landed on the chin might have even knocked him out. Carpentier tried to follow it up, but Dempsey landed his own right to the Frenchman's mouth, and immediately realized Carpentier wouldn't be able to stand up to his punches.

In the third round, Dempsey focused his attack on Carpentier's body to bring his guard down. In the fourth round, Dempsey nailed his man with a left hook to the head and Carpentier went down for a count of nine. Although Carpentier beat the count, he was groggy when he regained his feet. Dempsey landed another big left, and while the Frenchman was falling

---

426 Dempsey, Jack, *Dempsey*, Simon and Schuster, Inc., New York, N.Y. 1960.

he hit him with a right for good measure. Carpentier was subsequently counted out fifty seven seconds into the fourth round.[427]

The final preliminary bout between Billy and Jack Renault was postponed until after the Dempsey-Carpentier fight so the main event could begin at its scheduled time. Most of the crowd of 91,000 stayed to watch the beginning of the Miske-Renault contest, although the majority of the sportswriters paid it little attention, instead focusing their attention on recording their accounts of the heavyweight title fight.

By the end of Billy's match with Renault, there were threatening storm clouds in view, and most of the crowd had already started to depart. The *Ogden Standard Examiner* reported that Billy gave Renault a "very artistic trimming" over eight rounds.[428] Sports columnist Jack Keene questioned the Canadian's gameness, writing there was some feeling Renault got his fill of punishment during the bout, and was glad when the final bell rang.[429]

As the headliners for the event, Dempsey and Carpentier each received $302,000 from Promoter Tex Rickard. Billy and Gene Tunney, who fought Soldier Jones, were the two highest paid men of the preliminary boxers, and received $2,000 each.[430]

Billy was supposed to fight Captain Bob Roper next, on October 19, but wasn't feeling well enough to go forward with the bout and asked for a postponement until October 21. Roper and his team agreed to this, but shortly afterward Billy sent word he was going to have to cancel the match altogether.

Meanwhile, Billy's automobile business continued to struggle. When it became apparent he had no other choice, Billy finally relented to the urgings of his friends and family and filed a petition for bankruptcy in federal court. His liabilities were listed at $28,127 with total assets of $20,775.[431] The investment into the automobile business proved to be a financial disaster for Billy and his family, and it was one they never really recovered from.

About the same time the bankruptcy was announced, it was reported Billy would now devote all his time to fighting.[432] On November 11, Billy was back in the ring in Columbus, Nebraska where he faced a Chicago heavyweight named Tony Melchoir. Billy weighed in at 187 pounds for the fight, while Melchoir came in six pounds heavier, at 193. Billy didn't waste much time feeling his opponent out, sending him to the canvas in the first minute of the fight with a big right to the jaw. Melchoir took a count of eight from the referee before climbing to his feet. The round ended with Billy battering Melchoir against the ropes.

---

427 Dempsey, Jack, *Dempsey*, Simon and Schuster, Inc., New York, N.Y. 1960.
428 *Ogden Standard Examiner.* Terrific Blow to Vertabrae Wins For Jack, July 3, 1921.
429 *Olean Evening Herald.* Sport Snap Shots, June 18, 1924.
430 *Evening Republican.* Rickard Pays Performers, July 9, 1921.
431 *Bismarck Tribune.* Miske Files Bankruptcy, October 29, 1921.
432 *Bridgeport Telegram.* Couple Tips for the Unemployed, October 17, 1921.

In the second round, Billy was warned twice by the referee for holding Melchoir with one hand and hitting him with the other. Melchoir was bleeding from the nose at round's end.

Billy rushed from his corner at the beginning of the third round and the two men mixed it up furiously, Melchoir getting the worst of it. The Chicago heavyweight's left eye was closed by the end of the round.

Melchoir continued to take a beating in round four and was barely able to stand at its conclusion. The bell saved him from a sure knockout. Both of Melchoir's eyes were about closed at the end of this session. He was also badly cut over one eye and he was bleeding badly. The referee awarded the fight to Billy on a technical knockout when Melchoir claimed he could no longer continue as a result of either a strained, or torn, ligament in his left arm.[433]

By mid-December, Billy was lobbying for another shot at Jack Dempsey. He based his case on his recent win over Bill Brennan, after Brennan had given Dempsey such a difficult time the previous December, and the fact he had also defeated Lee Anderson, "Farmer" Lodge, Tom McCarty, Jack Renault, and Tony Melchoir since February. It was true, he had looked pretty impressive during his most recent return to the ring, but there was no one other than himself clamoring for another match with the champion after the way Dempsey has so easily disposed of him in Benton Harbor.

So, while his manager searched for other opportunities, Billy enjoyed the holidays with his family in St. Paul. Once the holidays were past, he began training for a match that would take place in Newark on January 16, 1922 with Charley Weinert. Billy had already defeated Weinert a couple of times, back in 1917, and he gave him a bad beating over 12 rounds on the 16th to earn a newspaper decision victory.[434]

While they were in Newark, Jack Reddy made every effort he could to get Billy booked to fight in New York's Madison Square Garden. He threw out challenges to Dempsey, Bill Brennan and Bartley Madden, among others, but the best he could do in the immediate future was land a return engagement with Jack Renault in the Rink Sporting Club in Brooklyn on January 28.

The bout with Renault proved to be a slow and uninteresting affair until the tenth round, when Billy opened up and punished the Canadian on the inside. After getting the worst of things during the eleventh and twelfth rounds, Renault attempted to become the aggressor in the thirteenth session, but was dropped to his knees by a right to the stomach. When he arose, he was sent sprawling through the ropes by a left to the chin and

---

433 *Nebraska State Journal.* Billy Miske Wins Decision. Tony Melchoir Forced To Quit In Fourth Round, March 12, 1921.
434 *Racine Journal-News.* Ticks From the Sport Mill, January 17, 1922.

Billy was awarded a technical knockout when it became clear Renault would be unable to continue.[435]

Billy's next fight took place against "Captain" Bob Roper in the Olympia Athletic Club in Philadelphia on February 20, 1922. Roper, a former captain in the Army, was born as William Hammond in McComb, Mississippi on March 2, 1894, and while he could boast of victories over a number of good men such as "Gunboat" Smith, Frank Moran and Bill Brennan, he'd come out on the short end of his contests against the top fighters of that era he'd faced - like Tommy Gibbons and Harry Greb. When Billy was ill in October of 1921 and had to call off his scheduled bout with Roper, there was some speculation the cancellation had more to do with Roper's quick finish of big Carl Morris in Tulsa, Oklahoma.[436] This would give Billy a chance to show what he could do against the former Army officer.

Roper looked anything but a world beater when the pair finally came together before the club members. Billy had everything pretty much his own way in the early rounds, in fact so much so, those at ringside were sure he was "pulling" his punches and there were hisses throughout the crowd. In response, Billy picked up the pace in the fifth round and landed combinations to the body and head, staggering Roper and leaving him groggy by the bell ending the round.

Billy opened the sixth round with a furious attack, driving Roper across the ring. It was at that point Roper swung a wild right that landed well south of the border, doubling Billy up, and prompting a disqualification from the referee, "Pop" O'Brien. Once again, Billy had checked the rise of a heavyweight contender and eliminated him from possible consideration as a challenger to Jack Dempsey's crown.[437]

Reddy and Billy accomplished their objective of obtaining a fight in New York's Madison Square Garden next, with a match against Al Roberts of Staten Island, on the undercard of a March 2, 1922 main event between Kid Norfolk and Harry Wills.

Roberts weighed in at 183 pounds for the fight while Billy scaled 188 pounds. The less-experienced Roberts had wins against Charley Weinert, Bob Roper, and "Gunboat" Smith to his credit, but found himself in over his head against Billy. Billy knocked him down for a count of nine with a left hook to the jaw in the first round, and generally knocked him all around the ring, before knocking him out with a combination to the jaw at the 2:53 mark of the second round.[438]

---

435 *Times Tribune*. Miske Knocks Out Renault, January 28, 1922.
436 *Reno Evening Gazette*. Fighting Center is Now Chicago, October 31, 1921.
437 *New Castle News*. Bob Roper Fouls Miske in Philly, February 21, 1922.
438 *Sioux City Journal*. Harry Wills Wins Over Kid Norfolk by Knockout in Second Round, March 3, 1922.

In late March, Billy was matched to face a fighter named Billy Shade in Youngstown, Ohio on April 10, 1922. Shade, born in Concord, California on May 2, 1900, was one of three brothers who fought professionally, the other two being George, and the most famous of the trio Dave.

Initially, managed by their father Charles, the brothers ultimately moved east and placed themselves under the management of Leo P. Flynn. Billy Shade had captured the light-heavyweight championship of Australia in March of 1921 and returned to the States that Fall in search of more lucrative opportunities. While he enjoyed some early successes against men like Fay Keiser and Homer Smith, he subsequently lost decisions to Harry Greb, Chuck Wiggins and Jimmy Darcy, before rebounding with a victory over Martin Burke. On the face of it, he didn't seem like he would present much of an obstacle for Billy, as long as Billy was healthy, but there were those who believed he'd take Billy's measure. The fans in Youngstown eagerly awaited the match and the Youngstown Athletic Club anticipated a record attendance for the event.[439]

It turned out Billy had too much heavy artillery for Shade. Shade entered the ring at an announced weight of 174 ½ pounds but some felt he may have been lighter. Billy appeared fit at 185 pounds.

As expected, the event drew a large number of fans, with hundreds of others left on the outside, unable to gain admittance.[440] The event lived up to its advance billing in terms of action but it didn't last long. Toward the end of the first round, Billy backed Shade into a corner, measured him with a left jab, and crossed a right to the jaw. Shade responded with a combination of his own to the head but Billy dropped him with a short right to the jaw. Shade rose at the count of eight, blood running from his nose, and attempted to fight back, but Billy walked right through his punches and dropped him again with a vicious combination. The referee's count had reached three when the bell rang, and Shade's seconds rushed into the ring to help guide him back to his corner.

Shade's corner men worked furiously to revive their man during the break. When the second round began the crowd anticipated Billy would rush across the ring to finish his man, but he walked calmly to the middle and waited for Shade to come to him. Once they came together, Billy delivered a right to the jaw, followed by a short jab, and then another big right to the jaw that sent Shade toppling to the canvas. He rose shakily at the count of seven, but he was out on his feet.

The crowd urged Billy to finish the fight. He backed Shade into a corner and sent him crashing to the canvas with another big right to the jaw. Using the rope, Shade struggled to pull himself back into an upright position. When he was halfway there, Billy reached forward and lifted him the rest of the way, and then stepped back.

---

439 *New Castle News*. Miske-Shade Go Looks Very Good, April 6, 1922.
440 *New Castle News*. Miske Kayos Shade in Second Chapter, April 11, 1922.

Many in the crowd thought the fight had come to an end. By all accounts, the referee should have stopped it right there since Shade was out on his feet. Billy mercifully stepped in and delivered a light tap to the head that sent Shade down for a final time. At that point, the referee stepped in and ruled it a technical knockout in Billy's favor. Billy reached down, helped Shade to his feet and said to no one in particular, "He's not big enough."

While Billy was no longer as fast as he had once been, it seemed as though he'd managed to increase his punching power a bit. Speaking on the subject, and punches that do the most damage, Billy said:

> The punch you see coming rarely inflicts great damage, regardless of where it lands. When I have a chance to see a wallop that's headed my way, I somehow seem to instinctively protect myself by involuntary muscular contraction. It's the punch that filters through your defense when you thought there wasn't a chance for one to get through, that sets your brain whirling and weakens the control of the legs.

Billy declared he had learned a lot about punching in the past six months. "Unnecessary exertion in delivering a punch is silly. When you have them timed correctly and you can sneak them in through a defense, you have started on a knockout career," he said.[441]

On April 27, 1922, Billy won a decisive victory over Martin Burke in 15 rounds before the Orleans Athletic Club in New Orleans. Burke was lauded for his gameness and stamina, while absorbing tremendous punishment over the course of the contest. Billy weighed 184 pounds to Burke's 179.[442]

Many believed Burke would not be able to go the distance with Miske. Billy claimed the Louisiana climate got the best of him and he wasn't able to acclimate himself to it. Burke withstood everything Billy had to offer and made an impressive showing in the final rounds.[443]

Afterward, Billy credited Burke with being a "tough nut" but said he believed he would have knocked him out had Burke opened up more. Burke held and clinched throughout the bout.[444]

The sporting editor of the *New Orleans Times-Picayune* wrote that Billy was either the biggest dumb-bell in the boxing game or the toughest and stoutest-hearted man he knew of when he learned Billy wanted another chance at Jack Dempsey. In the editor's opinion, Billy's natural style was to tear in to his opponent, and in his view any man who tore into Dempsey was either a dumb-bell, or possessed the heart of a reckless lion.[445] Anybody who knew anything about Billy Miske knew the latter was true of him.

---

441 *Ogden Standard*. Punch if Seen Lacks Damage, April 23, 1922.
442 *Winnipeg Free Press*. Burke Shows Gameness in Bout with Billy Miske, April 28, 1922.
443 *Ogden Standard-Examiner*. Wants Return Bout, May 19, 1922.
444 *New Orleans Times-Picayune*. Burke Takes Cruel Beating But Keeps Feet Against Miske, April 28, 1922.
445 *New Orleans Times-Picayune*. Miske All Grit, April 29, 1922.

The day after the Burke fight, it was reported that American light-heavyweight champion Gene Tunney's manager, Frank Bagley, had turned down a proposal of a fight between Tunney and Billy to take place in Canton, Ohio. Bagley reasoned his man was too light to face Miske. Billy had run off a string of 12 straight victories since his loss to Dempsey, and Bagley apparently didn't relish the idea of pitting his champion against the St. Paul Thunderbolt.[446]

In hindsight, Bagley may have wished he had opted to accept the match with Billy on Tunney's behalf. Instead, Tunney agreed to a match with Harry Greb in Madison Square Garden on May 23 and received a terrific beating, while suffering the only official loss of his professional career.

---

446 *Syracuse Herald.* Harry Greb Signs to Box Against Tunney, April 28, 1922.

CHAPTER 13

Gibbons Establishes His Superiority

When Gene Tunney's manager declined the offer of a match with Billy, Reddy arranged another meeting for Billy with "Captain" Bob Roper. The two men were signed to fight over ten rounds at the Dyckman Oval in New York City on May 29, 1922.

Billy earned a relatively easy victory over Roper, gaining the decision from all three judges, when they met before the members of the Academy Athletic Club. In the opinion of the *New York Times* reporter covering the fight, Billy won every round, and had Roper on the defensive throughout the contest.

Billy weighed in at 188 pounds, three to five more than Roper, depending on the source, and also enjoyed advantages in both height and reach. He punished Roper severely to the body with lefts and rights, but appeared somewhat wild when he switched his attack to the head. Roper was in danger of suffering a knockout in both the second and seventh rounds, but tenaciously clinched to Billy whenever he was in trouble in order to save himself.

The *National Police Gazette* characterized the bout as "exceedingly rough" and noted that referee, Artie McGovern, cautioned Roper several times for hitting low. They indicated Billy's attack to the body was a key to his success in the contest.[447]

Although it was a clear decision victory for Billy, and he showed flashes of the form he had demonstrated for New Yorkers in the past, it was noted there was little of the sustained attack, and punching accuracy, or agility, speed and cleverness he had demonstrated when he was considered one of the best light-heavyweights in the country.[448]

Billy's next opponent was Michigan's leading heavyweight, Homer Smith, on June 23, 1922 in Covington, Kentucky. Homer faced some of the biggest names in boxing during a professional career that began in 1914 and lasted over 15 years. A very competent fighter, but a cut below the better men in his chosen profession, Homer suffered defeat at the hands of some of the best in the business, including Jack Dempsey, Harry Greb, "Battling" Levinsky, Harry Wills, Luis Firpo, Jack Sharkey, and even an aged Jack Johnson in 1924, as well as many other quality fighters.

---

447 The National Police Gazette, "*Billy Miske Beats Capt. Bob Roper in Rough 10-Rounder*", June 17, 1922.
448 *New York Times*. Miske Wins Easily From Bob Roper, May 30, 1922.

Homer who never drank or smoked, and won more often than he lost, was good enough to go the distance with a number of the better fighters of his day. It was said he traveled approximately 300,000 miles during his career, and fought in France, Germany, Belgium, England, Cuba, Spain and Hawaii in addition to all of his contests in the United States.

Homer claimed the hardest hitter he ever fought was either Jack Dempsey or Luis Firpo. "They hit differently," Homer said, "you might say it's like the kick of a mule and the kick of a draft horse. Dempsey has the mule kick; his punches are short, sharp and quick, and jar you something awful. Firpo's come like the horse kick – slower and mighty heavy." He went on to say Jack Johnson, long past his prime by the time he fought him, was the hardest man for him to hit. "He knew more ways to keep from being hit than anybody I ever boxed with," Homer said.[449]

The fight didn't provide much of a workout for Billy, or even a run for the fans' money, as Billy knocked Smith out in the first minute of the scheduled 12-round bout.[450]

A third and final fight with Willie Meehan was next, on July 3. Billy accomplished a feat he had been unable to pull off in their first two contests, and Jack Dempsey couldn't do in five fights with the crafty Californian. He knocked Meehan out in Oklahoma City and in the first round no less. It was the first and only actual knockout Meehan suffered in a professional career spanning over 150 fights including sluggers such as Harry Wills, Jack Dempsey, Bill Brennan, Fred Fulton, Jack Dillon and many others.

The knockout occurred just two minutes and 40 seconds into the opening round. Billy landed a hard left jab to Meehan's body and forced him to the ropes, where the pair exchanged some light punches, before Billy broke through and landed a big hook to the jaw that put Meehan down for a count of ten. Meehan weighed 195 for the fight, to Billy's 190.[451]

The fight took place on a program including a four-round exhibition between the heavyweight champion, Jack Dempsey, and Andre Anderson of Chicago. Dempsey toyed with the badly overmatched Anderson. There was some talk of granting Billy another opportunity to fight the champion on the strength of Billy's recent performances. Jack Kearns, Dempsey's manager, said Billy would probably have an opportunity to meet Dempsey before Christmas.[452]

Meehan went on to fight until late 1926. After his boxing career concluded, he became a production electrician for Hollywood movie studies. He passed away in 1953 at the age of 59.

---

449 *Evening Independent*, Homer Smith Has Met 'Em All In His Time, March 6, 1927.
450 *Capital Times*. Billy Miske Kayoes Smith in a Minute, June 24, 1922.
451 *Galveston Daily News*. Miske Knocks Out Meehan In Initial, July 4, 1922.
452 *Vancouver Daily World*. Miske Kayoes Willie Meehan, July 4, 1922.

After his victory over Meehan, Jess Willard, Bill Brennan, Georges Carpentier, and Harry Greb were all being mentioned, in addition to Billy, as possible opponents for the champion. In his *Sport Snap Shots* column, Jack Keene wrote Billy had done much better against Dempsey than Willard, Brennan, or Carpentier, and suggested Billy was an "invalid" when Dempsey knocked him out in their third contest. Keene felt Billy was the most worthy opponent for Dempsey at the time based on his recent victories over men like Brennan, Roper, Weinert and men of a lesser note. The truth be told, Harry Greb, although a smaller man, or Harry Wills may have presented the most worthy opposition at the time.[453]

On July 10, Billy received a second opportunity to fight heavyweight Martin Burke, this time in Denver. There were those who claimed Burke should have received no worse than a draw in the April contest between the two. In fact, at least one writer said Burke should have been named the winner, a number of writers feeling he won four of those rounds, and the remaining rounds were even.[454] The *New Orleans Times-Picayune* had indicated otherwise, reporting the decision in Billy's favor in their first match was never in doubt.

Burke had only been fighting as a professional for a little over a year and was viewed as an up-and-coming heavyweight contender. Upon his arrival in Denver, local sportswriter Howard Vickery wrote his appearance reminded him of old Bob Fitzsimmons, with his long legs and "bulky" set of shoulders.[455] Another local scribe, Otto Floto, said of Billy, that he looked like the same man who fought Jack Dempsey in their first meeting in St. Paul, Minnesota in 1918, as opposed to the shell that faced the champion in Benton Harbor in September of 1920. "He looks like the Miske who battled Jack Dillon and Fred Fulton to a standstill up in St. Paul, and we no longer wonder how he forced Billy Shade, heavyweight champion of Australia, and Homer Smith of Michigan to kiss the rug in one round. He looks every inch the part of a champion," wrote Floto.[456]

Burke was confident of victory and, according to Floto, was also good and sore at Billy, claiming he was sick and had two boils on his neck that Billy insisted on working over the last time the pair fought. "I'll show that Minnesota lumberjack what I can do the next time we clash," Burke said to Floto.[457]

Both men had something riding on the outcome. A victory for Burke would mean a match with heavyweight contender, Bill Brennan, and possible fight for the title should he win over Brennan. And Billy's manager claimed he was in receipt of a telegram promising a potentially lucrative

---

453 *Olean Evening Herald.* Sport Snap Shots, July 18, 1922.
454 *Capital Times.* Sport Snapshots, June 3, 1922.
455 *Denver Post*, Burke Arrives And Trains For Monday's Fray, July 8, 1922.
456 *Denver Post*, Billy Miske Is Staging Real Comeback; Wants Chance At Wills, July 3, 1922.
457 *Denver Post*, Billy Miske Is Staging Real Comeback; Wants Chance At Wills, July 3, 1922.

fight with Harry Wills in Brooklyn should Billy decisively defeat Burke.[458] Denver fight promoter, Jack Kenner, added another element of interest to the fight when he announced he had posted a $1,000 bonus to be paid to either man should they knock out the other in Monday's matchup.[459]

When the pair met in Denver, Billy weighed 189 pounds, while Burke tipped the scales at 182. Billy earned a decisive newspaper decision, winning ten of the 12 rounds per the reports out of Denver.[460] Reporting on the contest for the *Denver Post*, Howard Vickery wrote it was Billy's fight all the way, with Burke having claim to winning only one of twelve rounds, the sixth session, and that round by only a shade. "The rest of the time he was busy on the defensive, keeping out from under Miske's hooks and swings," said Vickery.

Billy had Burke in danger of suffering a knockout in the seventh, eighth and final round according to Vickery. Billy dropped Burke to his knees in the eighth round with a right to the stomach that almost brought an end to the contest. Burke was lauded for the gameness he exhibited under the punishment doled out by Billy.[461]

Two weeks after the Burke fight, Jack Reddy managed to arrange a long awaited rematch between Billy and big Fred Fulton. The pair had fought to a ten-round draw in St. Paul over four years earlier and there had been quite a bit of speculation as to the outcome of a second fight between the two. The rematch was scheduled to take place outdoors in St. Paul's Lexington Park.

Like Billy, Fulton had suffered a knockout to Jack Dempsey since their previous meeting, Fulton suffering the fate in July of 1918, roughly a year before Dempsey became champion. But, Fulton had enjoyed a very successful run since the loss to Dempsey, losing only once in 37 fights over the next four years, the loss coming against Harry Wills in July of 1920.

It was expected Billy would weigh anywhere from 185 to 190 pounds for the bout, while Fulton would come in around 210 pounds. Fulton was generally conceded to be the better boxer by critics and, as he did in their first fight, would enjoy significant advantages in height and reach. However, it was anticipated those advantages would be mitigated by Billy's aggressiveness and body attack.[462] A number of people were of the opinion Billy had improved since their first meeting, while Fulton had been traveling the other way. None were stronger in expressing this opinion than *The Boxing Blade*, a weekly Minneapolis based periodical edited by Fulton's former manager, Mike Collins. There were hard feelings between Collins

---

458 *Denver Post*, Burke Arrives And Trains For Monday's Fray, July 8, 1922.
459 *Denver Post*, $1,000 Bonus Posted For Fighter Crossing Kayo Monday Night, July 7, 1922.
460 *Boxing Blade*. Billy Miske Winner Over Martin Burke, July 1922.
461 *Denver Post*, Miske Laces Burke Thru Twelve Furious Rounds At Stadium, July 11, 1922.
462 *Daily Glove*. Billy Miske to Box Fred Fulton, July 31, 1922.

and Fulton, and Collins was not shy about criticizing his former boxer and questioning his fighting heart in print.

While training for the upcoming bout, it was arranged for Billy to provide an exhibition on the lawn before a group of disabled American soldiers at the Aberdeen Hospital in St. Paul on August 3. Several hundred veterans watched him spar under the shade of some nearby trees, while another 150 or so were moved closer to their windows in their beds so they could view the action.[463]

As the date of the fight came closer, the Miske's received a telegram addressed to their second oldest son, Douglas, from Billy's friend and actor, Douglas Fairbanks. Fairbanks, who had requested his friend name the boy after himself, asked the youngster to "Tell your dad I am pulling for him and know he will lick Fulton next Friday."[464]

The fight between Billy and Fulton was originally scheduled to take place on August 11, but was postponed when Fulton developed a boil on his nose and the boxing commission ruled against him fighting with it. The promoters gave serious consideration to having Tommy Gibbons take Fulton's place, but a week of heavy rains prompted them to postpone the event until August 25 instead.[465] Fulton advised fans he was in top form and said to look for him to knock out Billy inside seven rounds.[466] Despite Fulton's confidence, Billy was considered the favorite. The contest generated quite a bit of interest and the expectation was the winner would issue a challenge to Jack Dempsey.[467]

On August 13, it was reported there were rumors circulating the real reason for the fight's postponement on the 11th was efforts had been made to get Fulton to throw the fight, and when he rejected the idea, certain individuals who had bet heavily on Billy to win insisted the fight be called off. But, members of the commission investigated the matter and were satisfied the postponement was primarily due to Fulton's nose, as well as the rain.[468]

A day before the fight, Billy was listed as a 10 to 7 favorite to defeat the big fellow. "Fulton would like to box me," Billy said, "as he believes he's a better boxer than I am. But, he will have a hard time boxing me for I'll be in there close. He will have trouble in fancy stepping."[469]

When Billy and Fulton finally came together in the ring on the night of August 25, 1922, Billy weighed in at 188 pounds while Fulton came in 19 pounds heavier, at 207 pounds. *The Boxing Blade* voiced their opinion Fulton's best fighting weight was 215 pounds, and suggested his lower

---

463 *Minneapolis Tribune*, Miske to Show Wares Before Disabled Vets, August 3, 1922.
464 *Minneapolis Tribune*, Doug Fairbanks Sends Hopeful Message to Son of Billy Miske, August 7, 1922.
465 *Oakland Tribune*, Fulton and Miske to Meet Friday, August 12, 1922.
466 *Appleton Post*, Fulton and Miske Will Battle Friday Night, August 11, 1922.
467 *New Mexican*, Billy Miske Fights Fred Fulton Tonight, August 11, 1922.
468 *Minneapolis Tribune*, Mitt Directors Ignore St. Paul Scrap Rumors, August 13, 1922.
469 *Minneapolis Tribune*, Heavies Take Final Sprints Before Battle, August 24, 1922,

weight for the fight with Billy was brought about as a result of worry.[470] More than 7,500 fans were in attendance, generating total gate receipts of $20,000.[471]

The fans saw plenty of action, but it was all on Billy's part. The bout was scheduled for ten rounds but all Billy needed was one. He rushed out of his corner at the sound of the opening bell and wasted no time feeling his larger opponent out, immediately landing a vicious left to Fulton's midsection. Fulton was plainly surprised and hurt by the blow.

The two men then sparred for a bit, Billy initiating all the action, when approximately a minute into the fight, Billy bulled Fulton to the ropes and dropped his larger foe with a pretty left hook to the jaw. Fulton managed to regain his footing before Referee George Barton reached the count of ten, but Billy sprang forward and attacked with left and right hooks. Fulton was unable to produce any offense in response, doing all he could to fend off Billy's attack. Billy forced Fulton to the corner, found an opening, and landed another left to the jaw, followed immediately by a big right hand blow to the head that sent him down for a count he wouldn't beat.[472]

The Boxing Blade, while expressing a desire to avoid taking any credit away from Billy, reported it was the consensus of opinion of good judges at ringside that any second or third rate heavyweight with a little courage could have whipped Fulton. It was their reporters opinion, that while Billy's blows were punishing, and no doubt hurt, they didn't appear sufficiently damaging to stop a real fighter of the "class that Fulton pretended to be." They pointed to four other times in his career when Fulton had quit when the going became tough. The first time occurred in a contest against Al Palzer at Hudson, Wisconsin, and then again a short time later against big Carl Morris. The third and fourth times were said to have transpired in the first round of a contest against Jack Dempsey, and the third round of his match with Harry Wills.

It was after his short outing against Dempsey that Fulton initially suggested his manager, Mike Collins, had been involved in convincing him to take a dive. He later retracted that statement but it appears to have led to a permanent split in the relationship between the two men.[473] Collins vehemently denied there was any fix involved in the fight between Dempsey and Fulton, and said "there was no double crossing, excepting the left and right crosses which Dempsey put over on Fulton in the remarkably quick time of eighteen seconds."[474]

---

470 *Boxing Blade*, Fred Fulton goes to Fistic Dump after Lasting Only Two Minutes With Miske, September 9, 1922.
471 *Lincoln Star*, Fulton Floored In Single Round, August 26, 1922.
472 *St. Paul Pioneer Press*, Miske Knocks Out Fulton in First Round, August 26, 1922.
473 *Boxing Blade*, Fred Fulton Goes to Fistic Dump after Lasting Only Two Minutes With Miske, September 9, 1922.
474 *National Police Gazette*, Denies Fulton's Yarn That Fight Was Fixed, February 22, 1919.

After he was counted out in the match against Billy, Fulton was helped to his corner, and a melee broke out when his former manager, Collins, entered the ring and directed a remark to Fred that prompted Fulton's brother Whitey, and then Fred himself, to rush after Collins. Referee Barton, ringside fans and police, managed to restore order before anyone was seriously hurt.[475]

The Boxing Blade reported Collins had stepped into the ring to congratulate Miske, but Billy had already departed for his dressing room. It was at that point Collins looked across the ring and saw Fulton and decided to approach him for the first time in four years. Still sore about Fulton's implications of his involvement in a possible fix in the match with Dempsey, Collins said to Fred, "Is this the way Dempsey knocked you out a few years ago?"

The remark enraged Fulton and his brother, and set off the melee. Collins expressed his regret for his part in the incident afterward and Fulton maintained this fight with Billy was on the level.[476]

Jack Reddy wasted little time in voicing interest in another match with Dempsey after the win. Billy's recent wins over Weinert, Renault, Burke, Roper, Smith, Meehan and, now, Fulton among others didn't hurt his case, but there were others such as Harry Wills and Harry Greb who certainly seemed more deserving of a chance at the champion at the time.

Fulton went on to fight through 1925 and made brief one-fight comebacks in both years 1930 and 1933, but for practical purposes the loss to Miske marked the end of his career as a serious title contender. As Robert Ripley, of Ripley's Believe It Or Not fame, said about Fulton, he just seemed to have a "missing link." He had size, weight, strength, a punch, and boxing ability, but he just seemed to lack the one thing that would make him a champion. It wasn't that he lacked courage, but possibly he lacked spirit or fire in Ripley's opinion. [477]

Rather than rest on his laurels, Billy immediately agreed to a third match with "Captain" Bob Roper, to take place over twelve rounds in Oklahoma City on September 4, 1922. Fighting so far away from home and family, along with the uncertainty about how much time he had left on this earth, had to weigh heavily on Billy's mind. But, he was determined to provide for his family in the only way he knew.

Surprisingly, after such an impressive performance against Fulton, Billy produced a lackluster effort against Roper on Labor Day. It took a strong finish over the last five rounds for him to overcome the lead Roper had

---

475 *Vancouver Sun*. Bout is Followed by Free-For-All, August 27, 1922.
476 *Boxing Blade*, Fred Fulton Goes to Fistic Dump after Lasting Only Two Minutes With Miske, September 9, 1922.
477 *St. Paul Pioneer Press*, The Missing Link, May 20, 1923.

built up over the first seven rounds. It enabled him to earn a draw with his lesser regarded opponent.[478]

Despite the unimpressive outing against Roper, there were some who continued to maintain Billy deserved another chance with Dempsey. U.P.I. sports editor, Henry Farrell, was one of those men. He claimed Billy had a valid claim to fight the champion, and it was unfair to judge him on his performance in Benton Harbor against Dempsey since he was coming off a long siege of illness. Farrell felt Billy's performance over the last year, along with his first-round knockout of Fulton, made him a worthy challenger.[479]

On the flip side, sportswriter Bob Edgren was convinced Dempsey was Miske's master, and if Billy fought the champion again, the only question would be how many rounds Billy would stay on his feet. "And," Edgren wrote, "that doesn't make a very interesting bout."[480]

On September 29 of 1922 it was announced Billy and Tommy Gibbons had been matched for a fifteen round contest at New York's Madison Square Garden on October 13. All three of their previous meetings had been of the non-decision variety but Tommy was generally conceded to have the edge in those battles. He was one of the greatest light-heavyweights of all-time and had lost only two contests in more than 80 fights coming into this bout with Billy. One of those losses had come seven months earlier against Harry Greb in Madison Square Garden. Greb had made him look foolish in the bout but Tommy claimed he was just recovering from an illness and wasn't in his best condition.[481] It was reported that should Billy emerge victorious against Tommy he would be matched to meet Harry Wills.[482]

Billy arrived in New York several days before the fight and looked impressive in his workouts. One scribe noted he looked heavier and more rugged than he had in the past and he now fought as well as boxed.[483] Billy expressed confidence in his ability to beat Gibbons and even said he might do so via a knockout. He claimed he was in better shape than ever before and said he expected his speed and punching power to overcome Tommy's cleverness. He expected to weigh 185 for the fight.[484] Tommy was late to arrive, not appearing on the scene until late on October 11.

Tommy's father, Thomas Gibbons, Sr., was critically ill at the time Tommy departed St. Paul. His brother, Mike, later revealed Tommy had been hesitant about leaving, knowing his father's condition. But, he also knew boxing fans would view the announcement of a fight cancellation with skepticism. He believed his father would rather have him keep his

---

478 *Boxing Blade.* Billy Miske Gets Draw with Bob Roper, September 1922.
479 *Sheboygan Press-Telegram.* Farrell Chats About Football As A Profession, September 16, 1922.
480 *News Sentinel.* Sports Through Edgren's Eyes, September 11, 1922.
481 *Reno Evening Gazette.* Friday's Fight To Be Rattler, October 10, 1922.
482 *Lafayette Ledger,* Miske-Gibbons Bout on Tonight, October 13, 1922.
483 *Nashville Tennessean.* Gibbons Ready Friday's Big Battle, October 10, 1922.
484 *New York Times.* Miske is Confident of Beating Gibbons, October 10, 1922.

commitment, than be accused of running out of a fight. His 72-year-old father had been a fervent supporter of his sons' boxing careers, often offering support and advice, but he never attended any of their fights, apparently not relishing the idea of seeing either of them suffering any punishment.[485]

"Each time we signed for a fight, he promised that he would attend," said Tommy's brother Mike, "but at the last moment he always decided that he would rather stay at home. I can't remember that he ever discouraged us from boxing, but at the same time he never gave us much encouragement."[486]

Despite his late arrival and his concern over his father's health, Tommy claimed he was in the best shape he had been in a long time. He attributed this to spending most of his time in the woods. "All I need now is a little sharpening up work with the gloves," he said.[487]

The contest shaped up to be a very even matchup. Tommy was considered the cleverer boxer of the pair but Billy was viewed as having the edge in heart and hitting ability. Both men had a lot at stake. The bout was viewed as the beginning of an elimination tournament among heavyweight contenders for an eventual opportunity to challenge Jack Dempsey for the title.

Despite the fact Tommy held the advantage in their prior meetings Billy was viewed as the favorite heading into the fight on the basis of an increase in weight and his recent performances. Some thought Tommy had slipped a bit.[488] However, the *National Police Gazette* indicated the betting was 6 to 5 in Tommy's favor.[489]

On October 13, 1922, a crowd of more than 13,000 paid $39,392 to view the Miske–Gibbons fight at Madison Square Garden.[490] Billy weighed in at 187 pounds, while Tommy came in eleven pounds less, at 176.[491]

Once again, Tommy confounded Billy with his boxing ability and cleverness, but the bout came to a surprising conclusion in the tenth round. Billy landed first in round one, with a short right to the head. And, while the pair exchanged punches evenly from long range, both men were wild in the opening round. The *National Police Gazette's* reporter noted there was none of the lack of speed witnessed on Tommy's part in his contest in the Garden against Harry Greb the previous winter, and said the first two rounds were full of action.[492]

---

485 *Lincoln Star*. Gibbons Master of Billy Miske, October 14, 1922.
486 *Minneapolis Tribune*, News Withheld From Tom, 'Til Close of Bout, October 14, 1922.
487 *Logansport Pharos-Tribune*. Heavies Mix Tomorrow, October 12, 1922.
488 *Nashville Tennessean*. Miske Battles Gibbons Tonight In Big Bout, October 13, 1922.
489 *National Police Gazette*, "Miske Wins On Foul By Gibbons In Tenth", November 4, 1922.
490 Blair, George D., *Billy Miske, The St. Paul Thunderbolt*, Privately published, no date.
491 *New Castle News*. Tom Gibbons Loses to Miske, October 14, 1922.
492 *National Police Gazette*, "Miske Wins On Foul By Gibbons In Tenth", November 4, 1922.

In the second round, Billy caught Tommy with a left hook to the jaw. Both men landed left jabs to the head. While they maintained a lively pace throughout the round, there was little damage done to either man.

In round three, Tommy landed a hard left to Billy's jaw, after which Billy rushed Tommy to the corner and roughed him up along the ropes. Billy was extremely aggressive in this round, throwing a number of vicious punches and produced a stream of blood from Tommy's nose. He also opened a cut on Tommy's head that produced a second flow of blood. The session was considered even though, because of the number of stiff left hand jabs Tommy was able to land throughout the round.

Tommy landed several hard punches to Billy's head in round four, and opened a cut over Billy's left eye. Tommy had the better of the infighting, as Billy missed repeatedly with the majority of his punches, but the *Police Gazette* reported the round as even. As the fight progressed, the *Gazette* noted that while Billy's punches seemed to have plenty of steam behind them, Tommy was always going away, and more often than not, the punches found a missing mark.[493]

Round five found both men fighting cautiously, though Billy's left eye began to swell. Tommy continued to pound it with hard rights. Round six found Tommy continually landing lefts to Billy's head, while Billy was unable to connect with his own blows.

By round seven, it was clear Billy was puzzled by Tommy's footwork and defensive tactics. He missed badly, while Tommy seemingly landed with everything he threw. But, although he landed frequently, Tommy's blows seemed to lack steam and did little damage. It was during this round a uniformed messenger made his way to Gibbons' corner and delivered a yellow envelope to Eddie Kane, his manager. Gibbons saw it out of the corner of his eye as he continued to battle Billy.

When he returned to his corner at the end of the round he asked Kane, "What does it say?"

"What does what say?" replied Kane.

"Oh all right," said Tommy, "but I know." In his heart, he knew his father was gone.

Round eight found the fighters sparring for an opening while an impatient crowd appealed for more action. Billy was the aggressor, but Tommy dodged a number of punches, before sending in a series of blows, one of which Billy claimed was low. The *Police Gazette* reported the referee cautioned Gibbons against a repetition of the blow.[494] Tommy rained punches upon Miske's body, and knocked several teeth out of his mouth in this round and the *Police Gazette's* man thought Billy was close to going down. Still, Billy mounted a comeback and let loose a barrage of punches that sent Tommy to the ropes where he was forced to cover up. Tommy

---

493 *National Police Gazette*, Miske Wins On Foul By Gibbons In Tenth, November 4, 1922.
494 *National Police Gazette*, Miske Wins on Foul By Gibbons In Tenth, November 4, 1922.

finished strong, though, and they were trading punches at the bell, but Billy clearly came out on the short end of the exchanges during the round.

Tommy worked his left jab to perfection in round nine while Billy directed his attack to the body. Billy continued to attack while Tommy skillfully evaded the majority of Billy's punches and delivered his own counter blows.

Twenty seven seconds into the tenth round, Tommy delivered a short right to the body, and Billy fell to the floor, his face distorted in pain with his gloves clutching his groin. Referee McPartland wasn't in a position to see the blow land and sought the opinion of Artie McGovern, one of the judges at ringside. McGovern told him it was a foul, and McPartland, after a brief hesitation, disqualified Tommy and awarded the match to Billy.[495] The punch that produced an end to the contest was seen by very few. Gibbons, who had built up a seemingly insurmountable lead to that point, seemed dazed as he walked about the ring.[496]

McPartland helped Billy to his corner. Many in the crowd shouted for him to continue. Tommy walked over to Billy's corner, but Billy seemed too weak to acknowledge him. When the referee awarded the fight to Billy and announced the decision to the crowd, they booed it loudly. They also booed Billy when he was finally able to leave the ring.

When Gibbons returned to his own corner, his manager finally shared the telegram with him. "Read it Tom," he said. "Let's hurry and dress. I'm awful sorry." Tommy's father had died of cancer earlier in the day. Tears streamed down Tommy's face as he made his way up the aisle to the cheers of the fans.[497] On the way to his dressing room, Tommy acknowledged to a reporter the blow had indeed been low, but was accidental. "I don't think it was hard enough to hurt him much and I could not avoid it as he lurched when we came together," he added.[498]

Referee McPartland said he had warned Gibbons earlier in the bout to keep his punches higher, and added he was sure Billy had been struck by a foul punch in the tenth round. The club physician, Dr. Walker, examined Billy afterward and issued a statement saying he had failed to find any traces of the alleged foul blow.[499] However, he was also asked if the fact he found no evidence of swelling or abrasions in the region of the groin area provided indisputable proof that Billy was not hit low.

"No, it doesn't," he replied. "Very often it takes several days for external signs of injuries of the groin to show. An aluminum protector does not necessarily have to be dented when hit. Even a hard blow sometimes will

---

495 *Lincoln Star*. Gibbons Master of Billy Miske, October 14, 1922.
496 *Beloit Daily News*. Miske Gets Verdict Over Gibbons When He Claims A Foul, October 14, 1922.
497 *Lincoln Star*. Gibbons Master of Billy Miske, October 14, 1922.
498 *New Castle News*. Tom Gibbons Loses to Miske, October 14, 1922.
499 *Vancouver Sun*. Unknown article title, October 14, 1922.

make no impression on a cut, yet the jar or wrench of the blow will cause the recipient of the punch great agony."

Interviewed at his hotel after the contest, Tommy was asked about admitting he'd struck Billy low at ringside. "What I said was, if I hit him low I didn't mean it," replied Tommy. Then Tommy added,

> I can almost swear my punch was above the belt. I thought I hit him squarely on the belt line. But, I've fought Miske enough times to know that Billy is a game fellow and a sportsmanly one. If it was any one of a few other fellows I had fought, who acted as Miske did, I would be sure they had not been hit low and that they were yellow and were faking it. The only doubt I have of my punch not being above the belt was Miske going down under it and claiming foul. He is a game fighter and an honest one. I repeat, if I did hit him low it was absolutely unintentional.

The interviewer said his view of the blow in question was blocked, but three times during the contest he saw Tommy land low blows. Billy also landed two low blows, but only because in attempting to block the blows aimed for his stomach Tommy brushed them downward.[500]

The controversial ending to the fight prompted New York Boxing Commissioner, William Muldoon, to order the purses of both men withheld pending an investigation. Muldoon, the one-time famous wrestler and trainer of the great John L. Sullivan for his bareknuckle championship bout with Jake Kilrain in 1889, had been on hand to witness the fight. He declared emphatically Billy had quit in the tenth round. Muldoon said:

> There isn't the slightest doubt in my mind that Miske, realizing he was beaten, eagerly accepted the opportunity offered up in the tenth round and quit. I don't doubt that Miske was hurt but not so severely as to prevent him from getting on his feet before a count of ten had been finished. From my point of view, the blow wasn't below the belt but landed flush on the solar plexus, the same spot on which Fitzsimmons hit Jim Corbett at Carson.
>
> McPartland was deceived by Miske's grimaces into stopping his count and disqualifying Gibbons which was a great injustice to the latter. Gibbons put up a good fight and completely baffled Miske at every stage of the game. Gibbons is a much cleverer boxer than the other men that Miske has boxed. In a nutshell, Miske found his master and quit when the opportunity offered.[501]

---

500 *Evening Telegram*, Gibbons Loses to Miske on Foul. October 14, 1922..
501 *Bridgeport Telegram*. Chairman Muldoon Claims B. Miske Quit on Friday, October 16, 1922.

Muldoon said he wanted time to investigate the matter further, but promised he would reach a decision by no later than Tuesday.[502]

Clearly, Gibbons himself admitted the punch was a foul. But, the fact remained that until that point in time, the fight belonged to Gibbons. "At times, the crowd giggled at Miske's utter inability to place his fists on Gibbons' body," reported one writer.[503]

The Boxing Blade generally concurred with Muldoon's view of the fight. Their reporter, Clarence Gillespie, wrote most of the newspapermen at ringside agreed that Billy quit cold, and called it one of the worst cases of this kind he had seen in his twenty-five years of reporting fights. In Gillespie's view, Tommy had "punched Billy full of holes in every one of the nine preceding rounds, making him look foolish and bombarding him with an assortment of left jabs and right crosses." He said Billy failed to land half a dozen clean punches, and Tommy feinted him into knots and hit him when and where he pleased.[504]

The *National Police Gazette's* reporter said the punch appeared to land well below the legal line of the waist, and in his view landed squarely on Billy's groin.[505]

Ultimately, Muldoon authorized the fight's promoter, Tex Rickard, to go ahead and pay both Billy and Tommy. However, he once again voiced his opinion Billy could have continued, and surely would have had he been winning at the time of the alleged foul.[506] During the course of the investigation the judges, Artie McGovern and Charles Miles, Referee McPartland, the timekeeper and knockdown counter, and all other commission representatives who attended the fight were asked to express their opinions on the question of whether Billy had been fouled. The majority opinion was in support of the referee's decision to award the fight to Billy on a foul.[507]

The beating Billy took from Gibbons effectively ended any discussion of another match with Jack Dempsey. While Gibbons had looked impressive against Billy, most still considered he would be too small to defeat Dempsey.[508]

Less than a week later, Billy signed to meet a big heavyweight out of Atkins, Iowa named Bud Ryder on an American Legion boxing card on November 11 in Grand Forks, North Dakota. Ryder stood 6'3" and weighed approximately 235 pounds. Ryder provided little opposition for

---

502 *New York Times*. Miske Wins on Foul, October 14, 1922.
503 *New Castle News*. Tom Gibbons Loses to Miske; Admits Striking Unintentional Foul, October 14, 1922.
504 *Boxing Blade*, Tom Gibbons Victim of One of Those Queer N.Y. Decisions in Fight with Miske, October 28, 1922.
505 *National Police Gazette*, Miske Wins On Foul By Gibbons In Tenth, November 4, 1922.
506 *Nashville Tennessean*. Gibbons Did Not Foul Miske, Says Muldoon, October 17, 1922.
507 *New York Times*. Miske and Gibbons To Get Their Pay, October 17, 1922.
508 *Daily Democrat-Tribune*. Miske's Defeat Put Wills Ahead, October 25, 1922.

Billy when they met in Grand Forks. Billy knocked the big fellow down five times in the second round, the bell saving him from a sure knockout. He dropped Ryder with a right uppercut to the jaw in the third round and the referee mercifully stepped in and awarded the bout to Billy by a technical knockout in order to save Ryder from further punishment.[509]

Two weeks after the fight with Ryder, Billy and Tommy Gibbons were signed to fight for a fifth and final time, in a ten-round contest at the St. Paul Auditorium on December 15. It was agreed the two men would equally split a purse of $10,000. It was also decided an official decision would be rendered by two ringside judges, with the referee casting the deciding vote in the event of a disagreement. It would mark the first time an official decision would be awarded in St. Paul under the new boxing law.[510] George Sudheimer and Henry Lund were selected as the judges, while George Barton was named as the referee for the contest.[511]

The Boxing Blade, a Minneapolis based publication, indicated that while the contest was expected to draw a good crowd, there was no question Tommy would win, and noted the last time the two faced one another before a Minneapolis crowd it had been a rather tame affair.[512]

It was expected that the loser of this bout would be officially eliminated as a contender for the heavyweight championship. Gibbons' manager, Eddie Kane, predicted a knockout over Miske on the morning of the fight.

In response, Billy admitted Tommy was a better boxer, but maintained he was the better fighter. "I have fought them all and have been stopped only once by Jack Dempsey. I hope to force the fighting at such a pace that Tom will welcome the tenth round gone," he said. Others weren't convinced and speculated that the slight advantage Tommy enjoyed in reach, combined with his boxing skill and speed, would prove the deciding factor when the two men squared off again. [513] Billy expressed surprise the odds favored his opponent.

> I know Tommy is a cleverer boxer than I am, and he's faster on his feet, but Fulton also is a cleverer boxer than I ever was and he's about as fast as heavyweights ever are, but I finished him in quick order.
>
> I know that the only way I can beat Tommy is to fight him all the time and fight him hard. I purposely let him set the pace in our last fight in New York, but whether anyone believes me or not, I know I had him bewildered when I started cutting loose in the ninth and tenth rounds. I hit Tom often and hard in those rounds and it was

---

509 *La Crosse Tribune*. Unknown article title, November 12, 1922.
510 *Salt Lake Tribune*. Boxing Notes, December 14, 1922.
511 *Minneapolis Tribune*, Judges and Referee Are Picked for Gibbons-Miske Battle in St. Paul, December 14, 1922.
512 *Boxing Blade*, Gibbons And Miske To Box Again, December 16, 1922.
513 *Minneapolis Tribune*, Tom Gibbons to Meet Miske for Fifth Time Friday Night, December 10, 1922.

because I was pressing him so hard that he fouled me, unintentionally I know.[514]

"Billy will try harder for a knockout than he ever did before and that means a lot," added manager Jack Reddy.[515]

Both men had been examined by a physician and deemed to be in perfect physical condition.[516] The 28-year-old Miske weighed in at 196 pounds in his street clothes while the 31-year-old Gibbons weighed in at 182 ½.[517] Nearly 8,000 fans turned out to view the fight, generating total gate receipts of $18,699.[518]

Tommy gained an immediate advantage in the first two rounds, dancing in and out of range, and peppering Billy with blows that kept him from getting untracked. The third round was Billy's most productive of the night, as he rushed Tommy to the ropes and managed to land a number of solid punches. But from the fourth round on, Tommy resumed control and once again demonstrated he was Billy's master.

Billy didn't go down without a fight, however. He aggressively pursued Tommy in an effort to land the punch to turn the tide in his favor, and he landed enough punches to Tommy's left eye that it was closing by the end of round six. Tommy appeared to let up a bit as a result, passing up apparent opportunities to avoid risking damage to his other eye.

Despite fighting with greater caution, Tommy was able to maintain an effective offense during the final three rounds and Billy was often forced to clinch with Tommy in an effort to avoid too much punishment, or at least that's the way one ringside reporter viewed the final rounds.[519] Another writer noted that Gibbons' performance left no doubt he was Billy's master, and his punches to Billy's stomach and kidneys had Billy in distress and groggy upon the bout's conclusion.[520]

Earl Arnold of the *Minneapolis Tribune* wrote that while Billy was game and took his punishment like a man, always boring in looking for a chance to land a knockout blow, the opportunity never came and, upon the fight's conclusion, Billy's face was battered, swollen and covered with blood. He added that Billy was at least 10 pounds over his usual fighting weight and only in flashes did he look like the same fighter who had defeated Fulton so convincingly.[521]

---

514 *Minneapolis Tribune*, Bill Miske Puzzled By Odds on Gibbons Plans Surprise, December 11, 1922.
515 *Minneapolis Tribune*, Judges and Referee Are Picked for Gibbons-Miske Battle in St. Paul, December 14, 1922.
516 *Oakland Tribune*. Tom Gibbons – Billy Miske Meet Tonight, December 15, 1922.
517 *Sheboygan Press-Telegram*. Gibbons Wins Decision Over Billy Miske, December 16, 1922.
518 *Oakland Tribune*. Gibbons Wins From Miske in St. Paul, December 16, 1922.
519 *Sheboygan Press-Telegram*. Gibbons Wins Decision Over Billy Miske, December 16, 1922.
520 *Oakland Tribune*. Gibbons Wins From Miske In St. Paul, December 16, 1922.
521 *Minneapolis Tribune*, Gibbons Wins Decisive Victory Over Billy Miske in St. Paul Ring, December 16, 1922.

In a magazine article published in 1927, Tommy said of this fight that, in the ninth round, he felt as if he had Billy in a poor way, so he began to pour in a series of blows in an effort to finish him. And, then, out of nowhere, Billy hit him with a big left hook on the right eye that caused it to close. In Tommy's opinion, Billy came on strongly after that and more than held his own in the final round.[522]

Regardless, Tommy was awarded the victory by unanimous decision and it was expected he would challenge Dempsey for the heavyweight crown.[523] Any hope Billy had of another chance of his own with Dempsey had now officially ended. He was very complimentary of his conqueror afterward, issuing a statement to the press that he never saw a finer boxer and artist as Tommy Gibbons. "He can sock, not as hard as Dempsey, but not much less," said Billy.[524]

And, with that, another year in the ring was in the books for Billy Miske. On December 28, it was announced he would be one of the feature attractions on a January 12 bill in Omaha against Harry Foley of Hot Springs, Arkansas, but the balance of the month and early January 1923 would be spent enjoying the holidays at home with his family.

---

522 *Liberty Weekly Magazine*. Punches I Have Taken, March 5, 1927.
523 *Oakland Tribune*. Gibbons Wins From Miske In St. Paul, December 16, 1922.
524 *Capital Times*. Roundy Says, December 18, 1922.

CHAPTER 14

A Title Fight in Shelby, Montana

Billy found himself in a bind as the year 1923 began. While there were still plenty of opportunities for him inside the ring, his health was rapidly deteriorating. It was clear he wouldn't be able to continue fighting much longer. The medical bills were mounting, and he had Marie and three young children to provide for. Billy Jr. would be six in January, Douglas four in March, and Donna was now one-and-a-half years old. Scheduled to fight Harry Foley on January 12, Billy traveled to Omaha.

Foley billed himself as the heavyweight champion of the South. He was a strong believer of the methods of a French psychologist named Dr. Emile Coue. Coue, a pharmacist, originated the phrase, "Day by day, in every way, I am getting better and better." His method centered on the routine repetition of a particular expression in order to influence his patient's unconscious thoughts. When he dispensed medicine to his clients, he discovered that, although there was no difference in the medicines, the medicine that was praised to patients for its effectiveness produced much better results than the medicines he said nothing about. He theorized people could achieve similar results in other endeavors. Foley decided to see if it would improve his boxing results.

Both fighters put the finishing touches on their training with light workouts the day before the fight. They appeared on the main event of the Douglas County American Legion fight card on January 12, 1923. The bout proved disappointing to the local fight fans when Billy was awarded a technical knockout victory after just 42 seconds of fighting. Foley, completely outclassed, was knocked to the canvas no less than six times in that brief period of time. Finally, after the sixth knockdown, Foley's seconds realized the hopelessness of the situation, and mercifully threw in the sponge from the corner to signal surrender and bring an end to the debacle.

One writer who witnessed the fight joked that when Foley stepped out of his corner at the sound of the opening bell, he repeated over and over: "Round by round, as each bell sounds, I'm getting better and better," and after getting knocked down by Billy he changed his affirmation to "Blow by blow, as to the canvas I go, I get groggier and groggier."[525]

In February of 1923, the groundwork for an interesting side note in boxing history was laid in Shelby, Montana, when a young 23-year-old by

---

[525] *Lincoln State Journal.* Billy Miske Too Much For Foley, January 13, 1923.

the name of James W. Johnson came up with an idea for a way to generate publicity for the town.

James W. was born on his father's ranch near Shelby in May of 1899. As a young child, he was so sickly nobody expected him to live. All the neighbors said he was just a "little-bitty Body," and that's how he came to be known by the nickname "Body." His father, James A. Johnson, was one of the founders of Shelby. He raised cattle and sheep for a while, before moving into town where he owned and operated a number of businesses. He counted a store, hotel, newspaper and bank amongst his business holdings.

"Body" and his father became active in real estate after a few oil prospectors hit it big with an oil well north of Shelby in the spring of 1922. The discovery resulted in a big influx of oil people. To meet the increased demand for land, "Body" and his father began selling lots, and building small office space, homes and apartments during the summer of 1922. But, by the end of the year, business was declining.

One morning in February of 1923, "Body" and a friend were sitting in their real estate office trying to think of ways to generate publicity for Shelby. "Body" was thumbing through that day's *Great Falls Tribune* newspaper and came across an article concerning an offer of $100,000 to heavyweight champion Jack Dempsey to fight in Montreal, Canada. "Body" and his companion decided they should wire Dempsey's manager, Jack Kearns, and propose an offer of $200,000 for a championship fight in Shelby, Montana.

He arranged for two telegrams, the first to Kearns that read: "I am prepared to offer you a purse of $200,000 to be paid $50,000 upon signing of a contract and balance when you enter the ring for a 15-round championship fight against Tommy Gibbons to be held on July 4, 1923 in Shelby, Montana. Please wire your acceptance." The other telegram was sent to Mike Collins, who "Body" mistakenly believed was Gibbons' manager, when in fact it was Eddie Kane.

"Body" never really intended to follow through on the offer. He was only hoping the offer would produce a positive media response and bring some attention to the city. But before he knew it, Kearns replied and suggested a meeting. The whole thing just sort of took on a life of its own.

When Mike Collins received the initial telegram, he assumed it was just an advertising stunt, but decided the sender deserved a reply. So, he wired him back and said it would make a great fight and all it would require to stage would be plenty of cash. He was subsequently invited to visit the little town to discuss the matter further. As "luck" would have it, one of Collins fighters was scheduled to fight in Great Falls, Montana on March 17. After consulting a map and discovering Shelby was less than 90 miles away, he agreed to a meeting. He arrived in Shelby on March 11 at 5:30 in the morning.

Reflecting upon his arrival a number of months later, Collins said that if the train had arrived during the daylight, there never would have been a championship fight staged in Shelby. He would have quickly viewed the town and likely stayed on the train. When he departed the train, he was met by an enthusiastic crowd of approximately 750 folks who he decided made up just about the entire population of the little town. They whisked him off to the Silver Grill Café where he met a number of the leading officials.

Once he had completed breakfast, Collins walked outside and got his first good look at Shelby in the daylight. He recalled it being comprised of a few two-story business buildings, several houses, one depot, two small hotels and two small restaurants. That was the town as he saw it. Right then and there he became convinced it was all an advertising ploy, and there was no way the heavyweight championship of the world could be staged in this little place. He moved quickly to advance discussions and bring an end to the charade, but soon found himself in another meeting, this one involving the mayor, where he was asked what they needed to do in order to host the fight.

Collins told them they'd have to start with about $100,000 to show good faith and then come up with enough money to build an arena and another $25,000 to promote the show. The men sent for a local named Mose Zimmerman who had expressed a willingness to finance the show. Once the details were explained to Mose, he quickly backpedaled and stated he'd figured it was only an advertising stunt. He'd been playing his part in announcing a commitment to finance the event. It was at this point the County American Legion Boxing Association got involved.

The Association called in an attorney named Loy Molumby. After some discussion, it was decided it would be better if the American Legion on the state level put on the fight and have Molumby take over the negotiations with Kearns in the coming months. Molumby was a former star athlete at the University of Minnesota where he was captain of the 1915 track team. He graduated with a law degree and when the United States entered World War I he joined the air force and subsequently attained the rank of captain.

Molumby said there were 127 American Legion Posts in the state and suggested the committee lead a drive to raise the necessary $100,000 by appealing to each of the Posts to contribute a prorated share - on the basis of their respective sizes. Within a matter of minutes, there was $26,500 in cash and checks on the table. Although it still seemed highly unlikely the little town would be able to pull it off,[526] Molumby's suggestion kept the idea from dying a quick death.

Meanwhile, in early April, an initial meeting concerning the Dempsey–Gibbons fight proposal in Shelby was held between Lou Molumby, "Body" Johnson and Jack Kearns in Salt Lake City. At no time during the meeting

---

526 *Boxing Blade*, Mike Collins, Matchmaker of Dempsey-Gibbons Fight Tells How Shelby Came to Stage Contest, July 28, 1923.

was an amount any higher than $200,000 for Dempsey's share discussed, although Kearns did request the first $100,000 be paid to him in cash. "Body" and his father, James A., were confident the fight would be profitable if they paid Dempsey no more than $200,000.[527]

When Reddy caught wind of the movement to stage the fight in Shelby, he quickly sent the town's committee a telegram offering to match Billy against Dempsey for $50,000, with the provision the entire amount be donated to the American Legion should Dempsey knock Billy out. In response, he was told that Gibbons had received the first offer, and no action would be taken on his offer until final word was received from Jack Kearns.[528]

An advance sale of tickets took place in order to generate the initial payment of $100,000 required by Kearns. The telegram sent to Mike Collins in error, ultimately resulted in his being retained by the American Legion as the matchmaker for the fight. A second meeting was arranged in Chicago in early May between Dempsey's manager, Kearns, the matchmaker, Collins, Gibbons' manager, Eddie Kane and the American Legion's representative, Loy Molumby.

Molumby closed the deal but Kearns managed to convince him to sign a contract to pay Dempsey $100,000 more than originally intended. The contract called for Dempsey and Kearns to be paid $100,000 in cash at the time of the signing of the contract and $100,000 on June 15. A final payment of another $100,000 would then become due on July 2, two days before the fight. Gibbons was to receive a $10,000 advance for training expenses, and a percentage of the gate receipts after Dempsey received his $300,000.

Similarly to Dempsey's title fight against Billy, Kearns said his first choice to referee the upcoming contest was Jimmy Dougherty. He agreed to name another acceptable referee, but it seemed certain Dougherty would be chosen. Kane objected to the selection, but acknowledged he would probably have to go along with Kearns or risk losing the fight. "I don't like to have Dougherty shoved down my throat but I can't see any other way out of it," he said. "He's handpicked a friend (of theirs). He's a good fellow personally and a great booster for boxing, but I don't think much of him as a referee."[529]

Gibbons, who at this point was willing to yield on just about any point for the opportunity to fight for the title, added his view on the selection of Dougherty as the referee, saying: "Both Kane and I objected to Dougherty as the referee because he's a "pal" of Dempsey, but these Westerners who are backing the match have assured us we will have a square deal.

---

[527] Johnson, James W. (Body), *The Truth About '23*, Promoter Publishing Company, Shelby, Montana 1989.
[528] *Ogden Standard-Examiner*. Miske Sends Offer, February 13, 1923.
[529] *St. Paul Pioneer Press*, Fight Clinched As Kearns Receives $100,000, May 6, 1923.

Dougherty has never refereed a match of mine. At any rate, we won't miss the bout because of a squabble over the third man."[530] Gibbons had just purchased a new home in St. Paul, at 1517 Goodrich Avenue, and with three small children was no doubt hoping a good performance against the champion would lead to more lucrative opportunities in the future.

When Molumby returned to Shelby with the contract, the Shelby group's attorney, Jim Speer, reviewed it and pointed out that despite the fact Molumby had agreed to a figure $100,000 higher than the group intended, one bright spot was Dempsey would have to fight regardless of whether or not he ever received a dime beyond the initial payment of $100,000.

The contract was worded in such a way that even if he didn't receive the additional payments on June 15 and July 2, Dempsey would be required to perform his part of the contract before he could demand a settlement. Kearns understood this and knew that was the case. At no time, however, did he, or Dempsey, ever issue a statement to the media making it clear that was the case, despite the urging of the Shelby officials who desperately tried to sell more tickets as the date of the fight would eventually near. In fact, right up to the date of the fight, while applying the pressure to the town officials to make the last payment, Kearns kept telling the press if the last payment wasn't received, the fight wouldn't take place.

As a result, there was a lot of uncertainty expressed by the media as to whether or not the fight would actually take place right up until the night before the bout.

Once the contract was delivered, the towns' officials purchased the lumber and arranged for the construction of a 40,000-seat arena occupying twenty acres of land. Frantically, they began their efforts to come up with the additional $200,000 needed to pay Dempsey and his manager. Since the tickets were going to range from $20 to $50 each the most optimistic individuals believed a sellout would result in total revenues of as much as $1,500,000.[531]

On May 6, 1923, representatives of the Great Northern Railroad met in St. Paul to begin preparing for what was expected to be one of the greatest logistical challenges they had ever faced. The Great Northern was the only line serving Shelby at the time with four routes - one from the North Pacific Coast, another from St. Paul, a third from Sweetgrass, Montana at the Canadian border and the last from Great Falls. The problem of transporting thousands of fight fans to the little town was no small matter to overcome.

It was expected special trains originating from all parts of the country would carry the anticipated fans to Shelby and as many as 40,000 people would need to be accommodated by rail. The movement of that many

---

530 *St. Paul Pioneer Press*, Tommy to Get Chance Sought For Two Years, May 6, 1923.
531 *St. Paul Pioneer Press*, Dempsey-Gibbons Articles Signed For Shelby Bout, May 6, 1923.

passengers would require a fleet of 200 ten-car trains, which if connected end to end would make up a train extending from St. Paul to Chicago. The railroad further estimated the transport of this many people would need to take place over a two and one-half day period. Many other fans were expected to travel by car.

Upon the conclusion of their initial meeting the Great Northern officials issued the following statement:

> The Great Northern will see that there is plenty of trackage at Shelby to handle the greatly increased number of trains. If the attendance approximates 40,000 that means additional siding will have to be built. Undoubtedly, the trains would have to be held there for part of a day, or possibly more, and be used by the passengers for sleeping and dining.[532]

A few days later, it was announced that a number of executives from the railroad would travel to Shelby to study the situation there and prepare for the creation of facilities to handle the anticipated crowds. An additional depot, along with track, water capacity, telegraph equipment and other facilities would all be provided over the course of six weeks to enable the Great Northern to meet the needs of the thousands of people expected to attend the fight. Chairman Louis W. Hill gave his assurances the railroad's facilities would be expanded to meet all needs as fully as possible.[533]

While the officials in little Shelby, Montana continued their frantic efforts to raise the additional $200,000 promised to Jack Dempsey and his manager, speculation concerning the potential outcome of the contest between the two men began to garner more press. Most folks felt Gibbons had little chance to wrest the crown from Dempsey's head. The champion was considered near invincible, and in addition to the fact that he was six years younger, the champion was also expected to outweigh the challenger by 15-20 pounds.

In mid-May, Clare Shipman, of the *St. Paul Pioneer Press*, interviewed Tommy's wife in order to give the paper's readers some insight into the life of the wife of a heavyweight contender. Mrs. Gibbons advised her that cooking wasn't much of a challenge when her man was in training as all that was required for either breakfast or lunch was toast and tea and a couple of soft-boiled eggs. The second, and only other meal of the day, was a regular dinner and typically included either steak or lamb chops and the usual accompaniments and a simple dessert. In contrast to the fast life the champion and his manager lived, the Gibbons enjoyed a quiet family life. Like Billy's wife, Mrs. Gibbons enjoyed music and was an accomplished

---

[532] *St. Paul Pioneer Press*, Railroad Officials Here Plan Transportation Feat To Handle Shelby Crowds, May 6, 1923.
[533] *St. Paul Pioneer Press*, Officials Of Hill Road Will Go To Shelby To Study Fight Problems, May 12, 1923.

musician who sang as well. While the oldest of the couple's three son's bore a strong resemblance to Tommy, Mrs. Gibbons said the couple had no plans of making fighters out of any of their boys.[534]

On May 15, a group of Great Falls businessmen who had contributed $55,000 to the first $100,000 delivered to Jack Kearns optimistically predicted a gate of $600,000 and complete success for the upcoming title fight. They were busily making plans to accommodate as many as 25,000 more persons than normal as the date of the fight neared.[535]

A day later, on May 16, it was announced that Tex Rickard had finalized arrangements for a heavyweight title elimination contest to take place between former heavyweight champion, Jess Willard, and Luis Firpo in New York no later than July 7. He then planned to match the winner with the heavyweight champion on Labor Day. It was expected the fight would draw a gate of at least $500,000 and each fighter might be paid at least $100,000.

While the site of the event had not yet been finalized, it was believed it would take place in either New York's Yankee Stadium or Boyle's Thirty Acres in New Jersey. The New York Boxing Commission had a rule preventing men over 38 years old from competing that made it more likely the event would take place in New Jersey. Some hoped Willard's recent victory over Floyd Johnson in the boxing carnival would convince the boxing commission to reconsider their stance on this issue.[536]

On May 18, word came out of Great Falls that two twenty foot rings were being erected at Great Falls Park, which had been selected as the site of Jack Dempsey's training camp in preparation for the July 4 contest. He was expected to begin training within the week. Loy Molumby said $300,000 worth of tickets had already been sold, an additional $100,000 in reservations had been made and the event was already assured of being successful as a result.[537] Eventually, they claimed to have nearly $500,000 in advance ticket reservations. A total of 26 special trains were scheduled to carry fans to Shelby for the fight.

In response to Rickard's announcement, the champion's manager, Jack Kearns, said contingent upon a victory over Tommy Gibbons, his man would fight Harry Wills next Labor Day, and not the winner of the Willard–Firpo contest.

Explaining further, Kearn's said: "Neither Willard nor Firpo, whichever may win in their fight, would make a drawing card equal to Harry Wills nor be as hard to crack. Dempsey does not draw the color line and is willing to go against Wills Labor Day if a satisfactory offer is made, and Dempsey

---

534 *St. Paul Pioneer Press*, Mrs. Gibbons Says Tommy Will Train Better With His Family Along To Aid, May 13, 1923.
535 *St. Paul Pioneer Press*, Montanans See Complete Success For Title Match, May 15, 1923.
536 *St. Paul Pioneer Press*, Rickard Closes Match Between Jess Willard And Argentine Fighter, May 16, 1923.
537 *St. Paul Pioneer Press*, Dempsey Directs Erection Of Rings, May 18, 1923.

holds the belt against Gibbons in the Shelby fight." Dempsey had begun training and was working out with his sparring partner, George Godfrey. A large crew of men had begun working on the arena in Shelby with the aim of completing the work by June 30.[538] Wills, a 31-year-old African-American who weighed 215 pounds and stood 6'3" tall was a worthy opponent who never received an opportunity to fight for the title primarily because of the color of his skin.

Commenting on Tommy Gibbons as the guest of honor at a luncheon in Shelby a couple of days later, Kearns said, "Dempsey faces the hardest fight of his career. Gibbons is a hard hitter and the best boxer in the world."[539] In late May, Gibbons expressed his confidence for the upcoming battle saying:

> I have won thirty out of my thirty-four fights by knockouts and expect to win this fight. I have been trying two years to get the match – the one chance of my life to show my friends that I can fight and win from a champion. I do not care to boast, but I believe I am just as clever as the champion and can hit just as hard – and I have every confidence of winning.[540]

It remained to be seen if he would even get the opportunity.

---

538 *St. Paul Pioneer Press*, Dempsey To Meet Wills Next If He Defeats Gibbons, May 20, 1923.
539 *St. Paul Pioneer Press*, Faces Toughest Fight Says Kearns, May 24, 1923.
540 *St. Paul Pioneer Press*, Tom Gibbons Confident He Will Win Over Champ, May 29, 1923.

CHAPTER 15

Dempsey versus Gibbons

By July 1, 1923, Jack Dempsey and Tommy Gibbons were each putting the finishing touches on their training for their bout. Many fans and fight reporters were already in town for the event. Included among the masses was Billy Miske who had made the trek to Shelby to witness the title fight. Since he had fought both men on a number of occasions, his opinion on the outcome was solicited. Unlike most fight experts who believed Gibbons would be knocked out by Dempsey before the end of the sixth round, Billy said Tommy would last at least ten rounds with the champion, if not the entire 15 rounds. Few knew better than Billy did what a fine boxer Tommy was, and what an elusive target he could be.

> I wouldn't be surprised to see Tommy on his feet when the last round is completed. If Dempsey does stop him it will take at least ten rounds to accomplish the feat. In Gibbons he's going to meet a great fighter. The champion is not going to find Tommy so easy to hit and this is going to have a lot to do with the outcome.
>
> In all of his other bouts Dempsey has had slow moving targets. He has not had much difficulty in hitting them at will, but this fight is going to be a different story. The champion has not fought in two years and the old eyes are not going to be so good. Dempsey would have trouble hitting Tom if the champion were at his best and the fact that his eyes are not so good means he's going to have considerable difficulty in landing effectively.
>
> Dempsey will find that Tom will be going away with every blow and that is going to take the sting out of the champion's wallops. Tommy is a fast moving target and one has to be a sharp shooter to catch him. Take my word for it and just see how much missing Dempsey will do Wednesday.
>
> And another thing the critics are overlooking is that Tommy can hit. He has one of the greatest lefts of any fighter in the country and it is going to bother Dempsey. It hurts when it lands. I can vouch for that. Tommy keeps planting that wicked left right over the appendix all the time and it takes a lot of steam out of an opponent. If Tommy had a right that was equal to the left he would be one of the game's greatest fighters.

In picking Tommy to last at least ten rounds I am not doing so just because Tommy is a St. Paul boy. Dempsey is just as good a friend of mine as Tommy is. I am sincere when I say Gibbons is liable to be on his feet at the end of the fifteenth round.

Jack Reddy, who obviously didn't have the benefit of Billy's experience inside the ring with Tommy, was not as optimistic concerning Tommy's chances, and said he didn't believe the challenger would be able to go the distance with the champion.[541]

On June 30, as the Shelby group continued its struggle to raise the final $100,000 payment needed for Dempsey and Kearns, a reorganization of the events management was announced. Mayor J.E. Lane of Lewiston, one of the wealthiest men in the state was named as trustee of the fight, and Loy Molumby and Mayor Jim Johnson were removed from the management team. Lane was chosen to represent the twenty business men of the state who reportedly were going to contribute $5,000 each to make the final payment of $100,000.

Lane issued the following statement to the press:

> This morning before I had in reality accepted the trusteeship, I went to Kearns and laid the cards on the table. Both Kearns and I are satisfied the fight will go over. The guarantors will recover their money from the first $100,000 received from ticket sales.[542]

But, while Mayor Lane was offering his assurance the fight would take place, and as scheduled, there were many members of the press reporting there was serious doubt the fight would come off. For example, a prominent sportswriter named Heywood Broun wrote that while it seemed pretty certain Kearns would receive the final payment before midnight July 2, there were some rumors of a possible ten-day delay in the fight date.

Clearly news of this nature had to dissuade a number of fans from making the long trek to Shelby to view a fight on July 4 which may or may not take place. Broun predicted the event would be attended primarily by Montanans, the number of outsiders who would end up traveling to Shelby being relatively small.[543]

While railroad officials continued supervising work on landing places and smoothing out the track approaches to those sites, they reported very little of the increase in population in the town had arrived by rail thus far.[544] A crowd of 40,000 was no longer within the realm of possibility. Mayor Lane announced they were now expecting a total of at least 18,000, with the bulk of the late arrivals coming primarily via automobile.[545]

---

541 *St. Paul Pioneer Press*, Challenger's Chances Strong With Man Who Battled Both, July 1, 1923.
542 *St. Paul Pioneer Press*, New Manager Of Fight In Accord With Jack Kearns, July 1, 1923.
543 *St. Paul Pioneer Press*, Kearns Must Wait Until Last Minute For Money, July 1, 1923.
544 *St. Paul Pioneer Press*, Lunch Counters Once Idle Doing Thriving Business, July 1, 1923 .
545 *St. Paul Pioneer Press*, Gibbons Is Finely Drawn As Violin String, July 2, 1923.

As late as July 3, the day before the fight, there were media reports the fight was still in danger of not taking place because Kearns had still not received the final installment of $100,000. Mayor Lane had issued a statement concerning his groups' failure to raise the necessary amount which read as follows:

> This committee, of which I am the nominal head, entered the fight situation solely to raise the $100,000 due as a payment to Jack Kearns as the final installment of Dempsey's $300,000 guarantee. I was made trustee of this fund or whatever funds we were able to solicit. We have been unable to raise the necessary $100,000. That is all we have to do with the situation.
>
> Our mission is ended right now, but we will continue to function until midnight, when the time limit specified when we assumed responsibility expires. The continued existence of this committee for the remainder of the day, however, will be almost completely technical. By that I mean there appears to be no more active work confronting us.
>
> We tried every means possible, every source which occurred to us and every avenue which held out any hope of rescue has been followed without success. I am free to state I entertain no hopes of raising the money needed. So far as we are concerned the responsibility is lifted from our shoulders. We concede failure of our task. The matter is now in the hands of Promoter Molumby and Jack Kearns. It is they who will decide whether there shall be a bout on Wednesday afternoon. Our duties ended when we found we could not raise the $100,000 third payment.

Lane declined to reveal what amount of the necessary $100,000 payment had been raised.[546] The bottom line is a number of the men who had originally committed to contribute $5,000 each to raise the last of the necessary funds got cold feet and opted not to do so.

Ultimately, the fight was salvaged on July 3 when it was agreed Kearns and Dempsey would collect their final installment toward the $300,000 from the first $100,000 collected in cash at the gate from ticket purchasers. After that amount was collected, the Shelby group would be entitled to the revenues generated from any additional sales at the gate.

Sportswriter Grantland Rice noted nine out of every ten fight experts on-hand had picked Dempsey to win between the fourth and sixth rounds. Asked for a final statement concerning the upcoming fight, Gibbons said with a smile, "There isn't much more to be said now. I'm ready with the best I've got and as I won't collect a dime in chance for my share of the

---

[546] *St. Paul Pioneer Press*, Trustee Admits Inability To Raise Final $100,000, July 3, 1923.

purse I'll have to take my big shot in the ring." Rice felt the champion held too many advantages over the challenger and predicted Dempsey would retain his crown.[547]

Asked by another party for a pre-fight comment, Dempsey said:

> I am not one who regards Gibbons lightly. I regard every challenger as dangerous. They are all dangerous until they are on the floor. I am not going to take any chances with Gibbons. I'll make every effort to beat him in the first round if possible. Anything is liable to happen to a champion any time he goes into the ring.[548]

The fight didn't turn out to be particularly notable. There were no knockdowns, and it was generally viewed as a dull fifteen-round affair. Gibbons fought defensively from the start. Dempsey retained the title by a referee's decision and neither Gibbons nor his manager had any quarrel with the decision.

There was general agreement that the champion deserved the win and had earned 12 of the 15 rounds. Like Miske, Dempsey found Tommy Gibbons a difficult man to hit. At the end of the fifth round, when Dempsey returned to his corner, Kearns said to him, "Why the hell don't you go in and knock out that S.O.B.?" To which Dempsey replied, "How the hell can I knock him out if I can't hit him?"[549]

Grantland Rice reported Dempsey had slipped as a result of his inactivity over the previous two years, and Gibbons proved himself the superior boxer on the outside in the fourth through sixth sessions and forced the champion to fight the majority of the contest on the inside thereafter. He was unable to deliver any big knockout blows within that range, although he clearly punished the smaller man. Gibbons was able to land punches squarely on the champions chin or jaw with rights or lefts at least a dozen times but never with enough steam to stop him in his tracks for more than a fleeting moment or two.[550]

Badly tired near the end of the fight, Tommy repeatedly held the champion during the final two rounds in order to avoid a knockout. Rice also said Dempsey must now face the strong chance of losing his title to the next good hard-hitting man he meets unless he gets going again.[551]

Asked about the holding afterward, Tommy said:

> Perhaps I did do a little holding. I had to. Toward the end I became weary, my body became tired. He's a bigger, stronger man than I am

---

547 *St. Paul Pioneer Press*, 10,000 Will See Tom Try To Life Dempsey's Crown, July 4, 1923.
548 *St. Paul Pioneer Press*, Both Principals Confident On Eve Of Title Battle, July 4, 1923.
549 Blair, George, *Tommy Gibbons*, Self-published 1988.
550 *St. Paul Pioneer Press*, No Fighter Deserved Greater Credit Than Aspirant, July 5, 1923.
551 *St. Paul Pioneer Press*, Gibbons Best Man Dempsey Has Met, July 7, 1923.

and he punches hard. If I fight Dempsey again I'll fight him differently.[552]

It should be noted that Kearns' hand-picked referee, Jimmy Dougherty, did, in fact, end up working the fight, when, as he had for the Dempsey–Miske title fight in Benton Harbor during September of 192, Jack Kearns insisted Jimmy Dougherty officiate the match in Shelby or there would be no fight.[553] The *St. Paul Pioneer Press* account of the fight stated Gibbons fought under a big handicap as a result of Dougherty serving as the referee for the bout:

> Referee Dougherty permitted Dempsey to hit low four or five times during the bout, and never even cautioned the champion for his foul tactics. Twice the champion hit Tommy with hard blows after the bell had ended the round, but not once was he warned. And once Dempsey pushed Tommy through the ropes and then hit him while the St. Paul fighter was trying to get back in the ring. The fans did not approve of Dempsey's tactics or Dougherty's work, and time and again they roared their disapproval.[554]

The timekeeper for the contest, Richard Burke of New Orleans, added that early on in the contest while exchanging blows with Dempsey, Tommy addressed his foe concerning the low blows, saying, "For God's sake, Jack, get 'em up." According to Burke, Tommy was referring to three or four body blows that struck him in the groin area.

> I saw Gibbons this morning before I left Shelby," Burke said, "and he showed me the black and blue marks on his groin. I immediately said: 'Why, Tom, the press ought to know about this,' Whereupon Gibbons beseeched me not to tell the newspaper men. 'I don't have to have any alibi in this fight,' Gibbons said.

Tip O'Neill, a well-known oilman from Great Falls, told the same story in the lobby of the Glacier Park hotel saying he had also seen the marks on Tommy's body.[555]

Referee Dougherty replied that he witnessed no foul blows by either fighter and said he didn't think anybody else did either.[556] He went on to express his admiration for Gibbons, saying:

> Gibbons put up the most wonderful defense I have ever witnessed. Dempsey was fighting viciously for the body and he directed twenty to thirty punches right in the solar plexus, any of which would have

---

552 *St. Paul Pioneer Press*, Defeat Almost As Sweet As Victory To Tom Gibbons, July 5, 1923.
553 Kearns, Jack, *The Million Dollar Gate*, The MacMillian Company, New York, New York 1966.
554 *St. Paul Pioneer Press*, City To Celebrate In Gibbons Honor, July 5, 1923.
555 *St. Paul Pioneer Press*, Tom Is Marked By Low Blows, July 6, 1923.
556 *St. Paul Pioneer Press*, Couldn't See Any Foul Blows Says Referee Of Battle, July 5, 1923.

stopped Gibbons. But Gibbons had a peculiar way of defending the punches, so that they glanced up in his arms. I do not think there is any other heavyweight in the world that had the defense to ward off the attack of Dempsey as Gibbons has. He was fast as a bantamweight, and I want to say that Gibbons is the gamest man that I have had the pleasure of refereeing a contest for.[557]

Upon his return home after the fight, Gibbons remarked:

Dempsey is easy to feint, and easy to hit. He isn't the man killer you've heard about. Billy Miske hits just as hard. The trouble with Dempsey's hitting is that you can see 'em coming. If he had been a quick hitter he could have knocked me out of the state.

Gibbons went on to express his dissatisfaction with Kearns' hand-picked referee:

You can tell the world that Jim Dougherty won't referee for me again. Every time he broke us, he picked on me, and would set me back so that Dempsey would jump in and bat me. He didn't say anything about Dempsey's fouls, but when I accidentally got Dempsey with a back hand, Dougherty warned me.[558]

On the other hand, the sportswriter Heywood Broun expressed the opinion that under a strict interpretation of the rules, Tommy might have been disqualified in the closing rounds for not heeding Dougherty's orders to break from numerous clinches. "Dougherty had to tear him away from the champion to whom he clung like a drowning man," said Broun.[559]

Tommy's brother, Mike, surprisingly didn't make the trip to Shelby to watch his brother fight Dempsey. He went to Winton, Minnesota instead with a friend to keep his mind off the fight. But, afterward, he proudly pointed out his brother kept his word to be on his feet at the end of the final round.[560]

Dempsey expressed disappointment in his failure to knock out Gibbons, but then complimented the challenger:

In a way, I am disappointed with the result. I think I won clearly enough to dispel any doubt on the decision, but I felt sure when I entered the ring I could knock Gibbons out. I hit him often enough and hard enough to drop any ordinary heavyweight, but I guess everybody is convinced now that Gibbons is not an ordinary heavyweight. He certainly gave me a fight. He's one of the hardest

---

557 *St. Paul Pioneer Press*, Gibbons Alone Can Stand Jack's Attack, July 6, 1923.
558 *Eau Claire Leader*. Jubilant Crowd Welcomes Tom Gibbons Home, July 8, 1923.
559 *St. Paul Pioneer Press*, Shelby And Montana Win Victory Over Scribes Who Ridicule Town And State, July 5, 1923.
560 *St. Paul Pioneer Press*, City To Celebrate In Gibbons Honor, July 5, 1923.

men to hit cleanly or solidly that I ever boxed. He sure surprised me. He's a great boxer.[561]

Tommy fought for two more years, winning 11 of 12 fights, including victories over Georges Carpentier and Kid Norfolk. His final fight, a 12-round knockout loss suffered against future heavyweight champion, Gene Tunney, occurred on May 5, 1925 at the Polo Grounds in New York before 23,570 fans and effectively ended his chances of a return match with Dempsey. He received $110,000 for the fight, the largest payday of his career. But the knockout defeat, a nervous breakdown suffered by his wife, Helen, that April, and the loss of sight in one eye by his brother Mike, convinced Tommy it was time to hang up the gloves.

All the press concerning the difficulty Shelby was having raising the funds to make the additional payments to Kearns and Dempsey ultimately lead to a financial disaster for the little town. The bulk of the advance ticket reservations, as well as the special trains, were cancelled due to the uncertainty the fight would take place.

In the end it was estimated there were only 12,000 fans in the 40,000-seat arena on the day of the fight, July 4, 1923. Many of those crashed the gate in the last few minutes before the fight and watched the event free of charge.

"Body" and his father, James A., who stepped in and borrowed a considerable amount of money to contribute toward the second payment, lost a lot of money on the fight. "Body" claimed the amount lost by him and his father came to $169,000. Demonstrating he had a sense of humor on the same night after the fight despite his losses, James was heard to say, "Well, we saw a fight, didn't we? Slip me the price of a shave."[562]

The Johnsons eventually recovered, as a result of their successes in the oil business, ranching and other endeavors. But, they spent the next five years settling claims and fighting lawsuits.[563] At least two banks closed soon after the fight, the Stanton Trust & Savings Bank of Great Falls and James A.'s bank, The First State Bank of Shelby.[564]

While not entirely true, it has been widely written that Tom Gibbons received no income from the fight. In addition to the advance he received for training expenses, the town of Shelby built him a complete training camp for the fight. The camp was fenced in and he was allowed to collect daily ticket sales that produced a fair amount of income each day. Additionally, as a result of the publicity Tom received from the fight, he was given a 20-week vaudeville contract that paid him $2,500 per week. The

---

561 *St. Paul Pioneer Press*, Gibbons Different Says Champion Jack, July 5, 1923.
562 *St. Paul Pioneer Press*, Mayor of Shelby Loses Fortune in Staging Title Mix, July 5, 1923.
563 Johnson, James W. (Body), *The Truth About '23*, Promoter Publishing Company, Shelby, Montana 1989.
564 *Los Angeles Times*, Town in Montana Was Overmatched, February 5, 1989.

fight also cleared the way toward a lucrative contract to fight the Frenchman, Georges Carpentier, next.[565]

After boxing, Tommy became very successful selling insurance for a number of years. He later became the Sheriff of Ramsey County and helped rid the area of crime. After six years of serious illness, his wife Helen passed away in 1940 at age 46. Tommy remarried on February 15, 1941, and he and his second wife, Josephine, raised 12 children together, nine from Tommy's first marriage, and three from Josephine's. He retired from the sheriff's office in 1959 after 24 years of service. He spent his last year enjoying his many children and grandchildren. He passed away in St. Paul on November 19, 1960 at the age of 69.[566]

On July 12, Luis Firpo made his case for a match with Dempsey when he landed a big right to the jaw of the former champion Jess Willard in the eighth round of their bout at Boyle's Thirty Acres in New Jersey, and left Willard draped over the ropes where he was counted out. The total gate receipts generated from the crowd of almost 100,000 were estimated at $400,000. Willard received around $120,000 of that figure while Firpo took home approximately $80,000 for his share. Grantland Rice referred to the fight as a "battle between two one-armed men, Firpo with his crashing right and Willard with his jabbing left," and said in the end it came down to youth and speed over age.[567]

Dempsey went on to defend his title against Luis Firpo a short time later on September 14, 1923 in New York's Polo Grounds ballpark, and the two put on one of the wildest, albeit short, heavyweight title fights in the history of boxing. Firpo brought the crowd to its feet shortly after the bout began when he dropped the champion with a right hand. But Dempsey recovered quickly and proceeded to send Firpo to the canvas no less than seven times during the round.

There was no "three knockdown" rule in those days, nor was a fighter required to go to a neutral corner while the referee administered the count. So, Dempsey was permitted to stand over his opponent in the same manner he had against Willard four years earlier, and time and again the moment Firpo's knees left the floor he received another crushing blow that would send him back to the canvas.

Toward the end of the round, Firpo managed to trap the champion against the ropes and land a right to the chin that sent Dempsey crashing through the ropes and atop some ringside reporters. Dempsey was pushed back into the ring by those same men. He recuperated enough during the break at the end of the round so that he was able to drop Firpo two more

---

565 Johnson, James W. (Body), *The Truth About '23*, Promoter Publishing Company, Shelby, Montana 1989.
566 Blair, George, *Tommy Gibbons*, Self-published 1988.
567 *St. Paul Pioneer Press*, Thundering Right To Jaw Puts Giant Jess Dangling On Ropes, July 13, 1923.

times in the second round, finally bringing an end to the wild affair at the fifty-seven second mark of the round.

Some in attendance felt Dempsey had been the beneficiary of an awfully slow count when he had been knocked out of the ring in the first round, and still others believed he should have been disqualified as a result of the assistance he received when getting back up into the ring.

Dempsey took a three year break from the ring before returning in September of 1926 to lose his title to Gene Tunney in a driving rain over ten rounds in Philadelphia, Pennsylvania. He knocked Jack Sharkey out ten months later when the latter forgot the cardinal rule of boxing to protect oneself at all times. During the seventh round Dempsey landed a blow that Sharkey felt was too low. He immediately dropped his hands to his sides and turned to the referee to complain. It was a terrible mistake against a man like Dempsey. The former heavyweight champion immediately delivered a short left hook to Sharkey's jaw and he was counted out. The victory earned Dempsey the right for a return match with Tunney in Chicago's Soldier Field. The pair met on September 22, 1927 before a crowd of approximately 102,000 people.

The fight looked like a repeat of their first meeting. Tunney was firmly in control until the seventh round, when Dempsey caught him against the ropes and landed a combination of punches that sent Tunney crashing to the canvas. For a brief period, it looked as though Dempsey might become the first man ever to regain the heavyweight championship. But, of course, he failed to immediately move to a neutral corner as agreed upon by both men prior to the fight in the event of a knockdown. As a result, the referee's count was delayed for several seconds, and Tunney became the beneficiary of the famous "long count." He regained his footing before the referee's count of ten, and resumed control of the fight on the way to another clear-cut decision win over Dempsey.

The losses to Tunney, and the controversy surrounding the "long count" in their second fight, resulted in a tremendous increase in Dempsey's popularity. In retirement he enjoyed the adulation of his many fans, served in the Coast Guard during World War II, and later opened Jack Dempsey's Broadway Bar and Restaurant across the street from New York's Madison Square Garden, where he greeted guests, signed autographs and posed for pictures from 1935 to 1974. He passed away in May of 1983 at the ripe old age of 87.

Dempsey had many big wins as a fighter, but on February 17, 1923, when asked what fight he considered the greatest of his career, he surprised many with his answer:

> My first fight with Billy Miske, back in 1918, is the big event in my life as a fighter. Miske and I fought 10 rounds. No decision was rendered. Some of the writers gave Miske the edge, others favored me. At that time, Miske was a commanding figure in the fight game.

Some of the experts regarded his bout with me as easy picking. On the contrary, I gave Miske plenty of trouble. That bout convinced me that someday I would be champion, for had I not stayed 10 rounds with the great Miske, and at that time I was little more than a novice? The same year I also staged a six-round no-decision affair with him. In less than two years I was champion, winning from Willard, and had also stopped Miske in three rounds shortly afterward.[568]

---

[568] *Ogden Standard-Examiner.* First Miske Bout Is Termed Jack's Greatest, February 18, 1923.

CHAPTER 16

"Get Me a Fight"

When it became obvious there was no chance of Billy fighting the champion in Shelby, Montana in the summer of 1923, he was left to ponder what to do with whatever time he had left, inside and out of the ring. There were numerous newspaper reports of potential matches for Billy following his victory over Harry Foley in early January of 1923. Manager Jack Reddy tried to entice former heavyweight champion Jess Willard into fighting Billy in Minneapolis that February, offering the big fellow $10,000 if he could go four rounds with Billy, but Willard had already signed to fight Floyd Johnson in New York on May 4 and had agreed not to accept any other fights prior to the engagement. Willard was reportedly in much better condition at the time then he was when he lost his title to Jack Dempsey in Toledo in the summer of 1919.

Then, in March, Billy was mentioned as a possible opponent for Luis Firpo in the Milk Fund Boxing Carnival that promoter Tex Rickard was planning to stage at Yankee Stadium in New York on May 12. Many fight fans were as excited about two of the bouts scheduled on the fight card as they were about the title fight between Jack Dempsey and Tommy Gibbons that summer. The feature events on the Milk Fund's boxing card were matchups of former heavyweight champion Jess Willard against a promising young heavyweight named Floyd Johnson and Luis Firpo against Jack McAuliffe of Detroit, Michigan.

Although he was well past his prime at age 39, Willard was reported to be in first class condition for a boxer of his years. He still appeared to carry a big punch and at 238 pounds looked to be better prepared for battle than he had almost four years earlier when he lost the title to Jack Dempsey. McAuliffe, the 22-year old Canadian, now residing in Detroit, was also reportedly in good condition and expected to offer a stiff challenge to Firpo.[569] Fred Fulton, Jack Renault, Joe McCann, Bill Drake, Al Reich and "Tiny" Jim Herman were the others scheduled to appear in the ring.

Firpo, was a large 6'2½" tall and 214 pound heavyweight from Argentina nicknamed "The Wild Bull of The Pampas." He was fresh off a 12-round knockout victory over Bill Brennan on March 12 in New York's Madison Square Garden. He gave Brennan an awful beating in that contest. In fact, Brennan's wife was so alarmed at his behavior two days later she insisted he

---

569 *St. Paul Pioneer Press*, Milk Fund Boxers Complete Heavy Work For Bouts, May 9, 1923.

make a trip to New York's Jewish Memorial hospital where it was determined he had suffered a concussion.[570]

Firpo first became interested in the sport of boxing during the summer of 1916 when a number of professional fighters from the United States, including Sam Langford and Sam McVea, fought in Buenos Aires, Argentina. Firpo, a college student at the time, attended most of the bouts and later said he became so enthusiastic about the sport he decided to become a boxer himself.[571] He was a crude fighter, with little in the way of defensive skills when he arrived in the States in 1922 but he was extremely aggressive with a big punch, as Bill Brennan discovered.

At that period of time, many knowledgeable fight men viewed Firpo as Jack Dempsey's greatest threat and Grantland Rice provided the following assessment of him:

> Firpo is an offensive wonder. He can be hit, hard and rather often, and we doubt he will ever be a great defensive star. He put his entire soul into attack. To him, fighting means attacking – tearing in until at last he brings his man down. He may improve his defense a trifle, but as long as his entire soul is thrown into the charge it may be difficult to make him bother much with anything else. He will never have any rare enthusiasm for the defensive game. It will be a case of charge, counter-charge, give and take until somebody falls.[572]

There was no greater evidence of the truth of Rice's words than when Dempsey and Firpo came together in the ring later that year as mentioned in the end of the previous chapter.

Jack Reddy offered to send Billy against Firpo in the Milk Fund Carnival and donate Billy's entire purse to the fund if he failed to defeat the "Wild Bull." Firpo's handlers, however, declined the offer, preferring their man face another opponent.[573]

The boxing carnival turned out to be a big success, drawing 60,000–70,000 fans and netting a gate of $390,000. Thousands of bottles of milk were supplied to poor children as a result of the event. The event featured victories by Jess Willard over Floyd Johnson, and Luis Firpo over Jack McAuliffe. Their wins set up the future bout between the two mentioned in the preceding chapter for the right to face Jack Dempsey.

Reporting on the results of the Firpo–McAuliffe contest, Grantland Rice wrote that as Firpo stood glaring into the crowd after dispatching his opponent "one could look back a few thousand years and see again the type

---

570 *St. Paul Pioneer Press*, Brennan's Condition Not Serious Physician Says, March 15, 1923.
571 Moyle, Clay, *Sam Langford, Boxing's Greatest Uncrowned Champion*, Bennett & Hastings, Seattle, Washington 2008.
572 *St. Paul Pioneer Press*, Firpo Developed In Country Minus Athletic Events, May 20, 1923.
573 *St. Paul Pioneer Press*, Sport Gossip, March 24, 1923.

of man that fought the mammoth for existence and brought the saber-toothed tiger home to his mate."

Despite that comment, Rice added that much of the rawness Firpo had exhibited in his past performances had disappeared under the skillful direction of his trainer, Jimmy DeForest and he was closer to a finished product, and a "raging beserk who could hit straight and true, and with greater force than he had ever seen in any ring."[574] Rice's description of the man that faced Jack Dempsey in the ring in September of that year couldn't have been any more accurate.

Rickard, promoter of the Milk Fund Carnival, went on to stage a number of highly successful heavyweight championship fights over the balance of the decade. Included among those were Dempsey–Firpo, Dempsey–Tunney I, Dempsey–Sharkey and Dempsey–Tunney II. Undoubtedly, he would have promoted many more big fights if not for his death on June 6, 1929, at the age of 58, as a result of acute appendicitis.

In mid-April of 1923, Jack Reddy said that if he could get black heavyweight contender Harry Wills to agree to terms there was a good chance that a bout could be staged in St. Paul's Lexington Park between he and Billy that summer. Reddy, who said he'd been trying to arrange a bout between the pair for a long time but had continually run into obstacles, was now finally free to arrange a mixed race bout in the state of Minnesota. For many years, there had been a rule in place prohibiting boxing contests between Negroes and white persons, otherwise known as mixed bouts, but on April 4, Judge W.W. Bardwell permanently restrained the Minnesota boxing commission from issuing a license to any athletic association or boxing club permitted by the boxing commission to hold contests in Minnesota until the commissions rule was eliminated.

The judges' action left the commission with no other choice but to abolish the rule and brought to a successful conclusion a three-year effort lead by John A. Dickerson, Al. G. Johnson, and Hamlet Rowe, the latter being a writer for the African-American newspaper, the *Minnesota Messenger*.[575]

Other states, such as New York and Michigan, had already removed their own bans on mixed bouts. In making his case for the abolition of the rule, Rowe claimed it was unfair to the public and those interested in boxing to draw the color line, especially in a state where persons of both races were free to compete against one another in all other lines of athletics, were not prohibited by law from doing so, and prevented only because of a boxing commission rule.[576]

Tommy Gibbons was also mentioned by Reddy as a possible opponent for Wills, with the winner to be matched against the champion, Jack

---

[574] *St. Paul Pioneer Press*, Firpo's Heavy Fists Bring Kayo Conquest Over Jack McAuliffe, May 13, 1923.
[575] *Minnesota Messenger*, "Judge Bardwell Issues Injunction Against Boxing Commission". April 14, 1923.
[576] *Minnesota Messenger*, "2 City Delegation To Consult Preus On Boxing Rule." September 16, 1922.

Dempsey. But, Tommy's manager, Eddie Kane, later issued a statement in which he said that he and Tommy did not believe in fighting Negroes.

The statement was issued in response to a suggestion that Tommy be matched against black fighter "Battling" Siki, if Siki came to the United States. Siki had captured the Light-Heavyweight Championship of the World in Paris, France on September 24, 1922 with a stunning upset of the Frenchman, Georges Carpentier. He subsequently lost the title six months later in Dublin, Ireland against an Irishman named Mike McTigue on Saint Patrick's Day. While Rowe believed Gibbons would have no trouble defeating Siki, he wondered if Gibbons' stance against fighting Negroes didn't have more to do with a realization that if Tommy fought Siki he might also have to meet Kid Norfolk and Harry Wills as well.[577]

The *Minnesota Messenger* had a more positive view of Billy than Tommy Gibbons, pointing out that unlike some of the white fighters, Billy didn't draw the color line to avoid a tough opponent and that he had fought Kid Norfolk on two occasions. Although he had lost both contests, he gave a good account of himself.[578] The first mixed bout in the state ultimately took place on October 26, 1923, when an African-American named Clem Johnson met "Tiny" Jim Herman in a main event at the Armory in Minneapolis, Minnesota and suffered an eight-round technical knockout defeat.[579]

In May of 1923, Gibbons' manager, Eddie Kane, tried to engage Billy's services as a sparring partner to help prepare Gibbons for his upcoming fight with Jack Dempsey to no avail. The fact of the matter was that Billy was too weak to train, let alone do any fighting at the time, so he spent most of the first half of 1923 resting at the family's lakeshore home with his wife and children. Whenever he felt up to it, Billy also engaged in one of his favorite pastimes of playing golf.

In early July, Billy felt well enough to travel to Shelby, Montana to witness the Dempsey-Gibbons fight. Later that month, he traveled to Emmetsburg, Iowa to serve as a referee for a small boxing carnival. The event took place on July 24 in a new outdoor arena with a seating capacity of 2,000 and featured a bout between Louie Kelly and Archie Sheire.

A month later, Billy decided to buy a new home for his family. He purchased a Spanish-style bungalow in a relatively affluent area in St. Paul on 1387 Fairmount Avenue. Perhaps, it was that expense and the additional need for money to pay for the home that led to the discussions concerning a very surprising fight with former heavyweight champion Jack Johnson. In August, talks were held concerning the possibility of a match between the two men that would be sponsored by the Broad Athletic Club and take place in Newark's Dreamland Rink.

---

[577] *Minnesota Messenger*, "Why Dempsey Should Meet Wills for Heavyweight Title". July 28, 1923.
[578] *Minnesota Messenger*, "Billy Miske Dies." January 5, 1924.
[579] *Minnesota Messenger*, "First Mixed Bout In Minnesota." October 13, 1923.

Johnson had become the first black heavyweight champion of the world on December 26 of 1908. He had followed the current champion, Tommy Burns, around the world, finally forcing him to accept a match in Sydney, Australia when promoter Hugh McIntosh met Burns asking price. He subsequently dominated the champion over fourteen rounds at Rushcutter's Bay Stadium to win the title. Bitter about the way he was treated by the white establishment, Johnson flaunted his relationships with white women and ruled the heavyweight division for the next six-and-a-half years. His most famous victory occurred on July 4, 1910, when he dominated formerly undefeated champion James J. Jeffries before a huge crowd in Reno, Nevada.

On May 13, 1913, Johnson was found guilty of a technical violation of the Mann Act and less than a month later sentenced to one year and one day in the penitentiary. More specifically, he was found guilty of violating the White Slave Traffic Act, which came to be known as The Mann Act. The Act barred the transportation of women in interstate or foreign commerce for the purpose of prostitution or debauchery, or for any other immoral purposes. Johnson had been arrested on October 17, 1912 for transporting Lucille Cameron, a white woman he was seeing at the time, across state lines from Wisconsin to Illinois. Cameron later became his wife.

Rather than serve his sentence, Johnson chose to flee the country. On June 24, he disappeared. He turned up in Montreal, Canada and ended up in Paris, France in 1911. He defended his heavyweight title twice while in Paris, the first time in December of 1913, when he fought a draw with "Battling" Jim Johnson, and a second time in June of 1914 when he defeated Frank Moran in a twenty-round decision. He fought again on December 15, 1914, when he knocked out Jack Murray in Argentina.

The heavyweight crown finally changed hands on April 5 of 1915 when a big heavyweight, Jess Willard, knocked Johnson out in the 26th round of their title fight in Havana, Cuba. Johnson later claimed he threw the fight upon the assurances from the promoter, Jack Curley, that he would not only receive a sizable payment for doing so but Curley would use his personal connections to see to it Johnson could return to the United States without fear of going to prison. Whatever efforts Curley made on Johnson's behalf proved ineffective and Johnson and his wife spent the next five years living in exile.

Johnson ultimately returned to the United States in July of 1920, and was immediately arrested. In September, he was sent to Leavenworth prison, where he spent the next year. He was freed on the morning of July 9, 1921. By that time, Jack Dempsey was the reigning heavyweight champion. Dempsey's manager, Kearns, made it clear the champion would not give Johnson a fight. William Muldoon, the chairman of the New York Boxing Commission refused to issue Johnson a license to box, saying he was now too old at age 43. By February of 1923, the 45-year-old Johnson was working as a sparring partner for Luis Firpo.[580]

Unable to get a fight in the States, Johnson travelled to Havana, Cuba, where he defeated "Farmer" Lodge and Jack Thompson in May of 1923. Finally, on August 24, 1923, it was reported Billy and Johnson would fight in a 12-round no-decision contest in Newark on September 10th. It would be the first fight of any significance for the former champion since he lost his title to Jess Willard.[581]

Johnson was in New York where he was training at a local gymnasium when it was learned, on August 30, that the fight would not be allowed to go forward. The decision was announced by New Jersey's State Boxing Commissioner, Newton Bugbee. Johnson's conviction for violation of the Mann Act was provided as the reason. Although Johnson had served a prison sentence for his conviction the commission decided it was in the best interests of the sport to refuse him a license.[582]

Johnson would eventually get an opportunity to fight in the States again, but not until he was 48 years old in 1926. He'd lost five of his last seven bouts, his last fight taking place in September of 1938, when the 60-year-old man suffered a seven-round knockout to an unknown named Walter Price. He passed away in June of 1946 as a result of injuries suffered from an automobile accident in Franklinton, North Carolina (a small town near Raleigh), while he was on his way to New York to see the second Joe Louis–Billy Conn fight.[583]

The cancellation of the fight with Johnson left Billy without the income he'd planned for in September. The medical bills, purchase of a new home and months without any significant income during the year had left him financially strapped. He was convinced he didn't have long to live. Christmas would be arriving in a couple of months, in all likelihood his last, and he decided he wanted to make it a memorable one for his family. With that in mind, and despite his worsening condition, he went to the office of his manager, Jack Reddy, in October of 1923. His friend, and newspaperman, George Barton recounts what took place next.

"Jack," said Billy, "get me a fight."

"You must be kidding, you're in no condition to fight," Jack replied.

"Get me a fight anyway!"

Jack shook his head. "I won't do it."

"Look, Jack," pleaded Billy, "I'm flat broke. I know I haven't long to go, and I want to give Marie and the kids one more happy Christmas before I check out. I won't be around for another. Please get me one more payday. I

---

580 Ward, Geoffrey C., *Unforgivable Blackness*, Alfred A. Knopf, New York, N.Y. 2004.
581 *Massillon Evening Independent*. Bout for Jack, August 24, 1923.
582 *Bridgeport Telegram*. Jersey Will Not Give Jack Johnson License, August 31, 1923.
583 Moyle, Clay. *Sam Langford, Boxing's Greatest Uncrowned Champion*, Bennett & Hastings, Seattle, WA 2008.

want to make Christmas this year something Marie and the children will always remember me for."

"Look," said Jack, "you know as well as I do that if you were to fight in your present condition you might be killed."

"Sure, but I am a fighter and I'd rather die in the ring than while sitting home in a rocking chair."

Jack pulled out his wallet. "Let me help you. How much do you need?"

"No way," Bill put his hand up like a wall. "I've never take an handout, and I'm not gonna start now."

"Here's what I'll do," Jack said. "You go to the gym and start working out. If you get into any reasonable kind of shape, we'll talk about getting you a match."

"You know I can't do that," Billy replied. "It's impossible for me to train, but I've got to have one more fight for my family's sake. Please do it for me. Please."

Jack sighed. "I'll live to regret this." He stuffed his wallet back into his pocket. "Let me see what I can do."

After Billy returned home, Jack began looking into the possibilities. He found a willing opponent in Bill Brennan.[584]

At one time, Brennan had been a top contender for Dempsey's crown, and gave him one of his toughest fights. He had reeled off nine consecutive wins after losing a ten round decision to Billy in St. Paul in June of 1921, but then suffered two consecutive losses in early 1923. First, Floyd Johnson defeated him in a 15-round decision on January 12, and then Luis Firpo knocked him out in four rounds on March 12. Both losses had occurred in New York's Madison Square Garden. Firpo went on to seven more victories over the next five months, and a subsequent title shot against Jack Dempsey, while Brennan had remained inactive. By October of 1923, he was ready to launch a comeback.

George Barton, writing for the *Minneapolis Tribune* at that time, received a tip Billy was being matched with Brennan. He immediately phoned Jack Reddy. What are you thinking? If Billy fights, he could go down, permanently. I won't let you do it. You ought to be ashamed of yourself Jack. "

"You don't understand the situation."

"I understand well enough, and so will everyone else when I expose your despicable behavior."

"Hold everything," Jack said when George finally paused for a breath. "Don't write anything until I bring Billy to your office. We'll explain everything."

---

[584] Barton, George, *My Lifetime in Sports*, Olympic Press, Minneapolis, MN 1957.

When they arrived at George's office, Billy looked George in the eye. "I'm begging you, man, I gotta do this. Just keep quiet so I can have one more fight. Just one more."

George looked from Billy to Jack, then back to Billy. "I'll keep your secret. For one fight. And God help us all."

Billy's features relaxed, knowing he'd get to fight again. He also knew George feared the result.[585]

On October 17, it was officially announced Billy and Bill Brennan had been matched to meet in a ten-round contest to take place in Omaha, Nebraska on November 7, 1923.[586]

Brennan's manager, Leo Flynn, promised Brennan would surprise the fans when he returned to the ring. "He will be bigger and better," said Flynn. According to Flynn, Brennan had devoted time to getting into great shape, and was in better condition than he had been in years.[587]

On November 2, it was reported that after a month of hard training, Billy was going to begin a short series of fights beginning against Brennan. Once his bout with Brennan was completed, he was going to tackle a boxer named Joe Lohman in Grand Rapids, Michigan on November 13. It was claimed Billy was in the best shape of his career.[588] Clearly, he was anything but, having been inactive and unable to train for a number of months.

As the date of the fight drew closer, the *Omaha World-Herald* reported fans should expect to see a real battle between the two men on the main event of the American Legion's boxing card.

On November 4, the Sunday before Wednesday's scheduled fight between the two men, Brennan put in a hard workout before several hundred fans at Omaha's Business Men's gymnasium. He claimed he had been working hard at his residence in Long Island, New York; and was ready to face any heavyweight in the game. Billy reportedly worked out the same day in private at the home of a local resident.[589]

The truth was Billy's body wouldn't have been able to handle the strain of the type of training he would normally have undergone before a bout. When curious newspapermen and boxing fans asked Reddy why Billy wasn't working out in the Rose Room gymnasium in St. Paul in the weeks leading up to the fight, Reddy told them Billy was working out in a gym he had set up at his home on the shore of Lake Johanna. He was really at home conserving his strength and didn't even travel to Omaha until a couple of days before the fight.[590]

Both men passed the medical examinations given by the Nebraska State Athletic Commissions at the 3:00 p.m. weigh-in at the Business Men's

---

585 Barton, George, *My Lifetime in Sports*, Olympic Press, Minneapolis, MN 1957.
586 *Nebraska State Journal*, Brennan and Miske Matches, October 18, 1923.
587 *Syracuse Herald*. Bill Brennan Will Attempt a Come-Back, October 31, 1923.
588 *Bridgeport Telegram*. Billy Miske to Box Bill Brennan, November 2, 1923.
589 *Omaha World-Herald*. Gibbons, Brennan, Miske in Omaha, November 5, 1923.
590 Blair, George. *Billy Miske, The St. Paul Thunderbolt*, Privately Published 1988.

gymnasium on the day of the fight. The examinations weren't as strict in those days and Billy's was most likely only cursory at best. And, in terms of appearance, Billy appeared to be extremely fit. The fact he was suffering from Bright's Disease did not show on the outside. Brennan weighed in at 206 pounds, while Billy scaled 189 pounds.[591]

The *Omaha World-Herald* said a loss by Brennan would just about put an end to any remaining heavyweight title aspirations he might have, and predicted a victory for Billy based on the results of their previous fights.[592] The winner was expected to be matched with Jack Renault, Luis Firpo or Harry Wills, as that group of men continued to try and position themselves for an opportunity to fight Jack Dempsey.

Approximately 5,000 fans were on hand on the night of November 7, 1923 to witness the Miske-Brennan fight in the Omaha Auditorium. They began to express their dissatisfaction with the action, or lack thereof, early in the opening session. Billy was the aggressor and the first to score, landing a right to the jaw, followed by several body blows. Brennan landed two low blows, but they didn't appear to bother Billy and he didn't complain. Overall it was a slow round, with little damage done to either man. Cries of "Make 'em fight!" and "Throw 'em out!" were heard from the crowd. Brennan looked slow and fat. The round belonged to Billy.

Billy hurt Brennan with right and left punches to the jaw early in the second round and then chose to coast the rest of the way, clinching often, and using his shoulder to push Brennan away. He won this round as well.[593]

After the round, the referee, Leo Shea, went to Brennan's corner and warned him to put forth more effort.[594]

The referee's warning seemed to have the desired effect on Brennan, as he became the aggressor in the beginning of the third round, landing a number of blows to Billy's head. Billy covered up and clinched. When they were separated, Billy hurt Brennan with a hard left to the mouth. He rushed in and landed a series of lighter punches and Brennan fell to the canvas, rolling just outside the ropes. He rolled back inside the ring, and was attempting to rise as the referee's count reached five, when the bell rang to end the round, saving him from a possible knockout.

Brennan's seconds rushed into the ring and lifted him to his feet. He started after Miske, apparently unaware the round had ended, but his aides grabbed him and directed him toward his corner. As he turned he saw the referee, Shea, and shouted at him: "You hit me! What did you hold my hand for?

Shea walked toward Brennan's corner and replied, "You're crazy, sap, I wasn't near you at all!"

---

591 *Danville Bee*. Brennan Suspended After Being Floored, November 8, 1923.
592 *Omaha World-Herald*. Miske-Brennan On Winter Card Best of All, November 4, 1923.
593 *Omaha World-Herald*. 5,000 Fans Razz Terrible Fiasco, November 8, 1923.
594 *Danville Bee*. Brennan Suspended After Being Floored, November 8, 1923.

When the bell rang to start the fourth round, Brennan appeared groggy as he left his corner to meet Billy. When the two men came together, Billy threw a big right that landed on Brennan's jaw and he dropped like a rock. As Shea counted off the seconds, Brennan tried to rise, but he floundered about the floor, unable to regain the use of his legs.

At the count of ten, Billy, the referee, and others helped Brennan to his stool. Tommy Gibbons, who was in Omaha for a week's engagement at the World Theater, and who arrived midway through the fight, stepped into the ring and congratulated Billy on his victory. Then he hurried over to Brennan's corner.

"Can I help you any, Bill?" Tommy asked Brennan.

Brennan was still dazed and unable to answer at first. But, then he opened his eyes and saw Tommy. "Tom, did you see that referee hold my arm? He held me and Miske socked me right on the button. I wasn't right after that!"

Gibbons helped apply cold cloths to Brennan's head and then helped him out of the ring.

After the fight, Tommy told reporters he had been late in arriving, and had only witnessed the last half of the third round and what little there was of the fourth and final round. Tommy said:

> There was no fake about the knockout. Brennan was hurt. What went on before I got there, of course, I cannot comment on. But, Brennan was really hurt when I saw him. I've fought Miske five times and I've always had a lot of respect for his punching ability. Billy can sock![595]

The next morning the Nebraska State Boxing Commission advised they had suspended Brennan, along with a boxer named Harry Summers, who fought in one of the preliminary bouts, for their miserable performances. Summers went to the floor after receiving the first punch thrown by his opponent, and the sportswriters who witnessed the punch claimed there wasn't enough behind it to knock over a beer bottle.

Brennan was going to have an opportunity to state his case later that day. Unless he could convince the commission he had been in shape for the fight, as promised by his manager for the fight, he wasn't going to be allowed to box in the state again. If he was unsuccessful, it was expected his purse, amounting to $2,100 would be turned over to a community fund.[596]

Brennan said he fought the best he could and said he thought he was entitled to the money.[597] But, he was unable to convince the commission

---

595 *Omaha World-Herald.* 5,000 Fans Razz Terrible Fiasco, November 8, 1923.
596 *Beloit Daily News.* Charges Brennan Stalled in Bout With Billy Miske, November 8, 1923.
597 *Evening Independent.* Brennan Draws Suspension in Nebraska Bout, November 9, 1923.

and was forced to return to New York without any compensation.[598] Billy encountered no such problem; collecting the purse he'd been promised.

Drained from the fight, Billy didn't feel well enough to go forward with the fight he had scheduled to take place in Michigan on November 13 against Joe Lohman. He was forced to forfeit the $100 amount the Muskegon Athletic club had required him to post guaranteeing his appearance.[599]

There was some discussion over the next two weeks about the possibility of matching Billy with Jack Renault or Luis Firpo, in New York City in the near future, but there were doubts as to whether or not Billy was healthy enough to face a man as dangerous as Firpo.

And, while another battle with Renault looked like a real possibility for a while, he was managed by Leo Flynn, the same fellow who had just witnessed his other fighter, Bill Brennan, get knocked out by Billy. Flynn had hopes of negotiating a pairing of Renault with Jack Dempsey. Slim as those hopes may be, he knew another loss to Miske would eliminate the possibility altogether. "Tiny" Jim Herman was another fighter mentioned as a possible opponent for Billy, but nothing came of the talk.[600]

Once the fight was over, Billy returned to St. Paul to begin planning for Christmas. The money he received for the fight against Brennan, increased by the fact that Jack Reddy refused to accept a share for his managerial services, gave him what he needed to prepare for the kind of Christmas he desperately wanted to give Marie and the kids.

---

598 *Omaha World Herald.* Brennan Leaves Without Dough, November 9, 1923.
599 *Bridgeport Telegram.* Fight Club Returns Billy Miske's Forfeit, January 17, 1924.
600 *St. Paul Pioneer Press,* Chance for Miske to Meet Renault Faces Perceptibly, November 27, 1923.

CHAPTER 17

Billy's Last Christmas

Billy spared little expense during the final weeks leading up to the Christmas of 1923 as he purchased gifts for Marie and his three young children. The presents he purchased included a new baby grand piano for Marie, who had been studying voice upon Billy's urging, a tricycle for Billy Jr., one of the first kiddy-cars ever made for Douglas, and a doll for Donna, among many, many other gifts for the family.[601] By the time he completed his shopping, he felt good enough to enjoy one of his favorite activities: duck hunting. Unfortunately, he contracted a severe head cold as a result and it seemed to complicate his condition.[602]

Despite the cold and the fact he had been feeling so poorly for six months, Billy never complained. In the words of newsman George Barton, "There were days when he could scarcely stand on his feet but he always smiled cheerfully and told his wife and friends he was feeling fine."[603] Like many men in his chosen profession, Billy was a very tough individual. He endured his illness and the accompanying pain for a number of years and he wasn't about to let it take anything away from the Christmas he had planned for his family.

St. Paul experienced one of its drier Decembers in 1923, receiving only one-quarter total precipitation through the first 23 days of the month and, therefore, very little snow. The forecast for Christmas Eve called for partly cloudy skies with a temperature of approximately 25 degrees.[604]

When Christmas Eve arrived and the kids were all tucked in their beds, Billy and Marie piled all the presents high around the tree. Marie later said Billy's eyes were "aglow with love and happiness" as he surveyed the scene before him in their new house on Fairmount Avenue. It was the kind of Christmas he'd wanted. He had made it so."[605]

One can only imagine the thoughts that must have gone through Billy's mind at the time. Did he give thanks for the many blessings he had received during his short life? Did he wonder just how much more time he had and how Marie and the kids would get by when he was gone? Undoubtedly, he was saddened by the fact that he wouldn't be with them for much longer, but he must have been excited for Christmas Day to arrive and all the joy it would bring he and his family.

---

601 *St. Paul Pioneer Dispatch*, Unknown article title by Oliver Towne, December 25, 1963.
602 Blair, George, *Billy Miske, The St. Paul Thunderbolt*, Privately published, 1988.
603 *Minneapolis Tribune*, Illness is Fatal to Billy Miske, January 2, 1924.
604 *St. Paul Dispatch*, Today's Weather, December 24, 1923.
605 *St. Paul Pioneer Dispatch*, Unknown article title by Oliver Towne, December 25, 1963.

On Christmas morning, the Miske house was a joyful place as Billy saw the excitement in his children's eyes and listened to their cries of delight. There were songs of praise sung to the newborn Savior as Marie played her new piano and laughter filled the house.

Many years later, Billy Jr., who was almost seven years old that Christmas, remembered the sight of the new piano, the pile of presents and the sound of his father's laughter upstairs when Billy's mother's weight proved too great for a dressing room chair.[606] But, while Christmas Day was everything Billy had hoped for, he was in great pain and unable to enjoy the holiday meal Marie had prepared for the family.[607]

The day after Christmas fell on a Wednesday. Billy awoke in excruciating pain. When it didn't subside and when he could stand it no longer, he phoned his manager and friend, Jack Reddy and asked him to come over and drive him to St. Mary's Hospital in Minneapolis. Marie accompanied them and on the way to the hospital Billy finally revealed the extent of his suffering.[608] "I didn't know how sick he was," Marie said later. "I always thought because he was so husky and healthy looking –the doctors were wrong."[609]

A thorough examination by the physicians upon his arrival at St. Mary's disclosed the fact that Billy did not have long to live.[610] Marie, Jack and Billy's parents stayed with Billy at the hospital around the clock.

By Saturday, December 29, the news about Billy's condition had spread across the country. The day before, Billy physician, Dr. Andrew Sivertson, had issued a statement, saying Billy would not regain his health, and in all likelihood, would never leave the hospital.[611]

Billy lost consciousness around noontime on Saturday. On Sunday, it was reported that he hadn't shown any improvement and had only a slight chance of recovery.[612] By Monday, his doctors advised that Billy wasn't expected to survive the night.[613]

When New Year's Day arrived, Billy had been unconscious for most of the past few days and there was no hope for recovery. He rallied slightly that morning but his condition began to worsen around noon. Billy succumbed to the kidney disease at 8:00 p.m. with Marie and his manager and friend, Jack Reddy, by his bedside.[614] His long fight was finally over.

In addition to Marie, and his three children, Billy was survived by his parents, Herman and Bertha and his two sisters Florence and Mildred. A

---

606 *Sports Illustrated*, Reminiscences, December 3, 1984.
607 Barton, George, *My Lifetime in Sports*, 1957 Olympic Press, Minneapolis, MN.
608 Blair, George, *Billy Miske, The St. Paul Thunderbolt*, Privately published 1988.
609 *St. Paul Dispatch*, Unknown article title by Oliver Towne, December 25, 1963.
610 *Minneapolis Tribune*, Illness is Fatal to Billy Miske, January 2, 1924.
611 *Wisconsin Rapids Daily Tribune*, Billy Miske Will Never Fight Again, December 29, 1923.
612 *La Crosse Tribune*, Bright's Disease May Prove Fatal to Billy Miske, December 30, 1923.
613 *Beloit Daily News*, Billy Miske Can't Live Say Doctors, December 31, 1923.
614 *St. Paul Pioneer Press*, Ring Hero Loses Five-Year Fight to Regain Health, January 2, 1924.

funeral was scheduled to take place on Friday, January 4, at St. Adalbert's church in St. Paul.

Marie received telegrams of condolence from all parts of the country. Among them were messages from fighters Harry Greb, Gene Tunney, Mickey Walker, Benny Leonard, Pete Herman, Jack Dempsey and many others, in addition to a number of prominent boxing promoters and officials.

Tributes from many of the same men and others, printed by the press over the next two days:

Fred Fulton: "Deeply sorry about Billy Miske as he was a great boxer and gentleman. The game has lost one of the best men in the country."

Billy's manager, Jack Reddy:

> Words fail me when I try to tell how much I think of Billy Miske. We were more than manager and boxer. We were pals. During all my years in the boxing game as manager and promoter, I never met a finer fellow than Miske. He fought all comers and never quibbled over terms. I tried to persuade Billy to quit boxing when he first became ill, but he insisted upon continuing in order to recoup his losses in the automobile business. There were times I was tempted to inform the public and newspapers of Miske's true condition in order that they might pay proper tribute to a real fighter.

Mike Gibbons:

> Billy Miske was one of the greatest heavyweights I ever saw. If his health hadn't failed him I am sure he would have won the championship. He was a rare type of sportsman, being able to win and lose with equal grace. The boxing game would be better off if there were more men like Miske in it.

Tommy Gibbons:

> I always had the highest regard for Billy Miske, both as a boxer and a man. He was one of the nicest fellows I ever came in contact with in the boxing game or in any other profession. Although we engaged in five bitterly fought contests, our rivalry was limited to the ring only. We were the best of friends out of it. Billy always fought fairly. I don't remember a single occasion in all of our bouts that he violated the rules. Although I usually won from Miske, he gave me more trouble than any other boxer I ever met, and that includes Jack Dempsey. Miske was a credit to boxing.

George Barton:

> Miske was exceptionally popular with fistic followers everywhere he fought. He always battled on the level and gave the fans an honest run for their money. He was a gentleman in the ring as well as out of

it. As time rolls on and boxing fans discuss fights and fighters, those who knew Billy Miske personally will point with pride to the fact, for he was a MAN.

Billy's funeral took place at St. Adalbert's Catholic Church at 10:00 a.m. on Friday, January 4. Despite the freezing cold, hundreds of people, who were unable to gain entrance to the overcrowded church, stood outside to pay their last respects to the popular fighter.[615] Father Peter Roy provided the eulogy and paid tribute to Billy when he said "his stout heart will live on in the breasts of men who knew and admired him."[616]

The pallbearers were Eddie Reddy (Jack's brother), Alvin Stahl, George Studheimer, Tommy Gibbons, A.A. Lawson and George Barton. Billy's body was laid to rest in St. Paul's Calvary Cemetery. The motorcade to his final resting place stretched for several blocks.[617]

Billy's estate amounted to only $2,450. The majority of that amount was in the form of real estate holdings. It was left to Marie according to the will filed for probate.[618] A week after his death, the sportswriters of St. Paul and Minneapolis met to plan a boxing testimonial to honor Billy. Numerous boxers and others stepped forward to offer their services at no charge. Proceeds from the event would be used to purchase a monument for Billy's grave and to provide a nest egg for Marie and the children.[619] Jack Dempsey, who couldn't attend because of a previous business engagement, and his manager, Jack Kearns, donated $500 to the benefit.[620]

On Tuesday, January 15, thousands turned out to pay tribute to Billy and enjoy the fistic entertainment provided at the St. Paul Auditorium. Minnesota Lieutenant Governor Louis Collins served as the announcer of the event and the St. Paul Musicians Association and Rubinoff Jazz Orchestra each donated their services. Larry Hodgson, the former mayor of St. Paul, delivered a short eulogy on Billy and just before the first bout of the evening every person in the Auditorium stood in silent tribute, as the timekeeper, George Studheimer, rang the bell 10 times to signify the final count for Billy.

Harry Heilman, the batting champion of the American League's Detroit Tigers, was on-hand to auction off a baseball signed by Babe Ruth, and along with George Barton, Curley Ulrich, Jimmy Potts and welterweight champion Mickey Walker, served as referees for the evening's contests.[621]

The total gate receipts for the evening were $9,200. Donations produced another $800, and $500 was realized from the sale of the baseball signed by

---

615 *Minneapolis Tribune*, Body of Miske Leaves for Last Resting Place, January 5, 1924.
616 *Manitoba Free Press*, Billy Miske, Famous Boxer, Laid to Rest, January 5, 1924.
617 Blair, George, *Billy Miske, The St. Paul Thunderbolt*, Privately published 1988.
618 *State Journal*, Estate of Billy Miske, January 13, 1924.
619 *Manitoba Free Press*, St. Paul Sportsmen To Honor Billy Miske, January 8, 1914.
620 *Capital Times*, Unknown article title, January 12, 1924.
621 *St. Paul Pioneer Press*, Miske Benefit Raises $11,000, January 16, 1924.

Babe Ruth and auctioned off by Heilman. Overall, a sum of $10,500 was raised. Expenses came to about $2,000, leaving an amount of approximately $8,500 for the Miske family.[622] The Muskegon Athletic club also returned the $100 forfeit to Marie they had claimed in November when Billy had failed to appear in Michigan against Joe Lohman. "It will aid Mrs. Miske more than us," said their President, Joseph Riley.[623]

"Dago" Joe Gans of St. Paul outpointed Eddie Morris of Sioux City in six rounds in the main event. Tommy Burns of Detroit defeated "Gunner Joe" Quinn in the evening's other six-round event. Sammy Leonard of Minneapolis defeated Len Schwabel of St. Paul in a four-round go and Joe Burch of Milwaukee won over Johnny Noye of St. Paul in four rounds. Accompanying the aforementioned bouts were a three-round exhibition between the Mitchell brothers, Richie and Pinky, and a very entertaining four-round exhibition between locals Tommy Gibbons and Jimmy Delaney. Mickey Walker, who had originally planned to box in an exhibition as well, until developing a sty over his left eye while in route to Minnesota, refereed the Gibbons-Delaney exhibition.[624]

Marie had a big job ahead of her, raising three young children as a single parent, but the funds provided from the benefit, and the support of Billy's immediate family would prove very helpful as she went forward.

In the February 1924 issue of *The Ring*, Nat Fleischer, the magazines founder and editor wrote:

> Billy Miske has passed away and in his death pugilism has lost a stout-hearted, fearless and good-natured boxer. The boxing world will remember Billy Miske best as a light-heavyweight who came close to being not only the crown bearer in that division, but the heavyweight champion too. The fans the country over will remember Billy for his laughing face and his fighting heart. Those who were very close to the dead fighter will remember him as one of the gamest and one of the most unfortunate men in the annals of the ring. Miske lived up to the best ideals and died a victim of a seemingly cruel fate.

His friend and long-time Minnesota sportswriter, George Barton, called him the most courageous fighter he had known in more than half a century of his association with professional boxing.

Said George, "Maybe someone can name a gamer boxer than Billy Miske; I can't."[625]

---

622 *Minneapolis Tribune*, Testimonial Nets $8,500 for Family of Billy Miske.
623 *Bridgeport Telegram*, Fight Club Returns Billy Miske's Forfeit, January 17, 1924.
624 *Minneapolis Tribune*, Testimonial Nets $8,500 for Family of Billy Miske, January 16, 1924.
625 Barton, George, *My Lifetime in Sports*, Olympic Press, Minneapolis, MN 1957.

To "Fighting Billy Miske"

By Harlan Kentworth
of St. Paul, Minn.

Here's to a man who was game to the core,
Who'd go down to defeat, and come smiling for more;
And in this last battle he fought for his life.
But the odds were against him; now he's out of this strife;
He will long be remembered by those whom he knew,
As the finest of men. He was always true blue.

He has been in a hundred-ten fights, so I'm told,
But the sickness then came and secured a strong hold.
He thought it was nothing, t'would soon pass away.
It was only short months, and then came the day
When the "champ" of the fearless, the man of steel heart,
Was called by the Lord, from this earth to depart.

He gave up his life after long, weary nights:
And died like a hero, though he lost his great fight.
Four years "Billy" battled; he thought he had won.
He took a short rest, then his life work was done,
For fate overtook him, his conceptions were wrong.
So remember old "Billy," our pal who is gone.

The Boxing Blade, January 6, 1924

Epilogue

In a strange twist of fate, Billy's last opponent, Bill Brennan, lived only six-and-a-half months longer than Billy did. Brennan was shot down, just eight days shy of his 31st birthday early on the morning of June 15, 1924 in a New York cabaret he owned and operated, named the Tia Juana club. The fight between the two men in November of 1923 was the last one for both men.

Not long after the death of Billy Miske, his wife, Marie, sold the home on Fairmount Avenue. The family lived in a building located at 908 Ashland Avenue for a few years, but ultimately they moved into their lakeshore property on Lake Johanna.

Marie continued her voice lessons for a few years and reached a point where she was able to perform before a theatrical audience and appear on a St. Paul radio station. Ultimately, she was unable to earn a living at it. Billy's grandson, Bill Miske, said after her singing career failed to pan out, Marie operated a lunch counter in the St. Paul Public Safety Building for a number of years. It was there she met a firefighter named Alfred Peterson, whom she married seventeen years after Billy's death.

The couple continued to live in the Lake Johanna residence for the rest of Marie's life. Originally intended to serve only as a summer home, it was the last one on the lake to get running water and indoor plumbing. Marie's second husband, Alfred, used to carry home a 5-gallon can of water from work the family would use for drinking water, cooking and bathing. Bill remembers clearly what it was like to have to use the outhouse as a young boy during the freezing Minnesota winters when they visited grandma's home during the holidays.

Marie later worked as an undercover store detective for a Montgomery Ward department store for many years watching out for shoplifters. Over the years, several Hollywood studios called on her, wanting to make a movie of Billy's life. One movie mogul, along with the actor Dick Powell, wined and dined her in St. Paul in an attempt to gain her permission to make the film. But Marie refused, saying she wanted to let Billy rest in peace and after she was gone they could make the movie if they wanted to. She told a Minnesota boxing historian that she didn't want a lot of stuff said that wasn't true.[626]

A number of short stories about Billy's Christmas sacrifice appeared in periodicals such as *Readers Digest*, *Esquire*, and *Sports Illustrated* as well as many newspapers over the years, usually around the holiday season, but the movie was never made.

---

[626] Blair, George, *Billy Miske, The St. Paul Thunderbolt*, Privately published 1988.

Billy's father, Herman, passed away of kidney failure in 1927 at age 54.

Billy Jr. followed in his father's footsteps and became a professional boxer. He claimed the decision to become a fighter had more to do with the fact his home burned down and jobs were still difficult to find as a result of the depression.[627] While not as successful as his more famous father, he posted a winning record over his seven-year career and headlined a couple of local cards. He achieved success in sales and the insurance business after retiring from the ring. He passed away on January 19, 2000.

Billy's second son, Douglas, passed away in November of 1951 at the age of 32, when the plane he was flying for the Air Force during a training exercise hit some telephone lines along the Mississippi River in Minnesota.

The youngest child, Donna, received her Bachelor's degree in education and a Master's degree from the University of Minnesota. Until her marriage in 1954, she was the playground supervisor in St. Louis Park, a suburb of Minneapolis. She passed away on January 24, 2006 at the age of 83.

Marie passed away in the summer of 1978 in her early 80's while mowing the yard of her Lake Johanna home with an old push mower. According to Bill Miske, after Marie's death, her daughter Donna took the piano that Billy had purchased for Marie during their last Christmas together back to her residence in California. It was later donated to the nursing home where Donna lived at the end of her life.

Billy Miske was inducted into the International Boxing Hall of Fame in Canastota, New York on June 13, 2010.

---

[627] *Sports Illustrated*, Boxer Billy Miske Put Up The Fight Of His Life For One Last Christmas, December 3, 1984.

APPENDIX

BILLY MISKE
PROFESSIONAL FIGHT RECORD

1913

Mar	Soldier Gregory	Superior, WI	W KO 4	SPPP
Apr 29	Theodore Thompson	Superior, WI	W NWS 10	ST
Jun 6	Danny Ritt	Superior, WI	W KO 2	ST
Sep 30	Bill Scott	Superior, WI	L NWS 10	ST

1914

Feb 17	Spike Kelly	Superior, WI	D NWS 10	DNT
Mar 24	Tommy Gibbons	Hudson, WI	L NWS 10	SPPP
Apr 5	George Ashe	Philadelphia, PA	W NWS 6	PJ
May 26	Jack McCarron	Pottsville, PA	L PTS 10	PJ
Jun 3	Kid Griffo	Shenandoah, PA	W PTS 10	PPL
Jun 15	Theodore Thompson	St. Paul, MN	W KO 2	
Nov 14	Jimmy Dougherty	Philadelphia, PA	W TKO 3	
Nov 25	Ralph Erne	Shenandoah, PA	W KO 4	
Dec 10	Al Thiel	Pottsville, PA	D NWS 10	PPL

1915

Jan 1	Billy Maxwell	Philadelphia, PA	W NWS 6	PPL
Jan 9	Billy Maxwell	Philadelphia, PA	W NWS 6	PPL
Jan 12	Harry Greb	Philadelphia, PA	D NWS 6	PPL
Jan 16	Jack McCarron	Philadelphia, PA	L NWS 6	PJ

Feb 25	Mike Hirsch	Milwaukee, WI	D NWS 6	MFP
Mar 16	Gus Christie	Milwaukee, WI	W NWS 8	MFP
Mar 23	Eddie Nearing	Hudson, WI	W TKO 9	
Apr 6	Mike O'Dowd	Hudson, WI	W NWS 10	SPPP
Apr 27	George "K.O." Brown	Dubuque, IA	W NWS 10	CT
Jul 12	Tommy Gibbons	St. Paul, MN	L NWS 10	SPPP
Aug 24	Gus Christie	Dubuque, IA	L NWS 10	RJ
Sep 10	Jack Lester	St. Paul, MN	W KO 2	RJ
Nov 1	George "K.O." Brown	Winnipeg, CA	D NWS 12	MAFP
Dec 3	Terry Kellar	Superior, WI	W NWS 10	SPPP
Dec 17	Jack Clements	Minneapolis, MN	W KO 8	SPPP
Dec 28	Frank Hoe	Marshfield, WI	W KO 2	SPPP

1916

Jan 28	Jack Dillon	Superior, WI	W NWS 10	ECL
Feb 29	Dick Gilbert	Denver, CO	W PTS 15	DP
Apr 14	Jack Dillon	Minn., MN	L NWS 10	LTD
Jun 22	Jack Hubbard	Brooklyn, NY	W KO 9	NSJ
Aug 31	Johnny Howard	Brooklyn, NY	W KO 10	PHP
Sep 21	Jim Barry	Brooklyn, NY	W TKO 6	MFP
Oct 12	Battling Levinsky	Brooklyn, NY	W NWS 10	NYET
Oct 30	Battling Levinsky	Brooklyn, NY	W NWS 10	NYT
Nov 9	Tim O'Neil	Brooklyn, NY	W KO 6	NCN
Nov 17	Bob Moha	Brooklyn, NY	W NWS 10	NYET

| Nov 27 | Larry Williams | Philadelphia, PA | W NWS 6 | PPL |
| Dec 19 | Jack Dillon | Brooklyn, NY | D NWS 10 | NYET |

1917

Jan 1	George "K.O." Brown	Brooklyn, NY	W NWS 10	BE
Jan 12	Charley Weinert	New York, NY	W NWS 10	NYT
Jan 16	Jack Dillon	Brooklyn, NY	W NWS 10	NYT
Feb 27	Battling Levinsky	St. Paul, MN	L NWS 10	DN
Jul 24	Joe Bonds	Brooklyn, NY	W TKO 2	ODS
Sep 18	Bert Kenny	Brooklyn, NY	W NWS 10	PR
Sep 28	Carl Morris	New York, NY	W NWS 10	FWN
Oct 2	Charley Weinert	Brooklyn, NY	W NWS 10	NYT
Oct 16	Kid Norfolk	Boston, MA	L PTS 12	TET
Oct 30	Bert Kenny	Boston, MA	W TKO 5	BDN
Nov 13	Jack Dillon	Brooklyn, NY	W NWS 10	NYT

1918

Jan 18	Fred Fulton	St. Paul, MN	D NWS 10	MDN
Feb 27	Gus Christie	Superior, WI	W NWS 10	MT
Apr 8	Tom Cowler	Minneapolis, MN	W TKO 7	RJ
Apr 12	Gunboat Smith	Atlanta, GA	W PTS 10	WEM
May 3	Jack Dempsey	St. Paul, MN	D NWS 10	SPPP
May 31	Henry Hendricks	San Francisco, CA	W TKO 2	SFC
Jun 7	Willie Meehan	Los Angeles, CA	D PTS 4	OE
Jun 14	Ed. "K.O." Kruvosky	San Francisco, CA	W PTS 4	OT

Jul 12	Gunboat Smith	Jersey City, NJ	W NWS 6	NYT
Jul 15	Bartley Madden	Jersey City, NJ	W NWS 8	RJ
Jul 16	George Ashe	New York, NY	W NWS 4	NYT
Sep 14	Bill Hart	St. Paul, MN	W KO 1	SPPP
Sep 21	Harry Greb	Pittsburgh, PA	L NWS 10	PP
Nov 18	Tom McMahon	Pittsburgh, PA	W NWS 6	PP
Nov 28	Jack Dempsey	Philadelphia, PA	L NWS 6	PI
Dec 16	Fireman Jim Flynn	Tulsa, OK	W KO 2	GDN
Dec 27	Gus Christie	Milwaukee, WI	W PTS 10	NPG

1919

Jan 11	Tom Cowler	Philadelphia, PA	W NWS 6	PEB
Mar 28	Tom Cowler	Baltimore, MD	W KO 4	FWM
Mar 31	Harry Greb	Pittsburgh, PA	L NWS 10	PP
Apr 28	Bill Brennan	Tulsa, OK	W PTS 15	BDN
Jun 6	Willie Meehan	St. Paul, MN	W NWS 10	REG
Jun 9	Kid Norfolk	Pittsburgh, PA	L NWS 10	PP
Jun 19	Tommy Gibbons	Minneapolis, MN	D NWS 10	MT
Jun 25	Bill Brennan	St. Louis, MO	D NWS 8	DN
Jul 3	Battling Levinsky	Rossford, OH	D NWS 12	FWN

1920

| Jun 11 | Jack Moran | Minneapolis, MN | W KO 2 | SFC |
| Sep 6 | Jack Dempsey | Ben. Harbor, MI | L KO 3 | SPPP |

1921

Feb 9	Lee Anderson	Milwaukie, OR	W PTS 10	OET
Mar 7	Farmer Lodge	St. Paul, MN	W KO 4	EC
May 9	Tom McCarty	St. Paul, MN	W KO 2	ECL
Jun 8	Bill Brennan	St. Paul, MN	W NWS 10	MJ
Jul 2	Jack Renault	Jersey City, NJ	W NWS 8	NYT
Nov 11	Tony Melchior	Columbus, NE	W TKO 4	NSJ

1922

Jan 16	Charley Weinert	Newark, NJ	W NWS 12	PR
Jan 28	Jack Renault	Brooklyn, NY	W TKO 13	TT
Feb 20	Bob Roper	Philadelphia, PA	W DQ 6	NCN
Mar 2	Al Roberts	New York, NY	W KO 2	SCJ
Apr 10	Billy Shade	Youngstown, OH	W TKO2	NCN
Apr 27	Martin Burke	New Orleans, LA	W PTS 15	NOTP
May 29	Bob Roper	New York, NY	W PTS 10	NYT
Jun 23	Homer Smith	Covington, KY	W KO 1	TCT
Jul 3	Willie Meehan	Okl.City, OK	W KO 1	GDN
Jul 10	Martin Burke	Denver, CO	W NWS 12	NSJ
Aug 25	Fred Fulton	St. Paul, MN	W KO 1	SPPP
Sep 4	Bob Roper	Okl. City, OK	D PTS 12	BB
Oct 13	Tommy Gibbons	New York, NY	W DQ 10	LS
Nov 11	Bud Ryder	Grand Forks, ND	W KO 3	LT
Dec 15	Tommy Gibbons	St. Paul, MN	L UD 10	NYT

1923

Jan 12	Harry Foley	Omaha, NE	W TKO 1	LSJ
Nov 7	Bill Brennan	Omaha, NE	W KO 4	OWH

KEY:
BB *Boxing Blade*
BDN *Beloit Daily News*
BE *Brooklyn Eagle*
CT *Chicago Tribune*
D Draw
DN *Daily Northwestern*
DNT *Duluth News Tribune*
DP *Denver Post*
DQ Disqualification
EC *Evening Courier*
ECL *Ea Claire Leader*
FWN *Fort Wayne News*
GDN *Galveston Daily News*
JJ *Jersey Journal*
KO Knockout
L Loss
LTD *Lima Times Democrat*
LS *Lincoln Star*
LT *La Crosse Tribune*
MAFP *Manitoba Free Press*
MDN *Minnesota Daily News*
MFP *Milwaukee Free Press*
MJ *Milwaukee Journal*
MT *Minneapolis Tribune*
NCN *New Castle News*
NOTP *New Orleans Time-Picayune*
NPG *National Police Gazette*
NSJ *Nebraska State Journal*
NWS Newspaper decision
NYET *New York Evening Telegram*
NYT *New York Times*

ODS Oneonta Daily Star
OE   Ogden Examiner
OET Olean Evening Times
OT   Oakland Tribune
OWH Omaha World Herald
PEB Philadelphia Evening Tribune
PHP Philadelphia Press
PI   Philadelphia Inquirer
PJ   Pottsville Journal
PP   Pittsburgh Post
PPL Philadelphia Public Ledger
PPR Philadelphia Public Register
PR   Philadelphia Record
REG Reno Evening Gazette
RJN Racine Journal
SCJ Sioux City Journal
SFC San Francisco Chronicle
SPPP St. Paul Pioneer Press
ST   Superior Telegram
TCT The Capital Times
TEN Trenton Evening News
TET The Evening News
TKO Technical knockout
TT   Times Tribune
UD   Unanimous decision
W   Win
WEM Warren Evening Mirror

Index

Aberdeen Hospital, 144
Academy Athletic Club, 140
Albaugh Theater, 66
Alderice, Robert, 67
Allen, Tom, 11
Anderson, Andre, 111, 141
Anderson, Lee, 129, 135, 197
Andrews, Tom, 11, 47, 49
Armstrong, Bob, 46
Arnold, Earl, 154
Ashe, George, 15, 23, 57, 85, 193, 196
Auerbach, Al, 61
Austin, Sam, 44
Bagley, Frank, 139
Bardwell, W.W., 176
Barry, Jim, 27, 194
Barton, George, 22, 51, 70, 72, 94, 145, 153, 179, 180, 185, 187, 188, 189
Bauer, Joseph, 19
Benton, Thomas, 81
Bernstein, Ike, 106, 113
Bigger, Thomas, 116
Bonds, Joe, 38, 108, 195
Brady, William, 13
Brennan, Bill, 40, 49, 50, 51, 52, 68, 71, 72, 75, 77, 79, 130, 131, 135, 136, 141, 142, 174, 175, 180, 181, 184, 191, 196, 197, 198

Bright, Richard, 73
Broad Athletic Club, 177
Broadway Sporting Club, 26, 33, 35
Broun, Heywood, 165, 169
Brown, George, 85, 194, 195
Brunson, Sterne, 81
Buckley, Jim, 51
Bugbee, Newton, 179
Burke, Martin, 137, 138, 142, 143, 197
Burke, Richard, 168
Callaghan, Pat, 29
Cameron, Lucille, 178
Camp Gordon, 51
Carpentier, Georges, 73, 122, 127, 132, 142, 170, 171, 177
Cates, Maxine, 61
Choynski, Joe, 35
Christie, Gus, 16, 20, 23, 29, 37, 42, 49, 60, 63, 194, 195, 196
Clarke, Jeff, 42, 70
Clements, Jack, 22, 194
Clermont Avenue Rink, 26
Coburn, Fred, 22, 26, 37, 46, 48, 49, 53, 71
Coffey, Jim, 40
Coleman, Larry, 15, 16
Coleman, Tommy, 15
Collins, Mike, 17, 19, 43, 46, 70, 83, 143, 145, 157, 158, 159

Considine, Bob, 62

Corbett, James J., 35, 36, 68, 77, 151

Coue, Emile, 156

County American Legion Boxing Association, 158

Cowler, Tom, 25, 42, 50, 64, 66, 67, 195, 196

Cox, Monte, 4, 18, 61

Curley, Jack, 41, 178

Cusick, J.C., 19

Daab, Hyatt, 29

Daly, Al, 117

Darcy, Les, 32, 33, 37, 38

Death, 5

DeForest, Jimmy, 176

Deitsch, P.J., 19

Delaney, Jimmy, 9, 189

Dempsey, Jack, 24, 37, 38, 40, 45, 48, 49, 51, 54, 56, 57, 58, 59, 60, 61, 64, 68, 72, 75, 79, 80, 82, 94, 98, 103, 104, 109, 110, 111, 112, 114, 116, 120, 121, 122, 123, 124, 125, 126, 127, 128, 129, 130, 131, 132, 135, 136, 138, 140, 141, 142, 143, 144, 145, 148, 152, 153, 157, 161, 162, 164, 172, 174, 175, 176, 177, 178, 180, 182, 184, 187, 188, 195, 196

Dillon, Jack, 5, 15, 20, 22, 23, 24, 25, 26, 27, 28, 29, 30, 33, 34, 43, 56, 61, 65, 67, 93, 141, 142, 194, 195

Donovan, Mike, 12

Dougherty, Jimmy, 15, 116, 117, 159, 168, 193

Drake, Bill, 174

Dreamland Rink, 177

Duquesne Gardens, 66

Dyckman Oval, 140

Edgren, Robert, 107, 147

Elgin Motor Car Corporation, 78

Erne, Ralph, 15, 23, 193

Ertle, Johnny, 9

Espin, John, 49

Fairbanks, Douglas, 66, 144

Farrell, Henry, 147

Ferguson, Sandy, 111

Firpo, Luis, 125, 140, 141, 162, 171, 174, 175, 179, 180, 182, 184

Fitzsimmons, Floyd, 79, 116, 128, 129

Floto, Otto, 47, 54, 142

Flynn, Jim, 51, 60, 62, 63, 196

Flynn, Leo, 42, 181, 184

Foley, Harry, 155, 156, 174, 198

Forbes Field, 58, 69, 70

Frawley Law, 12

Fulton, Fred, 30, 33, 39, 41, 43, 44, 45, 47, 48, 49, 50, 57, 59, 79, 83, 93, 141, 142, 143, 144, 145, 146, 174, 187, 195, 197

Gans, Panama Joe, 109

Gehan, Mark, 131

Gibbons, Mike, 9, 14, 15, 19, 25, 26, 30, 36, 81, 82, 84, 187

Gibbons, Thomas, 147

Gibbons, Tommy, 9, 15, 18, 19, 20, 30, 38, 43, 70, 71, 75, 86,

201

100, 103, 110, 136, 144, 147, 148, 150, 152, 153, 154, 155, 157, 162, 163, 164, 167, 168, 169, 170, 171, 174, 176, 177, 183, 187, 188, 189, 193, 194, 196, 197

Gibson, Florent, 58

Gillespie, Clarence, 152

Godfrey, George, 163

Great Northern Railroad, 8, 9, 160

Greb, Harry, 15, 26, 29, 45, 58, 66, 68, 86, 112, 114, 118, 136, 137, 139, 140, 142, 146, 147, 148, 187, 193, 196

Gregory, Soldier, 10, 13, 193

Griffo, Kid, 15, 193

Grimson, Lew, 60

Guy, Richard, 58

Haack, Billy, 45

Haddock, William, 67

Hall, Jim, 10

Harlem Sporting Club, 33, 39

Hart, Billy, 58

Hart, Marvin, 58, 60, 196

Heinen, Jack, 109, 112

Heirnor, Walter, 75

Hendricks, Henry, 55, 195

Herman, Jim, 174, 177, 184

Hirsch, Mike, 16, 194

Hoe, Frank, 22, 194

Hoke, Billy, 22

Holt, Sterling, 23

Howard, Johnny, 26, 194

Hubbard, Jack, 26, 194

Igoe, Hype, 47

Jab, Jim, 58

Jeannette, Joe, 108

Jeffries, James J., 35, 60, 125, 178

Johnson, Clem, 177

Johnson, Floyd, 162, 174, 175, 180

Johnson, Jack, 4, 35, 36, 39, 41, 60, 73, 109, 140, 141, 177, 179

Johnson, Jim, 34, 70, 165, 178

Johnson, Lester, 61, 62, 70

Jones, Tom, 41

Kahn, Roger, 61

Kane, Eddie, 70, 149, 153, 157, 159, 177

Kearns, Jack, 37, 77, 108, 116, 128, 141, 157, 158, 159, 162, 165, 166, 168, 188

Keck, Harry, 58, 70

Keene, Jack, 75, 134, 142

Keiser, Fay, 137

Kellar, Terry, 21, 87, 111, 194

Kelly, Louie, 177

Kelly, Spider, 54

Kelly, Spike, 14, 193

Kenner, Jack, 143

Kenny, Bert, 39, 42, 89, 195

Ketchel, Stanley, 15

Kilrain, Jake, 151

Kruvosky, Edward, 56

Lane, J.E., 165

Lang, Fred, 22

Leonard, Benny, 80, 106, 113, 116, 187

Lexington Park, 131, 143, 176

Lodge, Walter, 130, 131, 197

Louis, Joe, 179

Lund, Henry, 153

Lynch, Mike, 26

Madden, Bartley, 57, 99, 135, 196

Madden, Billy, 35

Madison Square Garden, 57, 100, 107, 108, 135, 136, 139, 147, 148, 172, 174, 180

Malone, Jock, 9, 52, 86

Mann Act, 178, 179

Marburger, Sam, 25

Marshfield Athletic Club, 22

Martin, Bob, 130

Mason, V.A., 41

Maxwell, Billy, 15, 193

McAuliffe, Jack, 174, 175, 176

McCann, Joe, 174

McCarron, Jack, 15, 16, 85, 193

McCarthy, Tom, 131

McCauley, E.A., 117

McCoole, Mike, 11

McCoy, Al, 16

McCoy, George Jr., 58

McCoy, Kid, 59

McFarland, Packey, 89, 113

McFayden, Hugh, 19

McGoorty, Eddie, 129

McGovern, Artie, 140, 150, 152

McGovern, Terry, 52

McMahon, Hugh, 14, 16

McMahon, Tom, 196

McTigue, Mike, 177

McVea, Sam, 20, 42, 175

Meany, Tom, 108

Meehan, Willie, 38, 55, 56, 59, 69, 79, 93, 141, 195, 196, 197

Melchoir, Tony, 79, 134, 135

Menke, Frank, 109

Merriam, William, 10

Michigan State Boxing Commission, 116, 118

Miles, Charles, 152

Milk Fund Boxing Carnival, 174

Minneapolis Auditorium, 59

Miske Auto Co. Distributors and Dealers, 78

Miske, Bertha, 7

Miske, Herman, 84

Moha, Bob, 29, 31, 194

Molumby, Loy, 158, 159, 162, 165

Moran, Frank, 25, 26, 30, 40, 136, 178

Moran, Jack, 79, 196

Morris, Carl, 30, 36, 39, 40, 41, 42, 44, 45, 47, 49, 51, 52, 136, 145, 195

Muldoon, William, 151, 178

Murphy, Tommy, 16, 17

Murray, Jack, 178

National Athletic Club, 16, 64

Nearing, Eddie, 16, 194

Nelson, Walter, 19

Neu, Adam, 19

Neu, John, 18, 19

New Era Motor Car Company, 78

New Jersey Boxing Hall of Fame, 26

New York State Athletic Commission, 12

Nicollet Park, 70

Norfolk, Kid, 38, 41, 49, 69, 130, 131, 136, 170, 177, 195, 196

O'Brien, Jack, 15

O'Neil, Tim, 28, 194

Olympia Athletic Club, 136

Orleans Athletic Club, 138

Palzer, Al, 145

Pantages Theater, 130

Pelkey, Arthur, 42

Polo Grounds, 125, 170, 171

Price, Walter, 179

Reddy, Eddy, 19

Reddy, Jack, 19, 49, 51, 56, 59, 65, 66, 77, 80, 91, 106, 135, 143, 146, 154, 165, 175, 176, 179, 180, 184, 186, 187

Reich, Al, 174

Reisler, John, 33

Renault, Jack, 132, 134, 135, 174, 182, 184, 197

Rice, Grantland, 166, 167, 171, 175

Rickard, Tex, 52, 132, 134, 152, 162, 174

Riley, Jack, 111

Rink Sporting Club, 135

Ripley, Robert, 28, 146

Ritt, Danny, 13, 193

Roberts, Al, 136, 197

Rocap, Billy, 47

Roosevelt, Theodore, 12

Roper, Bob, 134, 136, 140, 146, 147, 197

Rothfuss, Carl, 82

Rowlands, Len, 38

Runyan, Damon, 116

Ryder, Bud, 152, 197

Schaaf, F.C., 19

Schaeffer, Willie, 16

Scott, Bill, 13, 111, 193

Shade, Billy, 137, 142, 197

Sharkey, Jack, 140, 172

Shea, Jimmy, 72

Sheire, Archie, 177

Simmer, John, 18

Slocum, Bill, 62

Smith, Ed, 47, 116

Smith, Harry, 55

Smith, Homer, 81, 111, 137, 140, 141, 142, 197

Smith, John, 11, 16

St. Joseph Hospital, 38

St. Paul Athletic Club, 19

St. Paul Auditorium, 19, 20, 44, 47, 49, 58, 94, 110, 130, 153, 188

Sudheimer, George, 153

Sullivan, John L., 12, 35, 36, 151

Sun Shipbuilding Company, 116

Taft, William, 12
Tate, Bill, 42, 70, 109, 112, 118, 119
Thompson, Johnny, 29
Thompson, Theodore, 193
Tillman, Johnny, 109
Tyrell, Frank, 30
Vickery, Howard, 142, 143
Walcott, Joe, 29
Walker, Ed, 128
Walker, Hugh, 64
Wegner, Jake, 4, 5, 6
Weinert, Charley, 33, 40, 130, 135, 136, 195, 197

Wells, Billy, 132
Wiggins, Chuck, 118, 119, 137
Willard, Jess, 25, 27, 30, 35, 40, 41, 44, 45, 46, 48, 49, 51, 52, 64, 68, 72, 79, 98, 109, 110, 111, 121, 123, 125, 142, 162, 171, 174, 175, 178, 179
Williams, Larry, 30, 195
Wills, Harry, 127, 136, 140, 141, 142, 143, 145, 146, 147, 162, 176, 177, 182
Wilson, George, 111
WWJ, 118
Youngstown Athletic Club, 137
Zimmerman, Mose, 158

www.ingramcontent.com/pod-product-compliance
Lightning Source LLC
Chambersburg PA
CBHW030411100426
42812CB00028B/2912/J